Abel Stevens

Madame de Staël

A Study of Her Life and Times, the First Revolution and the First Empire. Vol. 1

Abel Stevens

Madame de Staël
A Study of Her Life and Times, the First Revolution and the First Empire. Vol. 1

ISBN/EAN: 9783337246495

Printed in Europe, USA, Canada, Australia, Japan

Cover: Foto ©ninafisch / pixelio.de

More available books at **www.hansebooks.com**

MADAME DE STAËL.

VOL. I.

LONDON: PRINTED BY
SPOTTISWOODE AND CO., NEW-STREET SQUARE
AND PARLIAMENT STREET

MADAME DE STAËL;

A STUDY

OF

HER LIFE AND TIMES:

THE FIRST REVOLUTION and THE FIRST EMPIRE.

BY A. STEVENS, LL.D.

IN TWO VOLUMES.—VOL. I

WITH PORTRAITS.

LONDON:
JOHN MURRAY, ALBEMARLE STREET.
1881.

All rights reserved.

PREFACE.

I HAVE NOT been able to find, in any language, anything like an adequate biography of Madame de Staël—a woman who, more than any other, (not excepting Madame Roland) represents her epoch, and that the epoch of the modern history of Europe. The best of French critics, Sainte-Beuve, has accorded to her this pre-eminence. 'How incomplete,' exclaims Geffroy (Revue des Deux Mondes, tome vi. 1856), 'are the biographies of Madame de Staël!' Her gifted cousin, Madame Necker de Saussure, prepared for the first edition of her collected works (Œuvres Complètes de Madame de Staël, 17 vols. Paris, 1820–21) a 'Notice' on her 'Character and Writings' which is the best memoir of her yet given to the world: nearly all the facts of her early life, recorded by other writers, are borrowed from it; yet, of its more than three hundred and seventy pages, seven-eighths are devoted to general remarks on her character and critical remarks on her works. She complains of the paucity of her data, the difficulty of constructing a connected history of her friend. The writings of Madame de Staël, particularly her 'Ten Years of Exile,' her 'Considerations' on the French Revolution, and her sketch of her father introductory to his 'Manuscripts' (a sketch which Benjamin Constant pronounced her best self-revelation), are replete with allusions to her own life: but these are mostly detached and vague. The superabundant 'Memoirs' of her times, and the histories of the French Revolution, of the Literature, and of the Society of the epoch, abound in similar allusions, but they seem equally intractable to any attempt to reduce them to the correlation and consistence requisite for a biography of the usual form. Hence, probably, it is that, with almost innumerable biographical sketches, we have as yet no real biography of this greatest of literary women, greatest by the events of her life, if not by her literary productions.

Besides the elaborate 'Notice,' by Madame Necker de Saussure, Sainte-Beuve has given us (Portraits et Critiques Littéraires, 3 vols., Paris, 1841) a sketch of more than a hundred and twenty pages: Fr. Schlosser, a volume on Madame de Staël et Madame Roland (Frankfurt, 1830); Lydia Maria Child, a work with the same title (Auburn,

Me., 1861); Maria Norris, a Life and Times of Madame de Staël (London, 1843); Cousin (d'Avalon) 'Staëlliana' (Paris, 1820); Hortense Allart, 'Lettres sur les Œuvres de Madame de Staël' (Paris, 1824); Henri Baudrillart, an 'Eloge de Madame de Staël' (Paris, 1850), crowned by the French Academy. Philarète Chasles has made out an excellent *résumé* of her life and writings in the 'Nouvelle Biographie Générale,' and the sketch in the 'Biographie Universelle' is equally well done. Vinet has estimated, from his religious standpoint, her relations to the moral tendencies of our age: Villemain, Bonald, Quérard, Bauguelet, Chénier, and, indeed, nearly all other authorities on French Literature, have treated of her works and her character. Important publications, affording new materials for her history, have been multiplied in our day, but have been little used for the purpose —such as Madame Lenormant's 'Souvenirs and Correspondence of Madame Récamier,' and 'The Friends of her Youth and her Intimate Correspondence;' also 'Weimar and Coppet' (attributed to the same editor), with a considerable introductory sketch and numerous letters; Taillandier's 'Unpublished Letters of Sismondi,' and his 'Countess of Albany;' Geffroy's researches respecting her first husband, the Baron de Staël, and her own correspondence with Gustavus III. of Sweden, contributed to the 'Revue des Deux Mondes' (1856 and 1864-65), and others.

I gratefully acknowledge my obligations to Professor Albert Rilliet de Candolle, of Geneva, a relative of the companion of her childhood, Mdlle. Huber (afterwards Madame Rilliet-Huber), for some original data, and important suggestions; and most especially to Monsieur Pictet de Sergy (former Councillor of State, and author of a History of Geneva &c.), the only survivor of the personal friends of Necker whom I have been able to discover. His father (Pictet-Diodati) and his father-in-law (Pictet de Rochemont) were among the dearest friends of Madame de Staël, and familiar guests of Coppet. He, himself, was a still more habitual guest there, from the time of Necker down to the death of his distinguished daughter, and also of the *salon* of her friend, Madame Récamier, at the Abbaye-aux-Bois, Paris. He knew intimately the most noted characters of the Coppet *coterie*, and has entertained his extreme but genial old age by recording his 'Souvenirs' of them. This unpublished work, as also his manuscript 'Etude' on an important chapter of the 'Allemagne,' he has generously placed at my command, together with many other aids. Besides the citations from his manuscripts which will be found in my pages, I owe to him the right statement and proper colouring of many facts already given to the public with more or less inaccuracy.

But with all these abundant 'sources,' it has seemed impossible to make a satisfactory biography except on the plan I have adopted, as implied by my title—A Study of her Life and Times. Viewed *en famille*, and in her relations to her times—the era of the First Revolution and the First Empire— its Society, Literature, and Politics—her personality appears more distinctly, and in ampler and juster proportions, than it could be presented in any possible narration of the exclusively personal facts of her life.

She has been known abroad chiefly as the author of a couple of 'fictions,' or by French party criticisms and anecdotal disparagements; but critical students of her works and her times know that she was a profound ethical thinker; a political leader whose persistent liberal teachings have again ascendency in her country; a 'Queen of Society;' an oracle of the first minds of her age; the leader, as Lacretelle records, of the spiritualistic reaction against the materialistic philosophy of the Revolution; one of the principal promoters, as Lerminier asserts, of the literature and criticism of the Romantic school, in France, as contrasted with its old rigorous Classicism; the first, as Goethe affirms, effectively to break open the way for the outspread of German literature over Western Europe; the most genuine heroine of the Revolution; the most steadfast opponent of the despotism of Bonaparte— 'the last of the Romans,' as Lamartine says, 'under this Cæsar, who dared not to destroy her, and could not abase her;' the greatest woman of her times, as Macaulay asserted; the greatest woman in literature, as Byron said; the greatest woman yet produced by Europe, as Galiffe believed—a superb intellect, and a woman of loving and most lovable soul.

In a period of illness and retirement, amidst scenes consecrated by her memory, I have found agreeable occupation in attempting to reinstate her in her real historical position; to restore her *salon* at Paris, crowded with representative personages of the times; to revive her brilliant literary court at Coppet; to disinter, from old publications, the contemporary and later criticisms on her works; to trace her travels, and relations with distinguished men and women, in France, Switzerland, Italy, Germany, Russia, and England; and, above all, to ascertain her own intellectual (her interior) life. The task is beset with serious critical embarrassments, especially the liability that the frame may be too large for the picture. I have endeavoured to guard against this error, if not always with success, yet sufficiently, I trust, to obtain the indulgence of the reader. My work must necessarily be a mosaic; but the mosaic legitimately belongs to Art.

All writers on the life of Madame de Staël, especially her early life, are indebted to her cousin for a large proportion of their data; and, in any other than the French language, would naturally reproduce them in a style very like a free rendering of her narrative; there is, therefore, among them not a little similarity, of not only facts but of language. This should not, however, expose them to the suspicion of mutual plagiarism; it shows, rather, their common fidelity to the best original authority. In my use of her 'Notice sur le Caractère et les Ecrits de Madame de Staël,' I have not hesitated to follow their example.

As more than nine-tenths of my data have never before been presented in any consecutive form, I have given abundant marginal verifications.

GENEVA: *July* 14, 1880.

CONTENTS

OF

THE FIRST VOLUME.

CHAPTER I.

INTRODUCTION—PARENTAGE.

Coppet—Château de Necker—Madame de Staël—The Necker Family—James Necker—The Mother of Madame de Staël—Gibbon's Love—Character and Writings of Madame Necker—Moultou—Bonstetten—Voltaire—Salons of Paris—Madame Necker's Salon—Madame du Deffand—Marmontel—Madame Necker and Madame Roland 1

CHAPTER II.

CHILDHOOD AND EDUCATION.

Madame Necker's System of Education—Rousseau's Theory—Anecdotes of the Childhood of Mademoiselle Necker—Bonstetten—Raynal—Mademoiselle Necker in the Salon—Her first Literary Compositions—Grimm's Account of one—Morbid Effect of her Precocity—Necker's Resignation of Office—Tronchin's Prescription for his Daughter—Her Emancipation—Love for her Father—Her Mother—Madame de Genlis 32

CHAPTER III.

YOUTH AND EARLY WRITINGS.

First Travels—Visit to Buffon—His Egotism—His Rule for Style—Fine Sayings of Madame Necker—Journey to Switzerland—Lake Leman—The South of France—Retirement at Marolles—Early Literary Compositions—Dramas—Fictions—Criticism 60

CHAPTER IV.

EARLY WOMANHOOD.

Necker—His Daughter with him in Exile—Her Account of his Book on the Importance of Religious Opinions—Her Development—An early Portrait of her—Description of her in her Eighteenth Year—In her Twentieth Year—Her Manners in Company—Her *Bonhomie*—Her Conversational Powers—Her Religious Tendency—A Literary 'Portrait' of her. . . 74

CHAPTER V.

MARRIAGE—CORRESPONDENCE WITH GUSTAVUS III.

Baron de Staël—Count Fersen—Interest of the French Court in the Marriage—Staël's subsequent Career—His Wife's Correspondence with his King—French Court Life—Necker's Restoration to Office 86

CHAPTER VI.

LITERATURE—THE REVOLUTION.

Necker again in Office—First Publication of Madame de Staël—Letters on Rousseau—Her Opinion of Literary Life—Madame Necker de Saussure's Estimate of the Letters—Grimm's Criticism—Madame de Staël's Sympathy with the Revolution—Her Account of the Opening of the States-General—Necker's Dismissal—His Triumphal Return—Letter from Mlle. Huber—Riots of the People—Necker finally retires 100

CHAPTER VII.

MADAME DE STAËL'S HEROISM IN THE REVOLUTION.

Necker at Coppet—His Daughter's Correspondence with him—Parisian Society at this epoch—Influence of Woman—

Madame de Staël in the Perils of the Revolution—Heroic Efforts for her Friends—She is arrested—Terrorism in Paris—Her Escape to Coppet 121

CHAPTER VIII.

AT COPPET.

Coppet—Madame de Staël rescues Achille du Chayala—Mathieu de Montmorency—Fate of his Family—Scenery of Lake Leman—Lacretelle on the Heroism of Madame de Staël . 139

CHAPTER IX.

IN ENGLAND—THE ROYAL EXECUTIONS.

The French Mickleham Colony—Fanny Burney—Life at Mickleham—The Burney Letters—Necker and the King's Death—Madame de Staël pleads for the Queen—Execution of the Queen—Madame de Staël writes for Peace—Her Politics . 146

CHAPTER X.

DEATH OF HER MOTHER.

Madame Necker's Sufferings—Last Interview with Gibbon—Letter to him—Her Character—Posthumous Letters to her Husband—His Devotion to her—Moral Beauty of the Last Scene 165

CHAPTER XI.

IN PARIS AGAIN.

Political Condition of France—M. de Staël—Social Reaction in Paris—Madame Tallien—The Salon again—Madame de Staël and Talleyrand—She rescues Dupont de Nemours and Narvins de Montbreton—Her Efforts for Lafayette—Her Womanly Sensibility—Education and Career of her Son, Auguste—Her Treatise on the Passions 173

CHAPTER XII.

MADAME DE STAËL AND BONAPARTE.

PAGE

A new Epoch in her Life—Her Relations to Napoleon—The Cause of his Hostility—His Character—Anecdotes—Sophie Gay—Invasion of Switzerland—Scenes at Coppet . . . 194

CHAPTER XIII.

LIFE IN PARIS—BENJAMIN CONSTANT.

Necker—Madame de Staël's Separation from her Husband—Her Daughter Albertine — Lacretelle — Benjamin Constant—Madame de Charrière—Madame de Staël's Salon—Constant's Speech against the Government—Its Consequences—Madame de Staël's Work on Literature—It restores her Social Position in Paris 214

CHAPTER XIV.

HER WORK ON LITERATURE.

Its Scope—The Perfectibility of Man—Contemporary Criticism on the Book — Fontanes — Chateaubriand — Christianity—What she meant by Perfectibility—Vico's Theory—Noble Thoughts 230

CHAPTER XV.

DE GÉRANDO, THE PHILOSOPHER—MADAME DE KRÜDNER, THE MYSTIC.

Her Relations with De Gérando—Annette de Gérando—Spiritualism—Madame de Krüdner—Letter from De Gérando—Her Salon in Paris—Necker's 'Last Views'—Napoleon's Resentment—Conversation with Lacretelle—Kant—Return to Paris 247

CHAPTER XVI.

LITERATURE—'DELPHINE.'

Publication of 'Delphine'—Criticism on it—Madame de Genlis attacks it—Sophie Gay defends it—Madame de Staël's Defence of it—Talleyrand a Character in it—His *bon mot* respecting it—Madame de Krüdner's Criticism . . . 275

CHAPTER XVII.

COPPET AND ITS SOCIETY.

Glimpses of Coppet—Its Society—Madame Rilliet-Huber—Madame Necker de Saussure—Sismondi in Love—Madame de Staël initiates his Historical Studies—Bonstetten—Frederica Brun—Madame de Staël as a Mother—Daily Life at Coppet 286

CHAPTER XVIII.

EXILE—MADAME RÉCAMIER.

Madame de Staël returns to France—Her Persecution by Bonaparte—Madame Récamier—Her extraordinary Beauty and Character—Her first Interview with Madame de Staël—The latter seeks shelter with her—A Gendarme takes charge of Madame de Staël—Joseph Bonaparte—She departs for Germany—Madame de Beaumont—Letter of Madame de Staël to Chateaubriand 300

CHAPTER XIX.

MADAME DE STAËL AT WEIMAR.

Weimar—The Duchess Amelia—The Duke Charles Augustus—The Intellectual Circle of Weimar—Wieland, Goethe and Schiller—The Duchess Louise—Letters of Goethe and Schiller respecting Madame de Staël—Her Estimates of Goethe, Schiller and Wieland—Life at Weimar . . . 318

CHAPTER XX.

BERLIN—RETURN—DEATH OF NECKER.

        PAGE

Madame de Staël at Berlin—Her Reception at Court—Its Pageantries—Kotzebue—Augustus William Schlegel—Execution of the Duc d'Enghien—Death of Necker and Return of Madame de Staël—Effect of his Death on her—Her Publication of his 'Manuscripts'—Society at Coppet . . . 331

CHAPTER XXI.

LIFE AT COPPET.

Moral Effect of the Death of her Father—Her Religious Views—Letter to Gouverneur Morris—Her Sketch of Necker's Character and private Life—Society at Coppet—Bonstetten—Schlegel—Müller, the Historian—Her Opinion of him—Madame Necker de Saussure—Letter to Madame Récamier . 345

CHAPTER XXII.

ITALY—ART.

Madame de Staël goes to Italy—Her Love of Music—Schlegel's connection with her Works—Her Italian Tour—Observations on Art—'Corinne' 356

Madame de Staël.

Chapter I.

Introduction—Parentage.

Coppet—Château de Necker—Madame de Staël—The Necker Family—James Necker—The Mother of Madame de Staël—Gibbon's Love—Character and Writings of Madame Necker—Moultou—Bonstetten—Voltaire—Salons of Paris—Madame Necker's Salon—Madame du Deffand—Marmontel—Madame Necker and Madame Roland.

The tourist in Switzerland, passing on Lake Leman from Lausanne to Geneva, sees on the north-western shore a small village, nearly all the habitations of which seem clinging to a central stately structure: it is famous as the hamlet of Coppet, and the parent edifice is the Château de Necker, the 'home of Madame de Staël.' As the steamer approaches the pier, all eyes, of educated foreigners at least, are turned from the sublimer scenery of the opposite shore to gaze on the memorable site. Guide books are eagerly consulted, and it is seldom that groups of travellers do not leave the boat to pay their homage at this shrine of the genius of the greatest woman in literary history.

Colonnades of ancient oaks, horse-chestnuts, and sycamores extend from the landing up to the mansion. The latter is spacious, but presents an aspect more of comfort and good taste, than of magnificence. Its principal court, formed on three sides by the building, on the fourth by a lofty grilled fence with ample gates, is adorned with flower beds, and flowering vines climb its angles to the roof. From its open northern side extends a simple picture of landscape beauty, designed more by nature than art: a combined English garden and park, with sward, clumps of flowering shrubs, and stately trees; a crystal brook (flowing down from the Jura) on one side; a fish-pond in the centre; and gravelled walks, with stone seats, winding among the trees.

The interior of the mansion still retains, intact, not a few mementoes of its celebrated mistress, objects of eager interest to innumerable pilgrims,— a bedroom, with its antique furniture and tapestried hangings; a library with its crowded book-cases, writing desk, and pictures; a *salon* with works of art. Scattered through these apartments are busts and portraits, of herself, of her first husband, and her children; of Necker her father, of her mother, of Rocca her youthful lover and second husband, of Augustus William Schlegel, and other literary friends.

West of the château lies the family cemetery, entirely shut in from the sight of the visitor by high walls, and a dense copse of aged trees and entangled shrubs and vines. In its centre stands a small chapel, within which sleeps the illustrious authoress, with her parents, and around it rest her children and grandchildren—four generations of the family of Necker. It is a sombre enclosure, but the nightingales delight to sing in its deep shades, and the vine-clad Juras on the one side, the lake and snow-crowned Alps on the other, frame about it a picture of exceeding beauty befitting the memory of its chief tenant.

Far more interesting by its social and literary memories than by its picturesque scenery, this charming locality will be a centre of our narrative. It was an intellectual centre of Europe in one of the most eventful periods of modern history. We shall have occasion incessantly to return to it; we begin with it, and must end with it.

Madame de Staël was unquestionably one of the principal figures in the history of French literature and society, if not indeed of French politics, during the era of the first Revolution and the first Empire. Coppet, like Voltaire's neighbouring Ferney in the preceding period, was a sort of European court, a gathering place of literary and political notabilities; and the great captain of the day was as jealous of the pen of its châtelaine as of the sceptre of any regal court. Her character is a study of rare interest. She combined the heart of a woman with the intellect of a man. Her 'Corinne' is the ideal of womanhood endued with genius, while her 'Allemagne' is, says Sir James Mackintosh, 'the most elaborate and masculine production of the faculties of woman.' Mackintosh gave her precedence of all other women who have won a name in authorship. Byron said, 'She is a woman by herself, and has done more than all the rest of them together, intellectually; she ought to have been a man.' Both knew her, and judged her from personal intercourse as well as by her writings. Alison estimated her as 'the first of female, and second to few male authors.' Jeffrey expressed the same opinion of her literary rank. Macaulay still more emphatically said that 'she was certainly the greatest woman of her times.' Schlegel, intimately associated with her for years, pronounced her 'a woman great and magnanimous even in the inmost recesses of her soul.' 'She was,' says another authority, 'probably the most remarkable woman that Europe has produced.'[1] Her idolatrous filial affection, culminating in the elegiac pathos, the almost lyrical enthusiasm, of her biographical introduction to the 'Manuscrits' of Necker, is as unique in literature as the maternal passion which is immortalised in the Sévigné Letters. Her conversational powers have probably never been surpassed, and she was the Queen of the Parisian 'Salon' of her age. Her activity in the politics,

[1] Galiffe's *Notices Généalogiques*, tome ii. (4 vols.). Geneva, 1829–1857.

and in some of the most perilous scenes, of the French Revolution, invests her character with romantic heroism, and connects her name with the greatest epoch of modern European history. The travels of her long exile rendered her cosmopolitan in the literary and social life of Europe, and the study of her life must be a study of the politics, the literature and society of her times.

Anne Louise Germaine Necker, Baronne de Staël Holstein, was born at Paris on the 22nd of April, 1766.[2] Her father, James Necker, was a native of Geneva, and was educated according to the strict regimen established there by Calvin. His own father, Charles Frederick Necker, was a native of Prussia, but early became a citizen of Geneva, and distinguished himself as Professor of Law in the city 'Academy' or University, and as author of several elaborate publications. Another son, Louis Necker, became Professor of Mathematics in the same institution, was later a banker at Paris and Marseilles, but finally returned to his native city, and devoted the remainder of his life to physical and mathematical studies; he also

---

[2] There are two records of her baptism in the city archives: in one of them her parents bear the title 'noble.' Jahl's *Dict. Crit. et Biog.* Paris, 1872. The 'de' (d'Albert) belonged to the old French Huguenot family of Madame Necker's mother. It belonged also to the wife of Samuel Necker (advocate, of Custrin) Marguerite Saphrasine de Labahache de Stettin—the parents of the grandfather of Madame de Staël, Charles Frederick. Galiffe's *Notices Généalogiques*, tome ii.

attained some rank as an author. A son of this brother (James Necker) was sometime Professor of Botany in the Academy, and a city magistrate, but is better known as the husband of the accomplished daughter of the 'physicist' De Saussure (Madame Necker de Saussure), the authoress of an able work on Education, which was 'crowned' by the French Academy, and one of the dearest friends and best biographers of her cousin, Madame de Staël. She will also be one of the most interesting characters of our narrative.

Charles Frederick Necker founded, then, the Genevan family with good Teutonic blood,[3] and the best education of the times, invigorated rather than impaired by the more than Lacedemonian rigour of the contemporary Genevan life—a rigour which survived, with but slight relaxation, the first, if not the second quarter of the eighteenth century. The Neckers were nearly all eminent for their intellectual culture, their moral character, and their success in life. James, the father of Madame de Staël, gave historical distinction to the family—a distinction immeasurably enhanced by the genius of his only child. Though his domestic and academic training had predisposed him to literary and philosophic studies—including theology, the dominant intellectual tendency of his native city—his parents early destined him to

---

[3] The family has been traced to Ireland, where it had, however, an Anglo-Saxon origin.

mercantile life, and sent him, when about fifteen years old, to Paris, where he passed his noviciate in the banking-house of Vernet, a member of the distinguished Genevese family of that name, with whom the Neckers maintained intimate relations. It is said that 'the clerk soon became master,' by his brilliant superiority in all the problems of the business. A fortunate altercation with the chief of the house led to his crowning success. Vernet lived in the country, and appeared in the bank only at certain hours. A letter arrived from Holland in his absence, proposing a negotiation which was quite foreign to the usual transactions of the firm. The chief clerk revealed it to Necker, who forthwith wrote out its details, and calculated its probabilities, with elaborate fulness. Vernet, on arriving, was astonished and indignant at the presumption of the young subordinate, who thrust under his eyes voluminous documents sketching an immense scheme of business, as if he were master of the establishment. High words passed between them. Necker, affirming that, as nothing had been consummated, there could be no consequence to justify the severity of Vernet, suddenly threw his documents into the fire and retired. Vernet saw, after brief reflection, that the youth had mastered the whole subject with astonishing ability, and immediately promoted him to the head clerkship. Necker acquired, in three months, a knowledge of the Dutch language in order to be able to deal with the capitalists of Holland, and, when Vernet closed his successful business, he put at his command sufficient funds to enable him to join the Thellusons, as partner, in founding the most celebrated French banking-house of the times.

He devoted twenty years to the making of his fortune, and then gave his attention to more general and public interests. A syndic of the old East India Company, he so conducted its affairs as to attain an unrivalled fame for financial skill, and a large increase of his own wealth, which was further augmented by extensive negotiations in the corn market. The republic of Geneva was proud of the ability and integrity of her son, and appointed him her resident minister at the Court of Versailles, where his talents were highly appreciated, especially by the Duc de Choiseul. He had not only become one of the ablest financiers of the age, but had cultivated literature. The collected works of his pen fill fifteen volumes, and are characterised by profound reflection and a vigorous though somewhat peculiar style. His first publications were 'Mémoires' relating to the affairs of the Indian Company. His 'Eloge de Colbert' commanded much attention, and was crowned by the French Academy. His treatise 'Sur la Législation et le Commerce des Grains' produced a remarkable impression, and led, at last, to his elevation to the royal cabinet. His 'Compte Rendu au Roi' threw all France into agitation, and effectively helped to bring on the Revolution. His 'Administration des Finances' excited a still greater sensation. His 'Importance des Opinions Religieuses' was an able though cautious attempt to check the anti-Christian tendencies of his age, and an admirable expression of his own deeply religious character. If somewhat defective in its theology, it is nevertheless pure and sublime in its ethics. Buffon sent, from his death-bed, his emphatic thanks to the author. It was the last book read by the naturalist, and his letter was the last that he ever wrote or dictated. 'The book of Necker,' says Sainte-Beuve, 'had the honour to draw from this great mind the last words in which he recognised the Supreme Being and immortality.'[4] The fragments of his 'Manuscrits,' published by his daughter, show much insight and subtlety in his judgment of character, and prove, says his ablest critic, that 'Necker, as a moralist, was a writer very acute, very piquant, and too much forgotten.'[5] He had evidently been a student, though he was no imitator, of Rochefoucauld and Vauvenargues. His little essay on 'Le Bonheur des Sots' is not unworthy of La Bruyère; it amused his generation, and showed that, beneath his habitual gravity, there was a living source of humour. His 'Cours de Morale Religieuse' is another proof of his profound interest in religion,

---

[1] Sainte-Beuve, *Causeries*, tome vii. (14 vols.). Paris, 1862.
[5] *Ibid.*

at a time when it seemed to be losing entirely its hold on the mind of Europe. Necker's best religious writings preceded those of the author of the 'Génie du Christianisme,' and he ranks by the side of Chateaubriand in the reaction in favour of Christianity which followed the disastrous scepticism of the Revolution. Sainte-Beuve admits that his religious works are characterised by 'a perfect sincerity, an unction, a sensibility profound and persuasive, which pervade his style and which often replace metaphysics by touching moral sentiment.'[6]

When Necker's superior qualities, especially his financial ability and integrity, led to his call to the government of Louis XVI., it was hoped he might rescue the sinking State from the overwhelming financial difficulties which, at last, wrecked it in the Revolution, and from which no power on earth could save it. His policy of retrenchment and rigid integrity, as well as his Protestantism, arrayed against him hosts of courtly and official enemies. He was, as we shall hereafter see, repeatedly displaced and recalled, amidst the enthusiastic sympathies of the people, who, on his dismissal, closed the theatres, and bore his bust, draped in black, through the streets; and, on his

[6] For a detailed account of his writings, and also those of Madame Necker, see Sayou's *Le Dix-huitième Siècle à l'Etranger*; *Histoire de la Littérature Française dans les divers Pays de l'Europe*, tome ii. livre xiv. chap. iv. Paris, 1861. This author gives some interesting facts respecting Madame Necker in chaps. xiii.–xv. of livre xii. (vol. ii.).

return, drew his carriage in triumph and made all Paris jubilant.

His characteristic excellences were not unmarred by characteristic faults. He was ambitious of popularity, and too self-conscious, especially of his abilities and merits. His sentimentality, a virtue in his writings and conversation, was a fault in his politics. His style was too complicated, too abstract, too oracular. He has been called the father of the *doctrinaire* school of politics,[7] of which Royer Collard, Guizot, and the Duc de Broglie, have been the most distinguished representatives in our century—a school which proposed to 'impress a new direction on France, to reform her impetuous temperament, and to give constitutional equilibrium to her political life.' This school bore, more or less, the impress of both his Anglican political ideas and of his literary style.

In person Necker was as remarkable as in character. 'His features,' says his wife, in a literary 'Portrait,' 'resemble those of no one else; the form of his face is extraordinary. A high retreating forehead, a chin of unusual length; vivid brown eyes, full of tenderness, sometimes of melancholy, and arched by elevated brows, gave him an expression quite original.' His statue at Coppet, somewhat theatrical in its attitude, expresses grace and grandeur of both soul and person.

Such was the father of Madame de Staël. His

[7] Rey's *Genève et les Rives du Leman*, chap. ix.

style of both thought and language, relieved of its peculiar defects, and endued with richer vigour and elegance, reappear in her own writings. Her intellectual legitimacy is indisputable.

Her mother was hardly less remarkable than her father, for qualities rare among her sex in that day. Susanna Curchod was the daughter of a humble Swiss pastor of Crassier, a hamlet of the Jura mountains.[8] Hardly could a retreat be found better fitted, by its tranquillity, its scenery, or its unsophisticated society, for the training of a precocious child; and it was said that her father bestowed upon her as complete an education as fell to the lot of any woman in Europe. She was taught thoroughly the classic and modern languages, and became a proficient in most of the learning usually pursued by men destined to the career of science or letters. Her daughter tells us that during all her lifetime it was her delight to hear the ancient poets read in the original. Gibbon, the historian, says that her occasional visits, in her youth, to Lausanne, where he then resided, led to such reports of her beauty and intellect as befitted only a 'prodigy,' and awakened his curiosity to see her.[9] She was a favourite among the highest neighbouring families; a local

---

[8] Vuillemin's *Le Canton de Vaud.* Lausanne, 1862.

[9] Gibbon's *Memoirs of my Life and Writings.* See also the *Salon de Madame Necker, après des documents tirés des archives de Coppet,* etc., par M. Othenin d'Haussonville, in *Revue des Deux Mondes,* 1880.

writer records that the beautiful and *spirituelle* girl was often seen riding a mule along the roads, from château to château, to give lessons, and her charms and talents excited enthusiasm in the cultivated circles of Lausanne.[1]

With the characteristic good sense and economical forethought of the Swiss, her father knew that she could have no better provision for the future than a well furnished and well disciplined mind. Gibbon says that she was accomplished in manners as well, and that her wit and personal attractions were the theme of universal interest. She was not without worthy suitors; but her father chose meanwhile to secure her independence by qualifying her for the office of teacher or governess, assured that if she should never need to use her qualifications in this laborious service, they would not the less fit her for her own household, however opulent it might be. In preparing her to be a teacher, he prepared her to preside in the highest circles of Parisian life; to command the admiring homage of the Parisian men of letters; to stand, superior in intellect, as in character, among the courtly women of Versailles; and, above all, to give to France, in the person of her own thoroughly educated child, the most accomplished female intellect of her age.

Gibbon's story of his love for her, and its disappointment, is well known; but it is worth

---

[1] Rey's *Genève*, &c. xiii.

repeating, as not only characteristic of himself, but of Mademoiselle Curchod. 'I need not blush,' he says, 'at recollecting the object of my choice; and though my love was disappointed of success, I am rather proud that I was once capable of feeling such a pure and exalted sentiment. The personal attractions of Mademoiselle Curchod were embellished by the virtues and talents of her mind. Her fortunes were humble, but her family was respectable. Her mother, a native of France, had preferred her religion to her country. The profession of her father did not extinguish the moderation and philosophy of his temper, and he lived content with a small salary and laborious duty, in the obscure lot of minister of Crassier, in the mountains that separate the Pays de Vaud from the country of Burgundy. In the solitude of a sequestered village he bestowed a liberal and even learned education on his only daughter. She surpassed his hopes by her proficiency in the sciences and languages; and in her short visits to some of her relations at Lausanne, the wit, the beauty, and the erudition of Mademoiselle Curchod were the theme of universal applause. The report of such a prodigy awakened my curiosity. I saw, and I loved. I found her learned without pedantry, lively in conversation, pure in sentiment, and elegant in manners; and the first sudden emotion was fortified by the habits and knowledge of a more familiar acquaintance. She permitted me to make her two or three visits at her father's house. I passed some happy days there, in the mountains of Burgundy, and her parents honourably encouraged the connection. In a calm retirement, the gay vanity of youth no longer fluttering in her bosom, she listened to the voice of truth and passion, and I might presume to hope that I had made some impression on a virtuous heart. At Crassier and Lausanne I indulged my dream of felicity; but on my return to England, I soon discovered that my father would not hear of this strange alliance, and that, without his consent, I was myself destitute and helpless. After a painful struggle I yielded to my fate; I sighed as a lover, I obeyed as a son; my wound was insensibly healed by time, absence, and the habits of a new life. My cure was accelerated by a faithful report of the tranquillity and cheerfulness of the lady herself; and my love subsided in friendship and esteem. The minister of Crassier soon afterwards died; his stipend died with him; his daughter retired to Geneva, where, by teaching young ladies, she earned a hard subsistence for herself and her mother; but in her lowest distress she maintained a spotless reputation and a dignified behaviour.[2] A

---

[2] She had previously maintained herself and her mother by teaching schools in Lausanne and Neuchâtel; it is doubtful that she taught in Geneva, though she was there in the family of her friend Moultou some time before she went to Paris. See *Lettres diverses recueillies en Suisse*, par le Comte Golowkin. Paris, 1821. This writer gives some forty letters from her pen.

rich banker of Paris, a citizen of Geneva, had the good fortune to discover and possess this inestimable treasure; and in the capital of wealth and luxury she resisted the temptations of wealth as she had sustained the hardships of indigence. The genius of her husband has exalted him to the most conspicuous station in Europe. In every change of prosperity and disgrace he has reclined on the bosom of a faithful friend, and Mademoiselle Curchod is now the wife of Monsieur Necker, the Minister, and perhaps the legislator, of the French monarchy.'[3] Gibbon never married. He maintained throughout his life an intimate friendship, full of delicacy and esteem, for Madame Necker and her husband; he frequented their home in Paris, corresponded with them, and was proud of Madame Necker's appreciation of his great work.

Madame Necker de Saussure describes her as endowed with firmness of character, strength of intellect, and a remarkable capacity for labour; as not only educated to an extraordinary degree in both science and letters, but as especially having that 'spirit of method' which serves for the acquisition of all things.[4] With brilliant faculties and personal attractions she combined the highest moral qualities. Her religious principles were never shaken by the scepticism and licensed im-

---

[3] *Memoirs* &c.
[4] *Notice sur le Caractère et les Écrits de Madame de Staël*, vol. i. of her *Œuvres complètes* (17 vols.). Paris, 1820.

morality, which prevailed around her Parisian home. The lessons of the humble parsonage of Crassier remained ever vivid in her soul, sanctifying her life and consoling her death. Her essay entitled 'Réflexions sur le Divorce' is an example of luminous reasoning and original style. It is a plea for the sacredness of marriage, against the loose opinions regarding it which characterised the epoch of the Revolution. Its last chapter, on the mutual succours and consolations of the aged in married life, is pathetically eloquent. She wrote from her own experience, and, as she says, to lead others to desire and attain a happiness which she herself enjoyed. Her 'Mélanges'[5] are distinguished by good sense, acute and epigrammatic observations on almost every subject that she touches, and by a moral elevation quite in contrast with the tendencies of opinion around her. Necker said of her, that, 'to render her perfectly amiable, she only needed some fault to pardon in herself.' Her greatest fault was perhaps her moral rigour; the forbearance which she needed not herself, she was slow to accord to feebler characters. 'She could captivate,' says Madame Necker de Saussure, 'when she wished; she freely gave praise where it was merited; her blue eyes were soft and caressing, and her face had an expression of

---

[5] Miscellaneous Papers, published by Necker after her death: 3 vols. 8vo. in 1798; and 2 vols. 8vo. (*Nouveaux Mélanges*) in 1802. Geneva.

extreme purity, and of candour, which made, with her tall and rather rigid figure, a contrast sufficiently fascinating.'[6]

Such was the woman whom Necker chose for his wife, while flushed with his rising fortunes and fame, and when she was struggling, alone in the world, with poverty and labour. After the death of her mother, she continued to teach for her living; but her life of toil was consoled by the intimacy and admiration of many eminent characters, particularly by the dearest friendship of her youth, with Moultou, a clergyman of Geneva, whom even Voltaire could not fail to reverence, and of whom she wrote an enthusiastic eulogy or 'Portrait.'[7] The philosopher Bonstetten (the life-long friend of Madame de Staël, and an habitual guest at the 'little court' of Coppet) was one of her ardent admirers, and, in his old age, records the pleasant excursions which he made, on every Saturday, with her and Moultou, to Voltaire's neighbouring Château de Ferney.[8] The 'Patriarch of Ferney' could not but admire her intellectual accomplishments, notwithstanding their religious differences, and was her flattering correspondent through the remainder of his life. Voltaire's brave fights for toleration, extending through

---

[6] *Notice* &c.

[7] It is Moultou whom she describes in her 'Portrait of my Friend,' *Nouveaux Mélanges*, vol. ii.

[8] Bonstetten's *Souvenirs*. Paris, 1832.

many years, in the famous cases of the Protestant families of Calas and Sirven, and of the Protestant galley slaves, commanded for him the interest, if not the affection, of the Swiss and French Protestants generally, in spite of their profound repugnance to his anti-Christian writings. Moultou stood side by side with him, his most effective assistant, throughout those prolonged contests which moved all Europe; and Necker and his wife acknowledged the beneficent services of the 'Patriarch' through a life-long friendship.[9]

A lady of society and wealth, Madame de Vermenoux, travelling for health, took Mademoiselle Curchod to Paris to instruct her son in Latin. Necker had been paying his addresses to this fashionable widow; but she had deferred her answer to his proposal of marriage, hoping for a more aristocratic offer. While absent she wrote to him declining his proposal; but she now returned, with the young governess, intending to accept the wealthy banker, whose fortunes and reputation had considerably augmented during her travels. Necker, however, was so struck with the superior qualities of Mademoiselle Curchod, that he transferred to her his attentions and affections. They were married in 1764; he aged thirty-two, she twenty-five years. 'Their marriage,' says his biographer, 'caused

---

[9] The Pastor Gaberel shows that Moultou was worthy of the admiration of Mademoiselle Curchod. *Voltaire et les Génevois*, ix. Paris, 1857.

Madame de Vermenoux acute suffering, the traces of which were never entirely effaced from her heart, but her relations with them remained friendly.'[1] 'From her marriage to her death,' adds this authority, 'thirty years passed in a union the most virtuous and the most affectionate of which history, and, I will venture to say, fiction, can offer an instance.' 'From this moment,' remarks the Duchesse d'Abrantès, 'she became the guardian angel of Necker: her husband was proud of her, and he had reason to be.' 'He chose her,' says another authority, 'only for her virtues and her charms. He discovered in her an enthusiasm for success and distinction which gave, perhaps, the first impulse to the still higher career in which he was afterwards distinguished.'[2]

Notwithstanding Necker's rare financial genius, he had, as we have seen, aspirations above the

---

[1] Memoirs, by his grandson, Baron de Staël, tome i. of Necker's *Œuvres complètes* (15 vols. 8vo.), Paris, 1820-21. I prefer this authority to that of the Duchesse d'Abrantès, who (*Histoire des Salons de Paris*, page 58, tome i. Paris, 1837) represents Madame Vermenoux as promoting the marriage, and as even assisting the young couple with money to begin housekeeping. Necker had been two years a partner in the greatest banking-house of Paris, soon to be the greatest in Europe. It was in the year of his marriage that he revived the fortunes of the Company of the Indies. In a letter written by Mlle. Curchod, the day before her marriage, to Madame de Brenles, she says of Necker, 'His talents and prudence have procured for him more consideration than his fortune, though he has an income of 25,000 livres.' (Count Golowkin's *Lettres diverses recueillies en Suisse*, &c. Geneva, 1821.) Marmontel gives a very flattering account of Madame Vermenoux (*Mémoires*, livre x. *Œuvres Complètes*, 7 vols. Paris, 1820).

[2] *Biographie Universelle.*

pursuits of gain. These pursuits were indeed, at times, quite irksome to him. He early gave himself to literary composition, and his youthful essays (mostly poetic and dramatic) are said to have been marked by much vigour and spirit; but he had the good sense not to publish them. Detesting the monotony of the banking-house, he nevertheless devoted his chief energy to the completion of his fortune and his reputation as a financier, hoping that thereby he might at last find, opening before him, a career more befitting his better tastes. His accomplished wife shared his ambition, for she could appreciate his competence for its highest aims. Soon after their marriage she opened her house for the reception of the leaders of opinion and society in the capital, proud to have her husband known and tested among them. She became the presiding genius of one of the most influential *salons* at a period when the Parisian *salon* was still a centre of power, social, political, and literary—when Madame Geoffrin's circle shone as a constellation of the highest intellects of the metropolis; when the Marquise du Deffand was reigning, imperially, in her parties on the Rue Saint-Dominique; and Mademoiselle de Lespinasse had just revolted from the tyranny of the blind old marquise, and had set up her rival *salon*, under the auspices of D'Alembert, drawing with her, by the fascination of her versatile accomplishments and her Sapphic enthusiasm, the *savants* and *littérateurs* of the city. The company of Madame Necker's mansion soon included many of the most noted writers of the day—Buffon, Marmontel, Saint-Lambert, Thomas, Duclos, Diderot, La Harpe, D'Alembert, Grimm, Raynal, Delille, Morellet, Gibbon, Hume,[3] not to name a host of marshals, dukes, marquises, and counts. Madame du Deffand herself frequented the *salon* of her new rival, and has left many allusions to it in her letters to Walpole.[4] 'I supped yesterday,' she writes, 'at St. Ouen, with the Duchesse de Luxembourg, the Bishop of Mirepoix, &c. Necker has much intellect. He resembles you in some respects.' Again: 'He is a very upright man; has much mind, but is too metaphysical in his writings. In society he is natural and gay, has exceeding frankness, but says little, and is often absent-minded. I sup once a week at his country mansion at St. Ouen. His wife has intellect and merit. Her society is composed ordinarily of men of letters, who, as you know, do

---

[3] Hume is not usually named, in the enumeration of her guests, by French writers, but she often alludes to him in her correspondence. In a letter to Madame de Breules (1765) she says: 'As to Hume, imagine to yourself a very gallant giant, with eyes having the insight of the philosopher; with good features, though dull yet mild; tolerable conversational powers, but with an air of reserved thought as though not expressing all that he thinks, an air which does not belong to a frank character; and withal a *bonhomie*, in society, which astonishes and enchants, &c.' *Lettres diverses recueillies en Suisse*, &c., par le Comte Golowkin. Geneva, 1821.

[4] *Lettres de la Marquise du Deffand à Horace Walpole*, vols. iii. and iv. *passim* (6 vols.). Paris, 1812.

not like me; it is in spite of them that she has taken to me.'[5] Again: 'Both of them have intellect, particularly he; but he lacks one quality which renders talent most agreeable—a certain facility, which elicits thoughts from those with whom one converses; he does not aid in the development of one's own ideas; and one is more stupid with him than when alone or with others.' Still later: 'I supped yesterday with the Neckers. He is truly a good man. He has capacity without presumption, generosity without ostentation, prudence without dissimulation. It will be a good choice for the government to employ such a man, but his religion is an insurmountable obstacle.' Again: 'They are upright people; the husband has high intellect and truthfulness; the wife is rigid and frigid, but good.' The marquise was morally incapable of appreciating a character like that of Madame Necker, and seems to have become aware of the fact. She writes again: 'The wife has intellect, but is of a sphere too elevated for one to communicate with her. Her husband has more than she; the most perhaps of any man in our nation at the present time; but he has no pedantry nor self-sufficiency. One is embarrassed with him; but he has frankness, good-humour, and cordiality.' At another time she reports as present, 'all the ministers, secretaries of state, diplo-

---

[5] The aged and cynical Marquise had been a favourite of the Parisian *philosophes*; but Mlle. Lespinasse had drawn them away from her.

matists—entertained with music, *proverbes*,[6] all the pleasures combined. My opinion is that the government could not employ a more capable man than Necker, more firm, more clear-headed, more disinterested.' Still later, after his appointment to the finances, she alludes with prophetic sagacity to his persecution, and predicts that 'he will retire from office, that everything will then give way; the public credit will be ruined; all will fall into chaos, his enemies will be triumphant; they will fish in troubled waters; they will affirm that his system, his operations, were only chimerical visions. This is what I, and many others, foresee. A greater misfortune cannot befall this country.' We find in these voluminous letters no allusions to the precocious child of the family, though some of them were written after she had been admitted to the company of the *salon*, and had attracted the attention of the guests. These intimations, respecting her parents, are, however, of some value; they afford us glimpses of their characters by one of the shrewdest observers. Madame du Deffand, nevertheless, exaggerated the defects of Madame Necker. The higher intellectual culture and moral purity of the latter were a tacit rebuke of the character and frivolous life of the marquise—a character and life which she herself continually acknowledges, in these famous letters, to be without self-respect, and almost insupportably miserable. Her impartial

[6] Brief dramas for domestic theatricals.

judgments were always acute, but her prejudices were extreme, and rendered many of her estimates of character mere caricatures.[7]

Marmontel, who was the earliest literary guest of the house, excepting Thomas, fondly admired the genius of the daughter, and shared the prejudices of Madame du Deffand against the mother. Their loose philosophy could not brook her religious pertinacity. Nor did Marmontel regard more cordially Necker himself, though he admits repeatedly his ability and his perfect moral integrity. For years he ate heartily the suppers of the great financier, but left for publication, when the latter was in his grave, disparaging allusions to him. 'Necker,' he writes, 'was not my friend, and I was not his.' He was compelled to esteem, but could not admire, Madame Necker, though he acknowledges her to have been, at his first introduction to her, 'young, sufficiently beautiful, and of a dazzling freshness,' possessing the 'charms of modesty, candour, goodness,' of 'culture and an excellent natural disposition;' 'sentiment in her was perfect' —certainly a rare example of accomplished womanhood. All these admissions, however, are but conciliatory preliminaries to a series of detractions —exaggerations of undeniable but minor defects, which deserved kindlier treatment after so many

---

[7] Her opinions of Turgot and not a few others, and some of her 'Portraits' (notably of Madame du Châtelet, Voltaire's 'divine Emilie) are examples.

years of hospitality and, as he affirms, of affectionate partiality. She had ' none of the *agréments* of a young French woman ; ' 'she had no taste in dress,' no 'ease in her bearing,' no 'attraction of manners.' Buffon and Thomas were, in his estimation, authorities too absolute, with her, in literary matters : ' lacking accuracy of thought and style, one would have supposed that she reserved correctness for the rule of her duties ; there all was precise and severely compassed.' He even complains that ' it was not for us·guests, nor for herself, that she gave us the entertainments of her *salon*, but for her husband ' —for the relief of a faithful public servant upon whom leaned a falling State ! Marmontel had been too much addicted to the frivolous and libertine world of Paris to appreciate such conjugal sympathy. Her *morale* was incomprehensible to him. Though she lavished special attentions upon him, ' our minds and tastes,' he admits, ' were not in harmony. I attempted to oppose her high conceptions ; it was necessary that she should descend from her inaccessible heights to communicate with me.' It is not improbable that his admiration for ' la belle Vermenoux ' (as he calls her), whom the young wife had superseded in the affections of Necker, had something to do with these prejudices. The widow was a devoted friend of Marmontel, and especially of his wife. He portrays her with rapture. She was the ' image of Minerva, but her brilliant visage could readily assume that air of graciousness, serenity, and simple, decent gaiety, which renders wisdom amiable. She and my wife were in perfect harmony of mind, of taste, and of manners. With what pleasure did this woman, habitually solitary and self-collected, see us arrive at her country house at Sèvres! With what joy did her soul surrender itself to the tenderness and exhilarations of friendship at our little suppers in Paris!' Though Madame Vermenoux was a welcome guest at the table of Madame Necker, Marmontel's partiality for the former could hardly admit of impartiality for the latter.

The *mémoires* of the time abound in criticism on the Necker *salon*, as on the *salons* of the metropolis generally, biassed by the social and political partisanship of the day; but the most reliable authorities, while admitting the peculiarities of Madame Necker, show her to have been pre-eminent in character, talents, and social tact. The historian of the 'Salons of Paris' represents her as 'an angel of virtue amidst that Court of Versailles, the noise of which only could reach her;' as ' naturally *spirituelle*, and perfectly instructed;' as having 'a sustained vivacity of mind, an unfailing sweetness.' The *salons* of Paris 'were then true schools, whose discussions were without scholastic pedantry, and Madame Necker and Madame Roland were the two chiefs in these arenas, where intellect appeared in all its forms: Madame Necker for the defence of religious ideas,

Madame Roland for that of liberal opinions, which at this period had already caused a general movement. Both gave a new impulse to the times.' 'Contrary to what has been said of the stiffness of Madame Necker, she did the honours of her *salon* charmingly. It is false that she was affectedly lofty in her conversation. In short, one found oneself more at ease with her than, later, with Madame de Staël, notwithstanding the brilliant genius and wonderful readiness of the latter.' 'She had an exquisite politeness in conversation.'[8]

In a hoary tower of the château at Coppet is a room protected by an iron barred door, in which the old archives of the family are deposited. Among a mass of other documents are twenty-seven volumes of letters, mostly from distinguished *habitués* of Madame Necker's *salon*—from Buffon, Grimm, Gibbon, Marmontel, D'Alembert, Diderot, the Abbés Morellet and Galiani, and Mesdames du Deffand, Geoffrin, d'Houdetot, &c. Marmontel's letters, there, belie his Memoirs. He speaks of her conversation as ' one of the greatest charms of my life.' When she was travelling for health he wrote, ' I cannot be gay till I learn that you improve; then I shall be foolishly so. In order to be gay I must be happy, and this I cannot be while anything remains for me to desire for you.' Diderot, whose writings were so brilliant and so corrupt,

---

[8] Duchesse d'Abrantès' *Histoire des Salons de Paris* &c. tome i. (6 vols). Paris, 1837.

wrote to her: 'How many things you will find in them which would never have been written, nor imagined, if I had had the honour of knowing you earlier.'—'You certainly would have inspired me with a taste for purity and delicacy which would have passed from my soul into my works.' He wrote of her as 'a woman who possesses all the purity of an angelic soul joined to refinement of taste.' The brilliant Abbé Galiani, one of the gayest of her guests, wrote frequent and long letters to her from Italy. 'The Alps,' he said, 'separate us; but neither time nor Alps can efface the memory of the delicious days I have passed with you.' In short, the most polished men of these corrupt times, while wondering at her 'rigorous regard for decency,' as said the Abbé Morellet, admired her character and her talents.[9]

Never, since the *salon* became a social institution (if we may so call it) of France, never since the days of the Hôtel de Rambouillet, were these reunions greater centres of power than now, when vague presentiments of the Revolution were stirring all minds. Their influence was rapidly communicated to the entire nation. In those of Madame Geoffrin, of Madame du Deffand, of Mademoiselle Lespinasse, of the Duchesse de Choiseul, and particularly of the Duchesse de Luxembourg, the elegant world of the Court found itself on a footing of equality with the men of letters who

[9] *Revue des Deux Mondes*, 1880.

then dominated in French society. It was from the *salons* of Paris that, later, the speeches of the Constituent Assembly went to the tribune; in these reunions were sketched the attacks and replies of the great adversaries who combated in that memorable arena.[1] Madame Necker's continued in full power till within a few months of the opening of Madame Roland's: the former was a centre of what might be called the progressive-conservative opinions of the day; the latter of the more advanced liberalism. The simultaneous appearance of these two most admirable women of the Revolutionary epoch was one of its many anomalies. With marked contrasts, they had many traits in common. They were both highly educated, and, judging from their writings, of nearly equal intellect. They were both exceptionally pure, among their class, in their domestic life; both profoundly patriotic, both womanly in heart and manly in mind. The one was devotedly and intelligently Christian, and died, as we shall hereafter see, tranquilly amidst the dearest sympathies of her family, and with the highest consolations of her religion; the other rejected Christianity for the 'philosophy' of the age, and died with Spartan heroism on the scaffold. Their correspondences

[1] *Histoire des Salons de Paris* &c., Introd. More than half the first volume of this work is devoted to the *salon* of Madame Necker. Its characters are real, but its scenes are fictitious. The Introduction (more than eighty pages) is historical, and mostly relates to the Neckers.

and contrarieties of character may well suggest the necessity of a generous judgment of human nature.

It was in such times, amidst the intellectual provocations, and moral perils, of the *salon* life of Paris, and the alarming presages of the Revolution, that Madame de Staël spent her girlhood and received her education. 'She was,' as Sainte-Beuve says, ' a daughter of the Revolution.' It made her heroic in character, and left her liberal in her political opinions, and unchanged in her moral convictions.

CHAPTER II.

CHILDHOOD AND EDUCATION.

Madame Necker's System of Education—Rousseau's Theory—Anecdotes of the Childhood of Mademoiselle Necker—Bonstetten—Raynal—Mademoiselle Necker in the Salon—Her first Literary Compositions—Grimm's Account of one—Morbid Effect of her Precocity—Necker's Resignation of Office—Tronchin's Prescription for his Daughter—Her Emancipation—Love for her Father—Her Mother—Madame de Genlis.

MADAME NECKER early perceived the extraordinary mental capacity of her child, but could not so readily appreciate those susceptibilities of genius—the deep and varied and sometimes anomalous sensibilities—which distinguished her from other children. She set herself to work, not merely to subdue, but to extinguish them, as dangerous indications, though they were but the overflowings of that imaginative and moral vitality which afterwards matured into the richest qualities of her transcendent womanhood and talents.

The mother, trained to be an instructor, had her own theory of education, and it was the worst possible one for her peculiarly gifted daughter—who was, in fact, a beautiful but incomprehensible marvel to her. Madame Necker's religious nature had led her to repel Rousseau's educational system, which was founded on an abuse of Locke's philosophy, then common among French thinkers; and which taught that, as our ideas, in their primary forms, are all received through the senses, the first task of the educator should be the training of the faculties of perception and observation, if we would procure an intellectual and moral development, not irregular, unhealthy, and illusory. To Madame Necker, Rousseau's theory was materialistic: 'she took therefore,' says Madame Necker de Saussure (herself one of the best authorities on education), 'the contrary route, and wished to act immediately on the mind by the mind; she believed it necessary to fill the young head with a great quantity of ideas, persuaded that the intellect becomes indolent without this labour of the memory.'[1] It was the 'cramming system'—not the education (educing) of the faculties; and if, as Madame Necker de

[1] *Notice*, on the character and writings of Madame de Staël (*Œuvres complètes*, tome i.), a work to which we are indebted for most of our data respecting the early life of her cousin. George Ticknor, the American scholar, says (under date of Geneva, Sept. 19, 1817), 'I passed a couple of hours with Madame Necker de Saussure, a cousin of Madame de Staël, who is considered in Geneva but little her inferior in original power of mind, and of whom Madame de Staël said, "My cousin has all the talents that I am supposed to have, and all the virtues that I have not." She is about fifty, and resembles Madame de Staël a little, and is interesting in conversation from a certain dignity and force in her remarks. She has published a work, in three volumes, *On Progressive Education* &c., which, for wisdom, delicacy of discernment, and acute observation, is superior to any study of the subject of the time.' Ticknor's *Life* &c., i. 7 (2 vols.). Boston, 1876.

Saussure thinks, it did not actually injure the child, 'relatively to the development of thought,' she was saved only by the uncontrollable vigour and self-assertion of her genius. The same authority assures us that, notwithstanding the rare excellences of Madame Necker, 'the charms of childhood had little power over her; she had subdued and disciplined her own nature too much to have preserved the freshness of her instincts. She could only love what she could admire; and a tenderness founded in presentiment and imagination was somewhat foreign to her mind. Gratitude was to her the first of ties; she had, in consequence, cherished her father; and this exalted filial love, which appears like a distinctive characteristic of the family, had always been active in her. God, her parents and her husband, whom she adored also as her benefactor, had been the only objects of her ardent affections. Nevertheless she undertook the education of her daughter with a fervent zeal inspired by the sense of duty.' But the 'sense of duty,' however noble in the less intimate relations of life, becomes almost ignoble when, in the relations of a mother to her child, it takes the place of maternal instinct.

Madame Necker's rigour oppressed her daughter. Her daily, her hourly life was under rule, her sports were restrained, her attitudes regulated, her studies severely mechanical. But her ardent nature was ever spontaneously breaking away from this bondage, so foreign to its instincts. She was full of gaiety, of *abandon*, of frankness, of affectionate impulses, of the love of dramatic effects—not to say dramatic tricks. Marmontel says that 'she was at times an amiable little mischief-maker.' Bonstetten, in later years her admiring correspondent, says that, as he was walking alone in Necker's garden, he was rudely struck from behind a tree with a switch; turning to resent the blow, he saw the child, then five or six years old, gleefully wielding the stick. 'Mamma,' she exclaimed, 'wishes me to learn to use my left hand, and you see I am trying to do so.'[2] 'She stood in great awe of her mother,' writes Simond, the traveller, who knew her from her infancy, 'but was exceedingly familiar with and extravagantly fond of her father. Madame Necker had no sooner left the room, one day, after dinner, than the young girl, till then timidly decorous, suddenly seized her napkin, and threw it across the table at the head of her father, and then, flying round to him, hung upon his neck, suffocating all his reproofs by her kisses.' This was nature, rude yet rudely beautiful. Bonstetten tells the story with some variations. According to him, she fairly drew Necker into a dance around the table, and was arrested only by sounds of the returning steps of her mother, when they

---

[2] Simond's *Voyage en Suisse*. Paris, 1822.

resumed their seats at the board with the utmost sobriety.³

Never has paternal or filial love been stronger, down even to the grave, than between Necker and his daughter. The caresses of the father encouraged the child to act, and especially to speak, with a freedom quite contrary to the severe notions of the mother; and, says Madame Necker de Saussure, 'the applause which the sallies of her humour called forth inspired her continually to indulge it in new ways, and already she responded to the pleasantries of Necker with the mingled gaiety and affection which characterised all her later relations with him. The desire to give pleasure to her parents was an extremely active motive of her affectionate nature. For example, at the age of ten years, observing their great admiration for Gibbon, she imagined it to be her duty to marry him, in order that they might enjoy constantly his conversation.' She made seriously the proposition to her mother, in spite of the grotesque corpulence of the historian, the 'ugliest man of the United Kingdom.'⁴ Notwithstanding these childish sim-

---

³ *Charles-Victor de Bonstetten: Etude Biographique et Littéraire*, par A. Steinlen. Lausanne, 1860.

⁴ Gibbon was hardly five feet in height, but in revenge of his short stature nature gave him an almost spherical shape; he could not have been less than ten feet in girth, as M. de Bièvre remarked. 'When I need exercise,' said De Bièvre, 'I make three times the tour of M. Gibbon.' His physique was a burlesque on humanity. While in Lausanne he became amorous of Madame de Crauzas, afterwards Madame de Montolieu, and declared his love. His figure, kneeling

plicities, Madame Necker de Saussure says she 'has seemed always young, yet never a child. In all that has been recounted to me about her early life, I remember but one trait which bears the character of childhood, and even this showed the dawn of intellect. She amused herself by making paper kings and queens, and setting them to act scenes of an improvised tragedy. When this entertainment was prohibited by her scrupulous mother, she would conceal herself in order to enjoy it. To this early amusement was attributed the only singular habit she ever had, that of twisting a bit of paper, or a leaf, between her fingers.'

In her tenth year she was exceedingly attractive. Her natural gaiety was extreme, though at times touched by that poetic melancholy which ever after tinged her soul. Her manners, especially when relieved of the restraints of her mother's presence, were the simple outbursts of her natural sensibilities and frankness. She was fascinating to many of the thinkers who frequented her mother's

---

before her, was so ludicrously grotesque, that she could not repress her smiles. At last she exclaimed, 'Do, Monsieur, do rise, and say no more.' 'Alas! Madame,' he replied, 'I cannot.' 'What!' she rejoined, 'can you not get up?' In fine, he was so enormous that, even with the aid of Madame de Crauzas, he could not rise; she had to call a *valet de chambre* to replace him on his legs. Duchesse d'Abrantès' *Hist. des Salons de Paris*, tome ii. Paris, 1837. The English *philosophes* generally made awkward figures in the French society of these times. Hume's grim pleasantries are well known. Gibbon's stateliness was anything but French. Franklin's unaffected simplicity, nevertheless, made him a favourite in the most fashionable circles, except in his occasional taciturn moods.

salon, and could foresee the luxuriant genius and beauty with which her nature was already unfolding. The Abbé Raynal, the 'Historian of the Indies,' holding her little hand in both of his, would prolong her conversation with wondering interest. Her impromptu remarks already flashed with somewhat of the light with which her conversation, in later years, illuminated the best circles of Paris, Coppet, Weimar, Berlin, Vienna, St. Petersburg and London. She was a brunette, her countenance shone with animation, and her 'great black eyes were dazzling with intelligence and kindliness.'

Her parents were fortunate in procuring for her a household companion in Mademoiselle Huber (of the distinguished Genevese family of that name), afterwards Madame Rilliet-Huber, who now became, and ever remained, one of her dearest friends.[5] Mademoiselle Huber has recorded her first interview with the brilliant young girl, the 'transports' with which she received her as her habitual associate, and the promises she made 'eternally to cherish her friendship.' 'She spoke

[5] George Ticknor says, under date of Geneva, Sept. 10, 1817: 'This evening I passed at Madame Rilliet's, to whom the Duchesse de Broglie gave me a letter. She was a particular friend of Madame de Staël's, and is a lady of large fortune, much talent, and elegant manners. Benjamin Constant said of her, with that kind of wit peculiar to the French, and which he possessed beyond any Frenchman I met in Paris, "Madame Rilliet has all the virtues which she affects," for there is a certain stateliness and pretension in her manners that remind you of affectation.'—*Life* &c. of Ticknor, i. 7.

to me with an ardour and fluency which made her already eloquent, and greatly struck me. We did not play as children; she immediately asked what were my lessons? If I knew any foreign languages? If I ever went to the theatre? When I replied that I had been there three or four times, she broke forth in exclamations of delight, and promised me that we should frequently go there together, adding that, on our return, it would be necessary to write out the subjects of the pieces, especially those parts which had most interested us; that this was her habit. "And then," she exclaimed, "we shall write every morning." We entered the *salon*; by the side of the arm-chair of Madame Necker was a little wooden seat, where she had to sit, obliged to hold herself erect, without support. Scarcely had she taken her place, when three or four venerable personages approached her, speaking to her with the kindliest interest. One of them, who wore a small round perruque, detained her in a long conversation, talking with her as to a person of twenty-five years. This was the Abbé Raynal; the others were, Marmontel, Thomas, the Marquis of Pesay, and Baron Grimm. We were called to the table; it was a wonder to see how she listened there. She spoke not a word, but seemed to share in all the discussions by the vivid and varying expression of her features. Her eyes followed the looks and movements of each speaker. You could see that she anticipated his ideas. All topics were familiar to her, even those of politics, which were already among the chief subjects of interest in the Parisian salons. After dinner many more guests arrived. Each, in approaching Madame Necker, had something to say to her daughter—a compliment or a pleasantry. She always responded, not only with ease, but with grace. Some would entertain themselves in trying to embarrass her, or to excite the young imagination which already displayed so much brilliancy. The men who were most distinguished by their talents were those who hovered most about her, prompting her conversation. They inquired about the books she was reading, reported new ones to her, and inspired her love of study by discussing with her what she knew and what she did not know.'

The severity of Madame Necker's domestic rule was by this time so far relaxed as to allow more indulgence to her child's dramatic tastes. Minor or 'domestic theatricals' were even admitted among the entertainments of her villa at St. Ouen, as we have seen in the citations from Madame du Deffand. Among her daughter's earliest literary essays were attempts at dramatic composition. She had shown extraordinary talent in the Portraits, Characters and Eloges, which were a sort of social literary recreation of the day. Grimm had sent examples to his princely correspondents, in various parts of Europe, as marvels of intellectual precocity. He now wrote them an account of a drama, produced in her twelfth year, and acted by her and her young companions in the drawing-room at St. Ouen. 'While Necker,' he says, ' covers himself with glory in the government, and renders himself eternally dear to France, and his wife devotes herself to her charitable hospital in the parish of St. Sulpice, their young daughter, who has evinced extraordinary talents, amuses herself by writing small comedies, after the manner of the semi-dramas of M. St. Marck. She has just completed one, in two acts, entitled " The Inconveniences of Life in Paris," which is superior to her models, and astonishing for her years. Its characters are well delineated, its scenes well adjusted, and the unfolding of its plot is natural and full of interest.' He adds that Marmontel, who was ever enthusiastic for the daughter, though he could never appreciate the mother, was affected even to tears on seeing this juvenile performance at St. Ouen.[6]

At fifteen years of age her faculties, if not her style, showed the maturity usual with cultivated minds at twenty-five. In 1781, when Necker's ' Compte Rendu ' first appeared, exciting all France,

---

[6] Grimm's *Correspondance*, 1778. Many allusions to the Necker family, and several letters from them, are scattered through this curious collection—a work almost as important for the history of France in the eighteenth century as the *Mémoires* of St. Simon are for the preceding age. Grimm and Diderot's *Correspondance* (15 vols.), Paris, 1829-31; and *Correspondance inédite* (8 vols.), Paris, 1829.

she, proud of his triumph in his defeat, wrote him an anonymous letter of such remarkable ability that he recognised its authorship by its talent. Her genius had already its stamp.[7] At this early age she had mastered some of the profoundest works of French literature, studying, not merely reading them. She had made ample extracts from Montesquieu's 'Spirit of Laws,' and had commented on them with her own acute reflections. Raynal, then rejoicing in the extraordinary but temporary fame of his 'Histoire Philosophique,' solicited her to contribute to one of his works an essay which she had written on the Revocation of the Edict of Nantes. Necker himself discouraged these premature efforts; but the training to which she had been addicted by the system of her mother, her elaborate though versatile studies, her participation in the discussions of the salon, and in the performances and criticism of the 'domestic theatricals,' could not fail to prompt her faculties beyond their normal and healthful growth. Everything about her ministered to her intellectual life. 'Her pleasures as well as her duties,' says Madame Necker de Saussure, 'were all exercises of her mind. Her mental faculties, naturally energetic, underwent thus a prodigious expansion.' The wonder is that they became not as prodigiously morbid. Nothing but her native vivacity—the national temperament which she so abundantly shared

[7] Philarète Chasles, *Nouvelle Biographie Générale*, tome xliv.

—could have saved her from the worst effects of such mental excesses. Thoroughly French as she was, in the flexibility and elasticity of her nature, her sensibilities nevertheless began to suffer by this unintermitted tension of her intellect, and we may trace to this period that poignant sensitiveness to the miseries of human life, that ever-recurring strain of sadness, which characterise nearly all her writings, and which, in spite of wealth, fame, talent, travel, 'troops of friends,' and a career splendidly successful in most respects, rendered her life a continuous scene of restlessness, if not of melancholy, and led her to say on her death-bed, that but one of the capabilities of her nature had been developed to its utmost, the capability of suffering.[8] Her cousin remarks that her sensibilities were, at this early period, as excessively developed as her mind, so that the praises which she heard given to her parents would melt her to tears. 'That which amused her,' says her companion, Mademoiselle Huber, 'was that which made her weep.' Her attachment to Mademoiselle Huber became a sort of passion. The presence of celebrated persons would make her heart palpitate. Her reading, which Madame Necker, more severe than vigilant, did not always prescribe, often produced on her extraordinary impressions; years later she said that Richardson's description of the carrying off of

---

[8] Chateaubriand's *Mémoires d'Outre-Tombe*, tome viii. (12 vols.). Paris, 1849.

Clarissa made an epoch in her young life. Her faculties, of mind as well as body, began to yield under this excessive stimulation. Long sustained attention was ever afterwards difficult to her; and the success with which she always seemed to master elaborate intellectual tasks was more the effect of genius than of continuous labour. 'A singular sagacity bore her to a distant end, without your seeing her on the route.'

Her father's relations with the Court, about this time, particularly the events which prompted her anonymous letter to him, exasperated the excitement which was preying upon her health. Her extreme filial sympathy made his anxieties her own; and now fell upon the family a greater affliction than any which had thus far marred its prosperity. Though Necker was not formally 'dismissed,' he was forced by his enemies to retire from office. During five years he had administered the finances with a success unapproached by his predecessors for years. It would be irrelevant to discuss here the principles of his policy, his disputes with the economists at a period when political economy was yet mostly undefined as a science; his altercations with Turgot, the ostensible representative of its principles in the government. Partisans have applauded or disparaged him, according to their partialities for antagonistic theories; but his administration was at a time, and amidst exigencies, which should, in our day at least, relieve him from such criticism. Necker was a practical man, and he attempted practically to grapple with the difficulties which had overwhelmed his predecessors. His great personal credit enabled him to command loans for the government which perhaps no other man in the realm could have obtained; and he retrenched expenses on every hand. More than six hundred unnecessary charges on the Treasury were cut off. The policy of loans—in our day the policy of States generally—is inherently fallacious, and can be safe only when based on economical retrenchments, and the prospective creation of new resources. Necker's scheme comprised these conditions. It was the only conceivable policy. That it failed is attributable, not so much to his lack of talent, as to the invincible vices of the government and of the times. Other experiments were made, by the frequent change of the financial administration, but they were all failures, and worse than failures. He had to be called in repeatedly to relieve them. But his stringent reforms had raised up enemies all around him. His position in the court was hardly tolerable; he had but a qualified title as Minister, and was not admitted to the Royal Council, for his religion was in the way. He saw that he could not have the power necessary for his measures, unless he were relieved of these disabilities. Full powers were offered him if he would abjure his Protestant faith. He refused to do so. He retired from office with the maledictions of most of the nobility, but with the benedictions of the suffering people. He had effectively, though not permanently, relieved the national finances. He had incurred the hostility of his aristocratic enemies by cutting off sinecures and superfluous pensions, and by reducing excessive salaries. He had accepted no compensation for his services; had given no office to his kindred or personal friends.[9] He had advanced two millions of his own money, as a loan to the government, which was not repaid during his life, and was recovered by his daughter only after the downfall of Napoleon. His 'Compte Rendu au Roi' was his vindication. In that famous work he gave a complete account, to the King, of the financial disorders of the country. It was a bombshell thrown into the Court, and the explosion that followed resounded throughout the kingdom and over all Europe. No such report on the administration of the finances had ever been made. The country had been kept ignorant of this, one of its most vital interests. Its kings themselves had been habitually deceived regarding it. The nation had been reeling on the verge of hopeless bankruptcy; Necker alone had thus far prevented its precipitation into the abyss. The Revolution was inevitable, though few then perceived either its proximity or its terrible significance. His work on the 'Administration des Finances,' a sort of reproduction and justification

---

[9] Louis Blanc, *Hist. de la Révolution Française*, ii. 66 (12 vols.). Paris, 1847.

of the 'Compte Rendu,' deepened and widened immeasurably the impression of the latter. Eighty thousand copies were quickly sold, six thousand on the day of its publication, besides a simultaneous edition in England. The people were maddened by discovering how their debauched rulers had been for years wasting their resources. Necker showed that twenty-five millions of francs were yearly thrown away on useless or licentious gratifications and pensions; that the collectors received more than one-fifth of all the revenue; and that nearly all the national institutions of charity and penal reform were mismanaged—the prisons, hospitals, asylums. In many of these, six invalids slept in the same bed, and sometimes the slightly attacked patient found himself with a dying man on one side and a dead one on the other.[1] Necker proudly alluded to his wife's good work in hospital reform. She had not frequented the Court, though she received some of the courtly ladies at her *salon*; the depravity which still lingered from the Regency and from the reign of Louis XV. about the royal precincts was a sufficient reason to keep her away, though Louis XVI. had solicited her presence, and Necker had mentioned only her feeble health as the reason of her absence. She appeared now, like himself, as a true friend of the people amidst the immense crew of courtly and official depredators

[1] De Tocqueville's *Coup-d'œil sur le Règne de Louis XVI.* chap. ii. Paris, n. d.

on the public resources. They were outraged. What right had this untitled foreigner, this Protestant heretic, to invade their luxurious places, and abridge their revenues? What a national disgrace that this 'Swiss schoolmistress' (for so they called his wife) should be able to hold up her pedantic head, pre-eminent above the aristocratic, free-living ladies of the court, the daughters of the old noble families of France? Pampered, infatuated parasites of power, they knew not that they were refusing the only help which could mitigate their coming fate—a fate which was soon to sweep them from the face of their country and shake to its foundations the whole civil and ecclesiastical world of Europe.

Necker's daughter observed his anxious preoccupation, notwithstanding his seeming tranquillity. The evening before his resignation he accompanied her and her mother to the hospital of Madame Necker in the parish of St. Sulpice. 'He was in the habit of going to this asylum,' she writes, ' to take fresh courage against the cruel difficulties of his situation. The Sisters of Charity, who had charge of the place, loved him and Madame Necker, notwithstanding they were Protestants, and welcomed them now with flowers and the chanting of verses from the Psalms, the only poetry they knew. They called them their own benefactors, because they succoured the poor. My father this day was deeply affected, more so, I remember well, than ever he had appeared to be by similar testimonies of gratitude. Without doubt he regretted the power to serve France which he was about to lose. Alas! who at that time could have supposed that this man would one day be accused of hardness of heart, of pride, of arrogance? Never a soul more pure has traversed the region of storms; and his enemies, in calumniating him, committed an impiety; for the heart of a good man is the sanctuary of God in this world.'[2] The next day he returned from Versailles no longer Minister.

Necker retired to his country seat at St. Ouen with the sympathies and applause of the nation. Not a few of the higher classes, able to appreciate him—the Prince of Condé, the Dukes of Orleans and of Chartres, the Prince of Beauvais, the Duke of Luxembourg, the Archbishop of Paris, and, above all, the literary men of the Necker *salon*—hastened to visit and sustain him there.[3] Such moral support was grateful to his heart, but assuredly not more so than the sympathy of his

---

[2] *Considérations sur la Révolution Française*, i. 8: *Œuvres complètes*, tome iii. Paris, 1861.

[3] Marmontel was one of the most eager to proffer his doubtful sympathies. He hastened to St. Ouen before the family arrived; then hastened back, and meeting them on the road, mounted their carriage, and accompanied them to the house, not without something like relentings towards Madame Necker. 'I had always,' he says, ' for her the most sincere veneration, for I had seen in her only kindness and wisdom and virtue; and the particular affection with which she had honoured me well merited that I should share the sorrow which I doubted not deeply affected her.'—*Mémoires* &c.

devoted daughter, expressed in the anonymous
letter, the authorship of which he had identified by
indications the most consoling that could touch a
father's affections—its proofs of the superior intellect and overflowing heart of his child. Agita-
ting as these circumstances were to her sensitive
nature, she was cheered by the demonstrations
of almost universal regard for him which she
witnessed at St. Ouen. 'All France,' she writes,
'seemed anxious to visit him; the great nobles,
the clergy, the magistrates, the merchants, the men
of letters. He received upwards of five hundred
letters of sympathy from towns and provincial
corporations, expressing a respect and affection
surpassing any ever received before by any public
man of France.' 'There was,' says Grimm, 'for
some days a continual procession of carriages on
the two leagues of road from Paris to St. Ouen.
Never has a Minister borne in his retreat a purer
fame.' Meanwhile all Paris was struck by the
event. 'Consternation,' adds Grimm, 'was painted
on all faces. The promenades, the cafés, all public
places, were crowded, but everywhere an extraordinary silence reigned. The people gazed at one
another, and pressed one another's hands sadly as
in view of a coming public calamity.'[4] It was the
murmuring lull that precedes the tempest.

Before these exciting events the health of Mademoiselle Necker had seriously declined, and had

[4] *Correspondance* &c., 1781.

added much to her father's anxieties. Tronchin, of Geneva, an old friend of the Necker family, was the medical oracle of the day; his removal to Paris, as physician to the House of Orleans, produced a sensation in fashionable circles, among which *ennui* and the 'vapours' prevailed as epidemics, in spite, if not in consequence, of the frivolity and licence of the times; and his prescription of fresh air and early walks for the 'great dames' of the city had led to the adoption of a convenient walking dress which bore his name. Fortunately he was at hand to save the child of his old friend; and his authority was too great with Madame Necker, as with all her feminine associates, to be countervailed by her prejudices for her favourite theory of education. He prescribed no medicine for the young invalid; for he avoided drugs as much as possible in his practice; and it was a maxim with him that 'positive sins in medicine are mortal, while negative ones are venial.' He saw at a glance the fatal tendency of Madame Necker's system, in a case of such precocious development, such superabundant power and sensibility. He ordered its immediate and total suspension. All serious studies must be laid aside. The child must be allowed to grow, for some time at least, spontaneously, in mind as well as in body, in the open air, amidst the landscapes of St. Ouen. Never was prescription more acceptable to an invalid; her native vivacity burst into full liberty. The caged bird, let loose, took to wing through the surrounding groves and meadows. Accompanied by her young companion, Mademoiselle Huber, she exulted in her freedom, and roamed from morning till night. Madame Necker de Saussure (who, for many years, was more her sister than her cousin) believed that this rural freedom and gaiety had the happiest effect, not only on the health, but on the genius of the young girl.[5] It was a period of living, pastoral poetry in her life, hitherto cramped by mechanical habits of study and the social artificialities of Paris. It was precisely what such a mind needed. Her imagination, so splendid in its later disciplined power, and one of the richest charms of her works, now flowered healthfully amidst natural scenes. Her remarkable faculty of picturesque description was developed. Her sensibilities, tending to morbid sentimentalism, and never afterwards entirely exempt from a tinge of melancholy, were placed in better harmony with her vigorous powers of reflection and reason—a harmony by which was at last attained the chief distinction of her intellectual character, her almost anomalous union of sentiment and thought, of enthusiasm and reflection, of the heart of woman with the head of man. 'This liberty accorded to her mind,' says her cousin, 'enabled it to take its best flight. The two young girls, running at large in the woods of St. Ouen,

Notice &c.

clothed as nymphs or muses, declaimed verses, composed poems, made dramas of every sort, which they immediately represented.' The impression of such a happy season in early life never fades away; it lingers a 'thing of beauty,' an azure and radiant interval of sky, in the darkest storms of later life.

Her cousin tells us that the heart of the grateful girl turned now, in her emancipation, more than ever towards her father. She 'seized the least occasion of approaching him, and found extraordinary pleasure and advantage in his conversation. He was surprised, more and more each day, by her remarkable intellect, and never was that intellect more charming than when near him.' Her quick filial sympathy perceived his need of amusement and distraction in his trials and the literary labours he now began on his 'Administration of the Finances,' and his 'Importance of Religious Opinions.' She attempted to 'cheer him in a thousand ways; she would risk anything to obtain from him a smile.' She would beguile his occasional hours of leisure, at St. Ouen, by leading him to narrate to her his early life, especially the twenty years he spent in Paris, before his marriage, struggling with fortune. A quarter of a century later, when he was in his grave, she writes of the 'profound effect' on her young heart which this story, of labour and almost ascetic self-denial, produced; 'the story of that period,' she says, 'in which I could only imagine him as so young, so lovable, and so lonely,—that time in which, perhaps, our destinies would have united us for ever, if fate had only made us contemporaries.'[6] Strange fancy of filial love! Her affection for him became a passion, the strongest that ever swayed her heart; her reverence, a worship, an idolatry, which lasted through his life, and wept at his tomb till she herself was laid there by his side. Meanwhile Necker, gratefully admiring her mental superiority, did not endanger her by fond flatteries; 'his looks were more encouraging than his words.' 'He habitually corrected her faults by a gentle raillery which was not without its charm; no exaggeration, no inaptitude of any kind escaped his attention.' He knew the liabilities of such a luxuriant nature, and his very parental pride led him to prune it, and make the most of it. 'I owe,' she frequently said late in life, 'to the incredible penetration of my father the frankness of my character, and the naturalness of my mind. He unmasked all affectations, and I received from him the habit of believing that my heart was clearly seen.' One of the most charming qualities of her womanly character was derived from this treatment—perfect sincerity, a childlike frankness in conversation, and in all her conduct, which, as it left nothing disguised, allowed not only her faults, but all the riches of her heart and faculties to be seen and, therefore, appreciated.

[6] *Caractère de M. Necker et sa Vie privée: Œuvres complètes*, tome ii. Paris, 1861.

A singular effect, more curious, however, than serious, attended this extraordinary sympathy between the father and daughter. It led to something very like jealousy between the child and the mother. Necker must have been a man of surpassing fascination in domestic life; his wife and daughter seemed emulous of each other, not only in affection, but in a species of adoration for him. It may perhaps be soberly said that there is no record of intenser admiration and love, of woman for man, than Madame Necker has left in her 'Mélanges' and letters; no record of intenser love and reverence of a child for a father, than Madame de Staël has left in her 'Notice' prefixed to his 'Manuscrits.'[7] They became rivals in an affection so superabundant that it could not escape the infirmities of human nature. The mother seemed to fear that her child, inheriting her own remarkable faculties and deep sensibilities, might take her place in the heart of her husband; or, as Madame Necker de Saussure says, 'allow her to be loved by him only in her daughter.' The latter, after the death of both her parents, could not allude to this affectionate rivalry without commending and yet envying her mother. 'He chose,' she says, 'for his wife a woman of perfect virtue, and of extremely cultivated mind. From the

---

[7] Madame Necker's 'Portrait' of him, *Mélanges*, vol. ii.; and her posthumous letters to him, given in the Introduction to his *Œuvres*, p. 327; Madame de Staël's 'Notice,' introductory to his *Manuscrits*.

moment of their marriage to her death the thought of my mother dominated his life. He was not, like other men in power, attentive to her by occasional tokens of regard; but by continual expressions of most tender and most delicate sentiment. My mother, whose affections were passionate, would otherwise have been unhappy. God spared her the affliction of surviving him. Peace to her ashes —she deserved more than I to be happy.' Her own affection for him, like all love when it becomes passion, could never be contented. 'The difference of our ages,' she said, at his death, 'often troubled my happiness during the time I possessed him; and now, if he could be restored to me, I would give all my remaining years for six months;' and she broke out with passionate self-upbraidings, as if under remorse for not lavishing upon him more affectionate attentions.

Meanwhile she never forgot her filial duty to her mother. She admired her rare talents and pure character, notwithstanding the disparity of their tastes. In mature life she remarked to Madame Necker de Saussure, 'The longer I live, the more I understand my mother, and the more my heart feels the need of her.' This good authority assures us that 'the extreme sweetness of the character of Mademoiselle Necker was always manifest when her mother addressed to her any reproaches. Her respect for her was always profound and declared. Endowed from childhood with a rare power of apt and vivid repartee, she never said a word, even on the most trivial occasions, which could show her under an unfavourable aspect.'⁸

⁸ Still later she spurned with violent indignation the reflections of Madame de Genlis on Madame Necker. This lady, the authoress of the day, had been a guest of the Necker *salon*, but never a cordial one. (Duchesse d'Abrantès' *Histoire &c.*, tome i.) She afterwards found in Madame de Staël a literary rival whose transcendent success she could not pardon, but pursued her with bitter and harassing criticism, especially during her persecutions by Napoleon. Madame de Staël bore all patiently till the jealous critic attacked the memory of her mother, when, says her cousin, 'she showed the greatest irritation that I ever witnessed in her.' 'Does she imagine,' she exclaimed, 'that because I do not defend myself, I will not defend my mother? Let Madame de Genlis attack my works, and my character, as much as she pleases, but not my dead mother, my mother who has only me in the world to take her part. She preferred my father to me, and she had reason, without doubt; I feel the more that I have her blood in my veins, and so long as this blood runs in them, I will not allow her to be outraged.' She would have appealed to the public, had she not been convinced that any publication of the kind would have been obnoxious to the actual government of France, and would only increase its persecutions of her family and friends. Madame de Genlis' attack on Madame Necker was made in her *De l'Influence des Femmes sur la Littérature Française*, Paris, 1811. Neither Madame Necker, nor any of her friends, ever pretended that she belonged to the class of literary women; her little essay on *Divorce* was the only production of her pen published during her life; her *Mélanges* were but fragments published by her husband after her death. Yet of her volume of nearly four hundred pages, Madame de Genlis gives more than one eighth to Madame Necker, more than twice as many as she gives to Madame de la Fayette, five times as many as to Madame de Sévigné, six times as many as to Madame Dacier, sixteen times as many as to Madame Riccobini. She gives to her, in fine, more space than to any other character in the volume, excepting Madame de Maintenon. The book was apparently published by the malicious old countess for the purpose of disparaging Madame Necker, and afflicting her successful daughter. She caricatured the latter in her novel of *La Femme*

It was in such circumstances that the genius and character of the sensitive young girl were developed. Her education was entirely domestic, for she was never sent away to school; and these circumstances, so early and so stimulating, were among the strongest impulses of her life. They impressed her nature for ever.

Madame Necker felt no little chagrin at the defeat of her plan for the education of her daughter. In abandoning it now to the control of her husband, she abandoned nearly all hope of the future 'distinction' of the child. She could not, however, fail to be surprised at her continued and wonderful intellectual growth, and when, at last, she appeared in the literary world, prepared to claim a distinction unrivalled among her sex, the mother's pride could hardly console her for the failure of her original scheme. 'I remember,' writes Madame Necker de Saussure, 'that at the time when the *éclat* of Madame de Staël's fame was

---

Philosophe. She endeavoured, years later, according to Sainte-Beuve, to atone for her early malice by her *Athenaïs, ou le Château de Coppet en 1807*, a romance which is of no authority, either for events or characters. She long survived Madame de Staël, and in 1825 published her *Mémoires* of herself, in ten volumes, in which she again attacks her rival with senile and ridiculous jealousy. See particularly volumes iii. and iv. 'In this work, as in all her other publications, for twenty-five years, she followed only the impulses of her hatred. She seized this occasion to renew her attacks against Madame de Staël. Her judgments on authors and their works are all dictated by the disparaging spirit which always guided her pen.'— *Biographie Universelle*, tome xvi.

yet new to me, I expressed to Madame Necker my astonishment at her prodigious distinction. " It is nothing," she responded, " absolutely nothing, compared to what I would have made it !" This answer struck me very much, because it referred only to the qualities of her understanding, and expressed a sincere conviction.'

CHAPTER III.

YOUTH AND EARLY WRITINGS.

First Travels—Visit to Buffon—His Egotism—His Rule for Style—Fine Sayings of Madame Necker—Journey to Switzerland—Lake Leman—The South of France—Retirement at Marolles—Early Literary Compositions—Dramas—Fictions—Criticism.

It was in this period of the retirement of Necker that his daughter had her earliest experience in travel—afterwards so much the habit of her life. Her first journey was to Plombières (the waters of which had been prescribed for the health of her mother),[1] and it was particularly interesting to her, as it afforded a visit, at Montbard, to the old friend of the family, the naturalist Buffon, now a sage of seventy-five years, and of European renown not only as a 'scientist' but as a classic model of French literature. He had been a favourite authority in the Necker *salon* on questions of literary criticism as well as of science. His celebrated discourse, before the Academy, on 'Style,' had won for him this deference. Surrounded by his 'little court' of admirers and co-workers, he received his guests at Montbard with

[1] *Notice* by Baron de Staël: *Œuvres de Necker*, tome i.

ceremonious attentions, which could not fail to prove irksome to the young girl whom he had gaily flattered at her home in Paris, and whose late emancipation in the woods of St. Ouen had unfitted her for dignified restraints. Instead of rambles among his flowers and birds, she found three grand velvet-covered arm-chairs, elevated in his *salon*, for herself and her parents; another, less raised, for himself; and these circled by lower seats for his associates, who were silent listeners to his conversations and discussions with the late famous Minister and his accomplished wife and daughter. His guests were amused at the deferential etiquette of the well-meaning patriarch, and endured it patiently, 'rather than afflict an old man,' their ardent friend, by hastening on their way; for the simplicities of decaying but affectionate age, like those of childhood, have a charm of their own, and though we may regret them, it is usually with a smile. Meanwhile the aspiring girl could hardly fail to learn important precepts, for her own future use, in the conversation of the venerable author. His very egotism made it the more comprehensible and instructive to her. In an elegant studio, a pavilion, so constructed as to exclude all surrounding sights and distractions, he meditated his picturesque descriptions and polished his periods, following his well-known maxim that 'Genius is only patience.' 'I trace,' he said, ' a first sketch, and, in doing this, I do what a hundred writers in Europe can do. I copy it, and obtain a result which but twenty writers can obtain. I recopy a second and a third time, and thus achieve, at last, what Buffon alone can do.' Madame Necker, with her notable aptitude for epigrammatic sayings,[2] remarks on the simplicity of her old friend, that 'Buffon knows not the world, but he knows the Universe.' But with all her respect for him, and in spite of so fine a compliment, she cannot refrain from a sarcasm on his egotism. 'He always says "great men," "people of good taste," &c., using the plural: it is because he sees himself in a mirror which has facets.'

Much more agreeable must have been their journey, in the summer of 1784, to Switzerland, which ever afterwards seemed to Madame de Staël a sort of native country, for, though she was born, and was to die, in France, in Switzerland were born, and there died, not only her parents, but nearly all her kindred; there was her dearest asylum in the darkest periods of her life; there was to be her own grave; and, notwithstanding her thoroughly French temperament and the Teutonic element of her blood (so manifest in her more studied works), her moral nature was distinctively Swiss.

Crossing the Jura mountains (the geographical, though not the political boundary of France), the first picture of the glorious land lay extended and

[2] Her *Mélanges* are superabundantly rich in them.

radiant beneath her gaze—Lake Leman flashing in the midsummer sun; the declivities of the Jura, terraced with vineyards, and studded with thriving hamlets; Lausanne, on the one hand, with its ancient cathedral; Geneva, on the other, with the grey towers of St. Peter's, whence had gone forth influences still dominant in the thought of all Protestant Christendom. Defining the background of the magnificent picture, the Alps stretched their snow-covered summits along the south, Mont Blanc lifting his head to the heavens sovereign of them all. Far to the left quietly reposed, on the margin of the Lake, Vevey, Clarens, the Castle of Chillon, the rocks of Meillerie, scenes of Rousseau's most powerful romance—an author whom the young traveller was now, not only reading, but studying, with enthusiasm, and meditating her first published book —an essay on his genius and writings—which was soon to surprise the world by revealing the extraordinary though immature luxuriance of her own genius. On the western margin of the lake lay Coppet, with its humble church, its few habitations under the shelter of its spacious château, her future Swiss home.

They now sojourned near Lausanne, in which city Necker was about to publish his 'Administration des Finances.' His wife was suffering seriously from her life-long malady,[3] but she was absorbed in cares for the comfort of her husband. Her daugh-

[3] Fragments of her letters, *Mélanges*.

ter's happiness, she writes, is independent of her maternal attentions, 'she is carried along by the torrent of her pleasures.' Bonstetten visited them at Lausanne, and says, 'I saw there the future Madame de Staël, in all the charms of youth, of intellect, and of coquetry.'[4] Madame Necker was now in view of the scenes of her early life. Crassier looked down upon her. She wrote sadly to her literary friend, Thomas, that, in retracing her old tracks here, she has passed over, in one day, an interval of twenty years. 'I hardly know,' she adds, ' whether the memories I still have are my own, or another's. If my heart did not still cling, in all places, to the objects of my regret and affection, I should believe my youth a dream, and the present alone a reality. Are not, indeed, the first years of life only passing illusions?' And yet this poetic land is God's own temple to her, 'luxuriant nature, mountains green and peopled, their tops touching the sky, a grand lake regaling the eye, scenes upon which one's gaze may wander with rapture. It seems that God has interested himself here more than elsewhere for his creatures, obliging them to lift up their thoughts to himself without ceasing.'

This tour brought Mademoiselle Necker into more intimate acquaintance with the kindred of the family, now somewhat numerous on the shores of Lake Leman, especially at Geneva, where the

[4] Bonstetten's *Souvenirs*.

talented daughter of the naturalist De Saussure married, about this time, in her nineteenth year, James Necker, and became afterwards celebrated in literature as Madame Necker de Saussure. The friendship of the two young women was a lifelong consolation to both; and Madame Necker de Saussure became the best biographer of her cousin. Her own biographer says that 'in these youthful years the conversation of these two persons, so worthy of each other, had a degree of vivacity and interest which it is impossible to describe. It seemed then that all which the imagination could suggest of what is beautiful and good would soon be realised by the growth of their souls. The sad effects of the great Revolution had not yet shown how easily the noblest designs may be defeated, how the most upright and courageous wills may be broken. In their confidential intimacy they discussed the grandest subjects which can occupy the human mind. Ideas which were one day to be uttered in the " Corinne " and the " Allemagne," the treasures of thought and of sentiment, the inventions of the imagination, dazzled their souls in these familiar conversations. Madame de Staël dreamed without ceasing in the companionship of her young cousin. She was delighted with this exchange of views, which tranquillised and directed the restless ardour of her thoughts. It was indeed a beautiful spectacle —these two superior minds, at the entrance of life, looking towards the future; the one already peaceful and self-collected, the other ready to take flight towards the regions where storms, and yet light and glory, prevail.'[5]

After passing some time at Coppet, they prolonged their absence into winter, by travels in other parts of Switzerland and in the south of France; for Madame Necker was quite willing to keep her daughter, now advancing in her brilliant youth, as long as possible away from the moral atmosphere of Paris. She had written to Lord Stormont, the British Ambassador at Versailles: 'Paris appears to me more dangerous than ever, now that my daughter is growing into womanhood, and that I find myself obliged to war without ceasing, by individual example, against the general example— a combat of unequal strength, and of doubtful success. I am every day astonished at the moral perversion which withers all minds and all hearts. Vices or virtues, all are alike indifferent, provided only conversation is animated, and *ennui*, our most dreaded plague, is banished.'

They spent some time at Avignon, under a sky so pure and transparent that it seemed 'one ought always to pierce the azure veil, and find, beyond it, all the consolations one needs!' But the vices of Paris are rampant here also; 'they have even lost some of their polite disguises on the way.' The opinions and corruptions of the capital had long

---

[5] *Notice sur la Vie et les Ecrits de Madame Necker de Saussure*, prefixed to the second edition of her work on Education.

been inundating the provinces; social, and especially domestic life were dissolving; and the whole nation was hastening on towards the abyss of its political dissolution.

They go to Montpelier, in sight of the Mediterranean and the Pyrenees. They are deeply interested in the fervid life of the South. They hear impassioned eloquence from its pulpits—'from bishops and archbishops,' and especially from the Bishop of Narbonne. They receive refreshing letters from their Parisian literary friends. Madame Necker replies to one of them, who had visited the family in Switzerland: 'Monsieur Necker, my daughter, and I, constantly think of you. He often says that you have rendered our sojourn at Coppet delightful. It is in retirement that one feels the preciousness of genius and friendship, as one hears best in the silence of the night the sound of the sea, or the song of the nightingale.'

By tracing allusions in their letters, and by other obscure clues, we learn that they turned towards Paris in 1785, and lived for some time in comparative solitude at Marolles, not far from the city. Here their retreat was 'quiet, as no movement reached it. All things around being tranquil, the soul is also.' It befitted the studious habits of Mademoiselle Necker, who having, without the aid of schools, far surpassed the usual academic culture, and ranged over the fields of both ancient and modern literature, now aspired to authorship and literary distinction. Her occasional brief compositions—'Portraits,' 'Eloges,' 'Synonymes'—had been read with avidity in private circles of her friends, and some of them, as we have seen, had been sent by Grimm to his princely correspondents, as promises of extraordinary genius. Her conversation and letters now showed rapidly maturing powers. Madame Necker, still suffering in health, had devolved her correspondence upon her daughter, whose brilliant letters brought back replies full of admiration. The mother, answering one of these admirers, not without a tinge of jealousy (ironical, let us trust, in this instance), wrote: 'The first days after my arrival have been very sad; I have left to my daughter the happiness of writing to you, but she has received a too charming letter from you, and I do not wish that she should inherit my rights before I am no more. One can make little presents during life, but we give all our property only when we die.'

In the year after her return from her southern travels, Mademoiselle Necker completed a drama in verse, in three acts, entitled 'Sophia, or Secret Sentiments.' Its theme is love without hope; it is pervaded, says her cousin, by 'a sweet and melancholy sensibility;' though it has the excess, the sentimentalism, of a juvenile production, the whole piece is marked by presages of genius. It is characterised by great moral delicacy, but it did not escape the rigorous criticism of Madame Necker.

It presents four characters clearly delineated, four well-defined situations, and its style, though incorrect, as its authoress remarked when, in later years, she gave it to the world, bears, nevertheless, the stamp of that vigorous originality which was the distinguishing seal of all her mature works. The next year (1787) her genius, now restless in its aspirations, attempted a more ambitious flight; she composed her tragedy of 'Jane Grey' in the customary five acts, a few copies of which were printed, three years later, for private distribution. Its style, though defective, as she acknowledges in the preface, shows a surprising improvement on that of her 'Sophia,' as do also its characters, and indeed all the essential attributes of the piece. She has strictly followed history, except in the character of Pembroke. That of Northumberland has been admired as revealing astonishing power, 'if we consider the age of the writer.' There is genuine pathos in some of the scenes, and not a few passages are written with an energy of thought and feeling unsurpassed in her later writings. This, it has been remarked, is the only work of Madame de Staël in which we find 'a picture animated with happiness;' its early scenes admit of such a treatment notwithstanding its tragic conclusion. It reveals also that religious tendency which habitually characterised the heart of its writer; 'for, as she had always,' says her cousin, 'need of gratitude and, in consequence, of religion, in happiness, she has given to the character of Jane Grey a deeply religious colouring.' From her childhood she had an ardent sympathy with her heroine. 'In reading her history,' she says, 'her character has transported me. I was about her age when I attempted to paint it, and her youth encouraged mine. I longed to be able to make others share my admiration of that union of force and sensibility which enabled her to brave death while prizing life.'⁶ She recurs to her a quarter of a century later in her 'Reflections on Suicide,' to show that the prospect of a frightful death is not, to a true Christian, a sufficient reason for ending one's days. A second tragedy, entitled 'Montmorency,' quickly followed that of 'Jane Grey,' but it has never been given to the public.

These juvenile works are interesting, chiefly, as indications of her growing intellect; imperfect as they are, they are vivid with her genius. With them ended her attempts at versification on any considerable scale, if we except her 'Épitre au Malheur, ou Adèle et Edouard,' relating to the atrocities of the Revolution, and published in the year 1795. Before she was twenty years of age she composed three tales, which were published with this poem—'Mirza,' 'Adelaide and Theodore,' and 'Pauline.' She did not overrate them; their situations are rather indicated than developed; she says, in her preface, 'their only merit is their pic-

⁶ Preface to *Jane Grey: Œuvres complètes*, ii. Paris, 1861.

tures of some sentiments of the heart.' That tragic tone which pervades all her writings is extreme in these fictitious sketches. The chief importance of the little volume is in its introduction, which is a critical essay, of remarkable ability, on Fictitious Literature, written at a later date, but certainly in her early womanhood. It indicates an incredible range of reading, and equally incredible depth of reflection on her reading. Sainte-Beuve calls it 'a charming essay.' It reviews nearly all the great works of this kind which had appeared down to her day, in any language—classifying them, first, as Fictions, Marvellous and Allegorical; secondly, Historical; thirdly, those which have both Invention and Imitation, but are founded not so much upon fact as upon probability. She gives pre-eminence, as works of Art, to such as are truly natural romances, exhibiting the real action of human affections and passions, without allegory, without mythology, without fantastic or fairy machinery, and without an obtrusive philosophic or didactic purpose.

Her 'Eulogy on M. de Guibert' was written in her twenty-third year; extracts were given in Grimm's Correspondence, but it was not printed till after her death. It is characterised by much of the enthusiasm and nascent genius which pervade her letters on Rousseau. Guibert was the hero of the famous letters of Mademoiselle Lespinasse, a fact not yet known, however, to his young eulogist.

There was much nobleness in his character, and he had rare talent, as his writings show; he was an habitual and brilliant guest of the Necker *salon*, and was in full sympathy with Necker's political opinions—'one of the first,' says Sainte-Beuve, 'to conceive the ideas and means of public reform, the States-General, the citizen soldiery,' &c.; 'but,' adds this writer, 'I am the more pleased with him for having foreseen with certainty, and disclosed in advance, by a "portrait" the future greatness of Corinne.' She had, probably, a stronger reason for her interest in him. Years later, when in England, she intimated to a friend that 'Guibert had been very much in love with her before her marriage.'[7] If she could not reciprocate his affection, she could appreciate it, for a woman, especially such a woman, always feels herself complimented by love, though it may be from a man incapable of winning her heart, or perhaps even her esteem. It is at least a homage to her attractions, and that is a tribute which no woman can despise. The Eulogy on Guibert is the expression of a grateful, as well as of an admiring heart.

Such were the tentative productions of her juvenile pen, before she dared to send forth the superior, though defective, 'Letters on the Writings and Character of Rousseau,' which were to be the first published demonstration of her superb genius.[8]

---

[7] Wharton's *Queens of Society*, p. 369. London, 1867.

[8] Sainte-Beuve is evidently inclined to think that the earliest

We have anticipated a few dates in this connected view of her earliest works. Meanwhile other and important events have occurred. Her father, still pursued by persecution, has been banished from the vicinity of Paris, and she has accompanied him in his exile. She has grown into a rich young womanhood, physical and intellectual. Her admirable conversational powers have already been recognised in the best circles as something wonderful. Her unfortunate marriage has taken place. The increasing embarrassments of the national treasury have compelled the government to turn again imploringly to Necker, and he is about to be recalled to office, replacing the family in the dazzling excitements of Parisian life. And in the same year with his restoration she is to take her position, and take it for ever, in the literary ranks of her country by her first publication.

written of her printed works may have been the small volume entitled *Lettres de Nannine à Simphal*, which was attributed to her by M. Beuchat, but was disavowed by her family at the time of its publication (1818), after her death; if it is genuine, it was probably written about her fifteenth year. M. Bohaire, publisher at Lyons, and owner of the manuscript, insisted that, though not in the handwriting of Madame de Staël, the work is nevertheless hers. (Querard's *La France Littéraire*, tome ix. The *Biographie Universelle* inclines to the same opinion.) It differs little from her three other novelettes, except that it is more juvenile in style. It is a small, sentimental romance, such as an ardent, guileless young girl might readily imagine.

CHAPTER IV.

EARLY WOMANHOOD.

Necker—His Daughter with him in Exile—Her Account of his Book on the Importance of Religious Opinions—Her Development—An early Portrait of her—Description of her in her Eighteenth Year—In her Twentieth Year—Her Manners in Company—Her *Bonhomie*—Her Conversational Powers—Her Religious Tendency—A Literary 'Portrait' of her.

NECKER, on his late visit to Lausanne, published there his work 'On the Administration of the Finances,' vindicating his 'Compte Rendu,' and exposing more completely the wretched fiscal condition of France. It struck the nation, as we have seen, with astonishment, and startled Europe. His daughter says 'it made the fortune of three or four publishers; a hundred thousand copies were issued, and it is now [1809] esteemed the only classic in French literature on its subject.'[1] The Emperor Joseph II., the King of Poland, and the King of Naples, had invited him to take charge of the finances of their governments. Catherine of Russia and Frederick the Great had expressed surprise and regret at his treatment by the Cabinet

---

[1] *Du Caractère de M. Necker* &c. An edition was issued the same year, 1784, in London.

of Versailles. Declining all foreign overtures, he remained faithful to his adopted country. Calonne, his successor, convoked the Assembly of Notables, and attacked before it the 'Compte Rendu.' Necker replied through the press, and the immediate result was his banishment forty leagues from Paris. His daughter was inexpressibly afflicted by this new persecution. She says that 'a *lettre de cachet*, an exile, appeared to me the most cruel act that could be committed. I uttered cries of despair when I heard of it. I had no idea of a greater misfortune. All the society of Paris, that refined manners and a long period of peace had rendered unfamiliar with such suffering, crowded to my father with their sympathy, and with indignation against his exile. I passed the time of his banishment with him. How calm and serene he was! He now finished his work "On the Importance of Religious Opinions," a grand proof of the tranquillity of his soul in circumstances which might well agitate an ambitious man. This production could not serve his interests; on the contrary, he risked many distinguished partisans by it; for he was the first, and even the only one, among the recognised writers of the period who dared to signalise the irreligious tendency of the times. Unaided, he warred against that disastrous tendency, not with hatred for philosophy, but with noble enthusiasm for religion; religion without which reason has no guide, imagination no object, sensibility no depth, and virtue itself no charms.'

During these adversities of Necker, the interval between his first and second administrations, 1781–1788, his daughter passed through the most interesting period of her youth, from her fifteenth to her twenty-second year. By her keen sympathy with her father she received the salutary discipline of affliction; her retired life enabled her to prosecute extensive studies; and the country air restored her health.

Sainte-Beuve mentions an unpublished portrait which he had seen, representing her, in her early youth, with hair loose and floating in the air; eyes confiding and bathed in light; forehead high; lips open, speaking, and 'moderately thick in sign of intelligence and generosity;' complexion animated by sentiment; neck and arms bare; 'costume light, with a ribbon floating at the waist; bosom respiring with full breath. Such might be the "Sophie" of the "Emile," such the author of the "Lettres sur Jean-Jacques," accompanying her guide in her Elysium, excited at every step, constantly advancing and returning, now on the one side, now on the other.'

In her eighteenth year she is described as 'so mature a woman that they could justly pronounce her to be one of the most luminous spirits of the times; she eclipsed all who came near her, and seemed rightfully the mistress of the house.'[2] The same authority, speaking of her appearance in her twentieth year, says, 'Her figure was admirable; her shoulders, her bust, her arms and hands, were of rare beauty; she had in her mien and her features all that poetry of soul which she afterwards displayed in her writings. Without being beautiful, she was already the model after which Gerard painted his Corinne twenty years later, having the same richness of form and health, the same purity of lines—those contours, powerfully rounded, which express a poetic organisation.' Young as she was (in 1788), 'she had a very powerful fascination, felt by all who approached her.' Her cousin says that she was graceful in all her movements; her countenance, without entirely satisfying the eye at first, attracted it, and then retained it, by a rare charm, for it quickly displayed a sort of ideal or intellectual beauty. No one feature was salient enough to determine, in advance, her character or mood, except her eyes, which were truly magnificent; but her varying thoughts painted themselves in ever-varying expression on her face. It had, therefore, no one permanent expression; her physiognomy was, so to speak, created by the emotion of the moment. In repose her eyelids had something like languor, but a flash of thought would illu-

---

[2] Duchesse d'Abrantès' *Histoire des Salons de Paris*, Introd.

minate her glances with a sudden fire, a sort of lightning forerunning her words. There was, however, no unquiet mobility about her features; a kind of exterior indolence characterised her; but her vigorous frame, her firm and well adjusted attitudes, added to the great force and singular directness of her discourse. There was, meanwhile, something dramatic in her bearing; and even her toilette, though exempt from all exaggerations, gave an idea of the picturesque more than of the mode or fashion.

Some of those negligent caprices, or eccentricities, usually attributed to persons of genius, were reported of her about this period. It is said that, at her presentation at Court, the courtiers, who were familiar with her reputation, amused themselves over a fault in her 'curtsey and a slight derangement of her robe;'[3] and in a visit, a few days later, to the Duchesse de Polignac, a confidant of the Queen, 'she forgot her bonnet, leaving it in her carriage.' The feminine gentlemen, and masculine ladies, of the court, envious of her rising fame, found occasion for self-complacent criticism, for rebuke and sarcasm, in such barbarous defects. She herself repeated these reports to her friends with equal self-complacency.

When she entered a *salon*, her step was, according to her cousin's sketch, measured and dignified; a slight diffidence seemed to require her to aim at

---

[3] *Encyclopédie des Gens du Monde* &c. tome xxi. Paris, 1844.

self-control, especially if her introduction attracted many eyes. As if this passing cloud of embarrassment had prevented her from distinguishing, at first, the individuals of the company, her face became illuminated in proportion as she recognised them. A listener would suppose that she had inscribed on her mind all their names; and very soon those charming words, of which she was so generous, showed that the most distinguished acts, or qualities, of each were present to her thoughts. Her praises proceeded from the heart, and therefore reached it. She knew how to compliment without flattering. It was a maxim with her that politeness is the art of choosing among one's real thoughts.

Her whole demeanour was marked by a disposition to oblige; there were abundant wit and vivid repartee, but no chicanery, and, especially, no severity, in her expressions. 'Her cordiality imposed silence on self-love,' and her superior sense imposed it on self-conceit; but pride itself could not feel resentful towards her, for her perfect sincerity and instinctive kindliness and good humour won all hearts. A writer who knew her in her childhood and in her advanced life says that 'among her most remarkable qualities her *bonhomie* held perhaps the first rank.'[4] This extraordinary conciliatory power, united to an intellectual superiority which seldom fails to provoke envious criticism, was doubtless much enhanced

[4] Simond's *Voyage* &c.

by a certain tenderness and sadness, which habitually affected her thoughts, and often appeared suddenly in her gayest conversation. Her sensibilities were quicker even than her thoughts. Society, conversation, were a necessity of her nature; she needed distraction, for a certain pensiveness, not to say melancholy, hung continually about her; it was mitigated by years, but was never totally dispelled.[5] It was a powerful element of her genius, and gave rich poetic colouring to her writings. She usually retired from company, in which she had conversed much, with sensible relief. 'This relief,' says her cousin, 'was necessary to her very being. The conservative instinct of her talents repelled dullness or depression. Perhaps her constitution, more sensitive than was supposed, required the stimulus of diversion; for a sort of terror seized her at the thought of the stagnation of existence. In her youth she could not endure solitude; and the melancholy impressions, which are painted with so much beauty in her works, were with her formidable realities.' It was only very late in life, when she was able to hold in abeyance the phantoms created by her imagination, that she could, according to her own expression, 'live in society with nature;' consequently *ennui*, which in

---

[5] The last and unfinished sentence in her *Ten Years of Exile*, written in her forty-sixth year, reads : 'I have always been strangely subject to *ennui*, and, far from knowing how to employ myself in those entirely void moments, which seem appropriate only to study . . . .'

society or elsewhere is a solitude in which one has not even his normal self for company, was extremely dreaded by her. It sufficed not that her associates were intellectual, they must be animated. She could not be content if they spoke without interest. 'How can they expect me to listen,' she said, ' if they do not themselves the honour to listen to themselves?' She could endure better certain defects of character or manner, than heartlessness, or a lack of interest in the speaker. She said, one day, of an egotist, ' He speaks indeed only of himself, but this does not oppress me, for I am sure that he is at least interested in what he says.' She delighted in humour, though there is hardly a trace of it in her own writings, except one or two of her domestic dramas. She showed a sort of tenderness, a lively gratitude, for those who cheered her by their conversation. A *bon mot*, a comic story, a brilliant epigram, charmed her. Piquancy, originality, imagination—these pleased her above all else; they gave spring to her mind, wings to her genius. A single marked trait or talent was more valued by her than any combination of mediocre qualities, however numerous.

Talent in others always prompted her own. She was never dispirited in conversation by the brilliancy of competitors; but, with a simple candour, a charming *abandon*, she gave herself up to the inspiration of their powers, and shone the brighter for the combination of their light with hers. This simplicity, this utter frankness, was an infinite charm; never has the etymological significance of the word sincerity had a finer exemplification. Hence her self-reliance never appeared like egotism; it was perfect, and yet apparently without self-consciousness, like that of the ascending lark, which doubts not its power of wing because it thinks not of it. She had no reason to fear rivals in conversation; her superiority there was supreme. 'This illustrious woman,' says a good authority, 'personified the eloquence of conversation in the country where that brilliant gift was the most fully appreciated.'[6]

In the more strictly moral qualities of her nature we discern an habitual conflict between her conscience and her life. Though, during this period of her young womanhood, she showed no very positive disposition to self-assertion on religious subjects, her heart ever turned towards them in spite of its waywardness, and of the corrupt social influences which prevailed around her, and, at a later period, more or less infected her. The authority just cited says, 'The daughter of Necker, notwithstanding the energy and originality of her nature, received a strong impression from the philosophic society which surrounded her youth; yet the scepticism of that arid and railing philosophy was utterly repugnant to the fervour and loyalty of her soul; and,

---

[6] *Coppet et Weimar: Madame de Staël et la Grande-Duchesse Louise.* Preface. Paris, 1862.

with her all convictions, took, on the contrary, the intensity and ardour of faith. As she ripened in experience and was cured of the intoxications and illusions of youth, she was more and more led to the Christian belief, the precepts of which were blended in her soul with her filial affection.' 'She could not,' says her cousin, 'separate in her experience religion from happiness,' and that highly gifted woman adopted, as the motto on the title-page of her important work on Education, a sentence from Madame de Staël which expresses her whole theory of human life: 'Life is valuable only so far as it serves for the religious education of the heart.'[7]

Madame Necker de Saussure has preserved for us a sketch of her as she appeared about this time, to her admirers at least,—one of those 'portraits,' the reading of which in the *salons* of Paris was a favourite literary entertainment of the period. They are abundant in the fugitive literature of the times, and though they were, of course, generally eulogistic, their success depended on their *vraisemblance*. This one was from the pen of M. de Guibert, whom we have already had occasion to notice as a guest of the Necker *salon*, and eminent in both the society and literature of that day. He wrote it after the model of a Greek poem, but,

---

[7] *L'Education Progressive, ou Etude du Cours de la Vie.* 3 vols. Lausanne, 1838.

apart from its poetry, it may be pronounced a true likeness :—

'She is but twenty years old, but she is the most celebrated priestess of Apollo, and the favourite of the god—the one whose hymns and incense are the most agreeable to him. Her words bring him down from heaven to glorify his temple and mingle with mortals.

'From the midst of the consecrated maidens, the choir of the priestesses, suddenly advances one; my heart will always remember her. Her great black eyes are radiant with genius; her hair, of the hue of ebony, falls in floating ringlets on her shoulders; her features are more strongly marked than delicate—one sees in them something above the destiny of her sex. Such it would be necessary to paint the Muse of Poetry, or Clio, or Melpomene. See her! See her! all exclaim, when she appears; and they hold their breath to hear her. I had seen the Pythoness of Delphi; I had seen the Sibyl of Cumæ, but they were extravagant; their movements were convulsive; they appeared less inspired by a god than devoted to the Furies. This young priestess is animated without excess; inspired without intoxication; her charm is freedom, and her supernatural powers seem to belong to her own nature.

'Uniting her voice with the sounds of her lyre, made of ivory and gold, she began to sing the praises of Apollo. Her words and music were spontaneous. From the celestial fire of the poetry which kindled her aspect, and the profound attention of the people, we could see that her imagination created the song; and, astonished and enchanted, we knew not which most to admire, its facility or its perfection. Then, laying aside her lyre, she spoke of the great truths of nature, of the immortality of the soul, of liberty, of the charm and the danger of the passions. In hearing her one would be disposed to say that many persons, many experiences, were mingled in her one soul. On observing her youth, we were fain to ask how she had been able thus to anticipate life and to exist before her birth?

'I saw and heard her with transport; I discovered in her features charms superior to beauty. What a play and variety in her countenance, what modulations of her voice, what perfect accord between her thoughts and expressions! When she speaks, if her words cannot reach me, her tones, her gestures, and her looks suffice to convey to me her meaning.

'She pauses a moment: her last words sound through my soul, and I discover in her eyes what she has yet to say. At length she is silent, and the temple resounds with applause; her long eyelashes shade her eyes of fire, and the sun is veiled from our sight!'

CHAPTER V.

MARRIAGE—CORRESPONDENCE WITH GUSTAVUS III.

Baron de Staël—Count Fersen—Interest of the French Court in the Marriage—Staël's subsequent Career—His Wife's Correspondence with his King—French Court Life—Necker's Restoration to Office.

ATTRACTIVE by rare endowments of mind and heart, with personal charms greater than those of beauty, and, withal, one of the richest heiresses of France, Mademoiselle Necker could not fail of suitors. Her marriage, however, was a difficult family question. Her mother was not willing that she should marry a Roman Catholic, and the most eligible opportunities, apart from religion, seemed almost confined to the high Catholic families of the country. The daughter's passionate affection for her father led her to insist that she should not be separated from him. These difficulties were compromised at last by their accepting Eric Magnus, Baron de Staël Holstein.

There is evidence that Count Fersen, a Swede of higher pretensions, had hoped to win her hand. He was younger than Staël, and singularly handsome, belonging to a family in which personal beauty had long been an hereditary distinction.

He was a favourite with his King, and beloved by the Queen of France, whose intimacy with him became a popular subject of the scandals with which she was overwhelmed during the Revolution.[1] He spent some years in America, fighting for the colonial revolutionists, as aide-de-camp of Count Vaux and, later, of Rochambeau; and was present at the surrender of Cornwallis. He attempted to save the Royal family of France by the famous flight to Varennes, and conducted them, disguised as their coachman, as far as Bondy. Though he revered Washington, he was one of the very few Frenchmen that served in America who did not return with liberal principles. He was opposed to the republican tendencies of the times, and abhorred the French revolutionists. He disliked Necker's liberalism, and this, probably, was the reason why he failed to win the affections of his daughter. The Adonis of the Court, he cared little about his failure; her great fortune was probably her chief attraction for him; and it is said that he compromised this with his friend Staël, by accepting from him a large bonus and by zealously promoting their marriage. Fersen wrote to his father, 'Necker has at last made his decision: he gives his daughter to Staël; and I am

---

[1] Baron Klinckowström, a relative of the Count, has published (*Le Comte Fersen et la Cour de France*, 2 vols. Paris, 1878), the diaries, letters, and despatches of Fersen—affording important data for the history of the Revolution. There are in these volumes twenty-eight letters from Marie Antoinette to Fersen, and thirty-two from him to her.

delighted for his sake. He had many and powerful rivals, among whom was Mr. Pitt, who is now at the head of affairs in England; but the girl has preferred M. de Staël.'

The Baron de Staël was a Swede, of moderate fortune, but of generous character, of solid instruction, of philosophic tastes, and zealously devoted to the reforms which then occupied the attention of the enlightened classes of French society,[2]—a man of polished manners, and of good official prospects. He was born in 1749; was a military officer some fourteen years; was chamberlain to the Queen of Sweden, and a Chevalier de l'Epée. He was made a Councillor to the Swedish Legation at the Court of France in 1778; appointed Chargé d'Affaires in 1783; subsequently Minister Plenipotentiary, and, finally, Ambassador.[3] At the time of his marriage he was thirty-seven years old; his bride was but twenty; but the disparity of their ages was no serious consideration, especially in view of the marriages of *convenance* then customary in France, which usually made little or no account of the age of the husband. It was not, however, a marriage of love, on the part of the bride at least. It is supposed that her motive in consenting to it was her affection for her father, for whom she was always ready to make any sacrifice. Staël was a fervent advocate of Necker's

---

[2] *Nouvelle Biographie Générale*, xliv.
[3] *Biographie Universelle*, xl.

political opinions, and was devoted to his official interests. He was a Protestant; and willing to concede Mademoiselle Necker's demand that she should never be separated from her parents. Like his friend Fersen, he was a favourite at the Court of Versailles, especially with Marie Antoinette, and could probably promote the interests of Necker there. The Queen encouraged the marriage, and induced Gustavus III. of Sweden to promise the Baron a long continuance in the Legation at Paris, in order that he might fulfil his pledge to the family not to withdraw their daughter from the country. In short, the match seemed every way eligible, if it could only be one of real affection. Mademoiselle Necker may have been able to see no more worthy opportunity, in the French society around her; or she may have deceived her own heart through devotion to her father's interests.

The marriage was not a precipitate one; the negotiations for it had extended through some years. King Gustavus was in intimate sympathy with the Court of Versailles; his occasional visits to Paris were a special pleasure to him; he constantly received news from the capital, not only through his official representatives, but from the correspondence of Madame de la Marck, Madame d'Egmont, and Madame de Boufflers. The latter persistently promoted the interests of Staël, and managed, with the King, the preliminaries of the marriage. She induced Marie Antoinette and at last the King himself, to write to Gustavus favouring it. Creuts, the Swedish ambassador at Paris, looking for promotion at home, urged Gustavus to give his place to Staël. 'Your Majesty,' he wrote, 'cannot imagine to what a point the King and Queen are interested in him. The King loves him as much as the Queen, and treats him with real affection. He has, according to the avowal of the King himself, special audiences with the Queen, such as I cannot, as ambassador, obtain.'[4] Staël himself kept up an adroit and urgent correspondence with Gustavus on the subject. In these, as in all his subsequent official communications with the Court of Sweden, he showed himself an able diplomat. Gustavus came to see, at last, that though the terms demanded for the marriage were extraordinary, yet the wishes of the French Court, and the opulent dowry and distinguished talents of the bride, would be of great advantage, not only to his legation, but to himself, and he consented. A formal stipulation was made, guaranteeing not only the ambassadorship for twelve years, but also a pension of 25,000 livres per annum in case, ' by circumstances unforeseen, M. de Staël should lose his ambassadorship.'

The marriage took place on the 14th January, 1786. As her husband will seldom reappear in our narrative, we may here briefly anticipate the

[4] Geffroy, *Revue des Deux Mondes*, 1856. See also *Gustav III. et la Cour de France*, by the same writer, *ibid.* 1864-65.

principal subsequent events of his life. Favouring, like Necker, the liberal spirit of the times, he did not, like Necker, escape its radical tendencies. He entered with enthusiasm into the Revolution, and allied himself closely with members of the Constituent Assembly. His King was decidedly hostile to the new political ideas of France, and, becoming the royal leader of the foreign opposition to them, recalled him in 1792; but he was restored the next year, after the death of Gustavus by assassination. He arrived again in Paris about two months after the execution of Louis XVI., and was then the only ambassador from a royal government to the new republic. An astonishing change had taken place in a short time. Most of his old friends had fled from the country, or were in prison, or had perished on the scaffold; and Necker had escaped, with his family, to Switzerland. On entering the capital he sought the goodwill of the Revolutionists, by a donation of three thousand francs to the poor of the section of the Croix Rouge, then a hot-bed of the revolutionary spirit. He was alarmed at the tumults and atrocities around him; and returned to Sweden, bearing with him a treaty of alliance, which had been forced upon him by the Convention, but which was so objectionable that the Regent of Sweden rejected it. Not till the fall of Robespierre did his Government send him again to the French capital, for the negotiation of another treaty of alliance. He remained at his post, displaying at times not a little courage, through the vicissitudes of parties, down to 1799, when he was recalled by the young King, Gustavus Adolphus. Of the separation of his wife from him and the reasons for it, and of his death, we shall hereafter have occasion to speak.

Under the auspices of the new ambassadress the *salon* of the Swedish Legation immediately became 'the most brilliant of all the diplomatic *salons* of Paris. The ambassador was more favoured than all others, in his private audiences at the Court, and by the confidence of Necker, who was familiar with the Court news and possessed commanding credit. Staël was at the summit of his ambition; he was master of an immense fortune, and ambassador for life. Necker saw his daughter a baroness and an ambassadress; he could hold his head high at Court. Gustavus himself, besides the political advantages which this union promised him, had won a new and already celebrated feminine admirer, whose correspondence would outshine that of Mesdames d'Egmont, de la Marck, de Boufflers, and so many others.'[5]

The correspondence here alluded to, though affording few personal facts for our pages, is valuable to the historian of the Revolution, and has a curious history.

---

[5] Geffroy errs in supposing the Baron's appointment to have been 'pour toujours.' See M. d'Haussonville, in *Revue des Deux Mondes*, Aug. 1880.

Some years ago the public journals of Europe announced that an important discovery was made in the Scandinavian University town of Upsala. Two large cases, filled with letters and historical documents, had been brought out of a subterranean concealment, and were about to be revealed to the world. They had been left, by the will of Gustavus III., to the University, in 1788, on the condition that they should not be opened till fifty years after his death. He died in 1792; they were opened in 1842, in presence of a royal commission. These documents formed more than a hundred volumes—sixty-four in folio, and fifty-five in quarto. They had been all classified, catalogued, and carefully stitched. The Swedish historian Geijer was appointed by the Government to examine and edit the precious collection. One of the volumes (in quarto) bears the title of 'Letters from Foreign Ladies.' They are from Marie Antoinette, Mesdames d'Egmont, de la Marck, de Boufflers, but, above all, many are in the handwriting of Madame de Staël. Immediately after her marriage she became, at the solicitation of Gustavus, one of his private correspondents; and, under the title of 'Bulletins of News,' sent him abundant court and city gossip, relieved often by sagacious comments which show that she understood, better perhaps than those around her, the drift of opinions and events, and the tragic catastrophe to which they were tending. They give a picture of the last years of the *ancien régime*, and striking proofs of the intellectual vigour of the young writer. She attributes the growing agitations to the North American Revolution. Gustavus himself saw them in this light; and, in a letter to Stedingk, his representative at St. Petersburg, which was to be shown to Catherine II., he calls them 'an epidemic of popular effervescence—an epidemic which has had its real source in America, and is extending over France.' The reaction of the new on the old world had already begun: it was to be fearfully abused; sometimes temporarily counteracted, but never defeated. For good or for evil, it was to shape the future social and political history of Europe. Dumont, the coadjutor of Mirabeau, says, 'The National Assembly began with the famous Declaration of the "Rights of Man;" it was an American idea, and regarded as a necessary preliminary.'[6] The first placards on the walls of Paris, proposing a republic, were written by Thomas Paine, and were signed by a young nobleman, Duchâtelet, who had served in America. Condorcet and his circle were among the first to avow Republicanism. 'America,' says Dumont, 'appeared to them the model of good government, and it seemed easy to transplant into France the system of federalism.'[7] The primary cause of the Revolution was, doubtless, the ruined finances of

---

[6] Dumont, though he did not approve the document, helped to compose it. *Souvenirs sur Mirabeau*, chap. vii. Paris, 1832.

[7] *Ibid.* chap. xvi.

the country; its proximate cause was the character of the King;[8] its final cause was the republicanism of America. 'The American war,' says a Royalist historian,' developed in France new germs of revolt. It afforded at once the example and the tactics; confused ideas of liberty, of independence, of democracy, fermented in all heads, and prepared a general explosion.'[9]

Her title as Ambassadress brought Madame de Staël into immediate relations with the Court. 'The Queen,' she writes to Gustavus, 'has received me with kindness. She said to me that for a long time she had desired my acquaintance, and she thus distinguishes all who bear Swedish names. The repast was more magnificent than any yet given to an ambassadress. Eight days afterwards I was received at dinner, with the Spanish Ambassador, at M. de Vergenne's. He took us both by the hand, to make us pass together.' She goes to the Trianon—still so agreeable to the eye, so sad to the memory—to the Court at Versailles and at Fontainebleau. 'The Queen's balls,' she says, 'are very splendid. The hall is arranged as a fairy palace. The gardens of the Trianon are there, and fountains of water play continually; pastoral ideas, reveries that the country inspires, mingle with the splendours of the luxury of

---

[8] Dumont, chap. xvii.
[9] Bertrand de Moleville's *Hist. de la Révolution*, &c. i., Introd. Paris, 1801.

courts. In another hall you witness recreations but little pastoral—reckless gambling. Young M. Castellane has had to quit his paternal home for having lost here, in one evening, the whole of his fortune. The Queen sets an example of moderation; and it is not on her account that her Court is ruining itself. But the gamesters tire of every other occupation; they find everything else insipid. They have acquired the taste for great excitements; they cannot get on without gaming. The apartments of the King, and above all of the Queen, at Fontainebleau, are of an extraordinary magnificence. The cabinet of the Queen is beautiful in all its details, beyond anything that can be imagined. The Marshal, Ségur, makes no promotions; the Ministers all retain their places; suppers and dinners are the only events of the day. They sup three times a week with Madame de Polignac, three times with Madame de Lamballe, and once in the Cabinet. The Queen goes to Madame de Polignac and Madame de Lamballe daily at twelve o'clock, and plays at billiards: a game at which women succeed well. It has become fashionable. The houses of the Ministers, of the captains of the Guard, of the great officers of the Crown, are filled even till twelve o'clock; at this hour all leave for the house in which the Queen is to be found. At midnight they go forth to pass the time elsewhere. Games are the only secret they have yet discovered for the amusement of assembled people—or rather for their occupation. The greatest pleasure of the mistress of a mansion is to disembarrass herself of those who are with her, by enchaining them to tables of *quinze* or of *trictrac*.'

Such scenes were, however, an onerous official etiquette to the young ambassadress. Her own *salon* presented attractions infinitely superior to this courtly and vacant folly, for there she could gather *élite* minds, and hold high discussions on the noblest themes.

Whether by the influence of his son-in-law and of his son-in-law's friends at Court, or otherwise, Necker's political fortunes began again to brighten. Every experiment made by his successors in the national finances only involved them in deeper embarrassment. Calonne's failures and his persecution and banishment of Necker caused a reaction. The King dismissed him. The feebleness of the sovereign's character, his habitual vacillation, rendered the policy and the fate of any Minister precarious, and must be considered as one of the chief causes of the general downfall which was now at hand. The Marshal de Castries, Minister of the Marine, proposed the recall of Necker, but the King could not yet humble himself by reinstating a man whom he had exiled. M. de Fourqueux was appointed, of whom Madame de Staël said that 'Never did the perruque of a Councillor of State cover a poorer head.'[1] M. de Brienne, then Archbishop of Tou-

[1] *Considérations* &c. i. 9.

louse, later of Sens, followed ; he attempted vigorous measures, but all his endeavours served only to show the impossibility of conciliating the obstinate selfishness of parties and classes ; none would tolerate measures for the relief of the treasury which might bear unfavourably on their own resources. At last, after seven years of disgrace, Necker had to be recalled, though he himself at least saw that it was in vain. His daughter was the first to bear to him the news, which at any earlier and more hopeful period would have been most grateful to his wounded feelings, but was now only alarming. 'When I came,' she says, ' to announce it to him, he exclaimed, " Ah, if they had but given me these fifteen months of the Archbishop of Sens ! Now it is too late." He submitted to the order of the King with sadness. Seeing my joy, he remarked, " The daughter of a Minister has only pleasure : she rejoices in the reflection of the power of her father ; but the power itself is at present more than ordinarily a terrible responsibility." ' She, proudly believing him equal to any exigency, could not share his discouragement. She records her extreme delight ; and so intense was it, that its very excess excited her apprehension : it seemed too precious to last, and ominous of coming evils. 'In traversing the Bois de Boulogne, at night, on my way to Versailles,' she says, ' I had a terrible fear of being attacked by thieves ; for it seemed to me that the happiness which the elevation of my father caused me must be balanced by some cruel accident. The thieves did not attack me; but destiny justified, only too faithfully, my fears.' On paying her homage to the Queen she found new reason for anxiety. 'The niece of the displaced Archbishop of Sens paid her court at the same time. The Queen showed plainly, by her manner of receiving us both, that she much preferred the displaced Minister to his successor. The courtiers, however, acted otherwise; for never have so many persons offered to conduct me to my carriage. The disposition of the Queen became one of the greatest obstacles that M. Necker had to encounter in his official career. She had protected him during his former ministry, but, whatever he did to conciliate her during the second, she considered him always as nominated by public opinion, and princes in arbitrary governments accustom themselves, unfortunately, to regard public opinion as their enemy.'[2]

Meanwhile Necker's restoration, though to himself hopeless, had an extraordinary effect on the nation. In one day the funds rose thirty per cent. Though only two hundred and fifty thousand francs remained in the treasury, capitalists immediately offered considerable loans. 'Such an effect,' exclaims his fond daughter, ' produced on the public credit, by confidence in a single man, is without example in history.' But his anticipation was correct; it was now too late for any scheme to save the nation from bankruptcy and revolution.

[2] *Considérations* &c. i. 12.

CHAPTER VI.

LITERATURE—THE REVOLUTION.

Necker again in Office—First Publication of Madame de Staël—Letters on Rousseau—Her Opinion of Literary Life—Madame Necker de Saussure's Estimate of the Letters—Grimm's Criticism—Madame de Staël's Sympathy with the Revolution—Her Account of the Opening of the States-General—Necker's Dismissal—His Triumphal Return—Letter from Mlle. Huber—Riots of the People—Necker finally retires.

NECKER was recalled to office in August 1788. He was now more than ever the idol of the nation. The vague sense of impending disaster—the general, though unacknowledged suspicion that the national condition was hopeless, seemed to give way before a man who, if he had not great abilities, had nevertheless great character. Corrupt as the nation was, it appeared to hope that virtue, if not talent, might yet save it. Again the Minister's family shone amidst the *éclats* of Parisian life. Again the Necker *salon* was thronged in the metropolis and at St. Ouen. If the devoted wife, thoughtful of coming events, moved more gravely, more reticently, in the brilliant circle, the daughter, the freshness and charms of whose girlhood were only enhanced by her recent matronhood, became its happy presiding genius. Proud of the restored honour of her father, and hopeful of all things in spite of all omens, exhilarated with genius and the homage of distinguished men, she not only led its conversations, but assumed there her first honours as an author.

In the year of her father's restoration her 'Letters on the Writings and Character of Rousseau' were printed for private circulation. Only twenty copies were issued, but it was reprinted and published the next year. To us this little volume is interesting as her first published work, an index to her youthful mind. To herself it always had another interest. In her second preface, written more than a quarter of a century later (1814), she says : ' It was published without my avowal, and by this chance was I led into the career of literature. I cannot say that I regret it ; for the cultivation of letters has afforded me more consolations than chagrins. One's self-love must be intense, if unfavourable criticism gives more pain than eulogies give pleasure ; and, besides this pleasure, there is in the development and perfection of one's mind a continual activity, an ever renewed hopefulness, that the ordinary course of life never affords. All things move towards declension in a woman's life, except the power of thinking, the immortal nature of which tends always to its own elevation.'

After all deductions for its juvenile enthusiasm

and occasional excesses of style, this first of her
printed writings is a very remarkable production
for so young a mind. It was a sudden apparition of a new star in the intellectual heavens.
However open to criticism, no critic could mis-
take its significance as an indication of rare
genius. Madame Necker de Saussure justly, and as
finely, remarks that 'in it we see all the vivacity
of a youthful intellect, and the highest charm
of such a mind, namely, both what it is and
what it will be. There is deposited the germ of
all the opinions that Madame de Staël has since
developed. We see in it a thinker, a moralist, a
woman, who can paint the passions, though as yet
confusedly. She ranges over an immense field of
ideas; she illustrates, in passing, a crowd of subjects; and though her steps are directed by those
of Rousseau, she accompanies him with a movement
so light and so rapid, she deviates from and surpasses
him so often, that one sees she has been prompted
rather than sustained by him. She always speaks
from the exuberance of her mind, yields to the uncontrollable expansion of her soul; and we acknowledge that if she had chosen another theme she
might have written with as much facility and as
much eloquence. With whatever influence Rousseau inspires her, she maintains the independence
of her mind. She scatters her opinions profusely
with the graceful embarrassment of a young woman
who evidently fears that she has displayed too

much force. In short, notwithstanding some immature judgments, she is already astonishingly herself in this book.'

Baron Grimm was favoured, as a guest of the Necker *salon*, with one of the twenty copies of the first edition of the 'Letters.' His antipathy to Rousseau, founded in personal recollections, was intense; but he could not fail to admire the genius of the young eulogist, and sent pages of her book to his correspondents.[1] 'It is a production,' he says, 'which in any circumstances, or by any author, would be important; but which is especially admirable as coming from a young woman of twenty years.' He cites, as proofs, her criticism on Rousseau's style, and her analysis of his several works; and especially the letter on his 'Emile,' as 'presenting a crowd of fine and profound ideas.' The first four letters cannot fail to excite the astonishment of the reader by the extent and maturity of mind they display; but still more surprising, he thinks, is her criticism of the 'Contrat Social,' and of similar speculations of Rousseau. Grimm cannot withhold 'his sentiments of admiration,' and pronounces the book 'a charming work;' its critical judgments cannot, however, be accepted in our day. Time has determined more justly the character and influence of Rousseau's writings; Madame de Staël herself would doubtless have

[1] Some twelve pages of the *Correspondance*, Jan. 1789, part iii. tome v. Buisson's edition of 1813.

given a very different estimate of them, had she written the Letters in her maturer life.

Her sympathy with Rousseau's political speculations led her to sympathise with the early tendencies of the Revolution; for Rousseau was the oracle of the leaders of that great movement, and his 'Contrat Social' was their text-book. Fundamentally erroneous as his theory of government may be, it nevertheless included many of the essential principles of political justice and liberty, and never had they been more clearly formulated, or more enthusiastically advocated. Her young soul caught his enthusiasm, and, like many of the best thinkers of the period—like Jefferson and most of the American statesmen, and Fox and Mackintosh in England—she saw, in the attempt of the French to embody some of his doctrines in the Revolution, a new epoch in history; an epoch of liberation and regeneration for Europe. She had, sadly enough, to qualify her hopes amid the frantic excesses which soon drove her from her country, but she never materially qualified her opinions. She lived and died an advocate of the rights of the people, as co-ordinate with the rights of their rulers. She was a conservative liberal, and never ceased to assert the claims of liberty against the usurpations and tyranny of Bonaparte.

Reinstated in the highest society of the metropolis, an ambassador's wife, a minister's daughter, and a recognised writer, she entered heartily into the political excitements and events of the day. The meeting of the States-General, in May 1789, was to her one of the most signal of these events. In her volume on Rousseau she had anticipated it, with patriotic enthusiasm ; and described ' the great nation which was soon to assemble to consult on its rights, as astonished at recovering, after two centuries, the power to do so.' It was to achieve, in peace, she believed, what ' other nations had reached only through fields of blood.' She invoked the spirit of Rousseau to ' witness the imposing spectacle that France was about to present of a grand event, prepared in advance, and with which for the first time no hazard would mingle.' This was but six months before the session of the assembly.

'I shall never forget,' she says in her work on the Revolution, ' the moment I saw the twelve hundred deputies of France pass in procession to the church to hear mass, on the eve of the opening of the Convention. It was an imposing spectacle, new to this generation of Frenchmen. All the population of Versailles and eager multitudes from Paris assembled to witness it. This novel sort of authority in the State, the nature and power of which they knew not yet, astonished most of those who had not reflected on the rights of nations.' [2]

It was indeed a splendid scene. ' From the

---

[2] *Considérations* &c. i. 16.

church of St. Louis,' says Carlyle, ' to the church of Notre-Dame, one vast suspended billow of life —with spray scattered even to the chimney-tops! For on chimney-tops too, as over the roofs, and up thitherwards on every lamp-iron, sign-post, break-neck coign of vantage, sits patriotic courage, and every window bursts with patriotic beauty; for the deputies are gathering at St. Louis' church to march in procession to Notre-Dame, and hear sermon.—This, the baptism day of Democracy, sick Time has given it birth, the numbered months having run.—The extreme unction day of Feudalism.—The procession of processions advancing towards Notre-Dame; shouts rend the air, one shout at which Grecian birds might drop dead. It is indeed a stately solemn sight. The Elected of France, and then the Court of France; they are marshalled and march there, all in prescribed place and costume. Our Commons in plain black mantle and white cravat; Noblesse in gold-worked, bright dyed cloaks of velvet, resplendent, rustling with laces, waving with plumes; the Clergy in rochet, alb, or other best pontificalities; lastly, comes the King himself, and King's household also, in their brightest blaze of pomp, their brightest and final one—some fourteen hundred men blown together from all winds, on the deep errand.'[3]

'I stood,' writes Madame de Staël, ' at a window near Madame de Montmorin, wife of the Minister

[3] Carlyle's *French Revolution*, iv. 4.

of Foreign Affairs, and abandoned myself—I acknowledge it—to the most exultant hope, in seeing for the first time in France, Representatives of the Nation. Madame de Montmorin said to me, with an emphatic tone, "Do not rejoice; out of this day will arise frightful disasters to France and to us."' The presentiments of this unfortunate lady were too true: she perished on the scaffold with one of her sons; another died prematurely by an accident; her husband was killed in the massacre of September; her eldest daughter died in the hospital of a prison; and her only surviving child, an accomplished, lovely woman, whom we shall hereafter repeatedly meet, sunk under the weight of her griefs before her thirtieth year. 'The family of Niobe,' continues Madame de Staël, 'was not more cruelly struck than that of this poor mother. One would say she prophesied amidst the splendours of the scene at Versailles.'[4]

The patriotic young writer witnessed, the next day, the opening of the States-General, with enthusiasm unchecked by the forebodings of her friend; for her own father was a chief actor in its proceedings, and, when he entered, 'was overwhelmed with applause.' His popularity was then entire. But 'when the King came to present himself on the throne, in the midst of the assembly, I experienced,' she says 'for the first time a presentiment of fear.' She remarked in the aspect and

[4] *Considérations* &c. i. 16.

bearing of the monarch, and of the Queen also, something that led her to apprehend discord between the Government and the deputies, and disaster to the nation. These apprehensions were too well-founded. Day by day 'confusion worse confounded' involved all public affairs. Necker's counsels in the royal cabinet were overruled by the influence of his enemies. He sent in his resignation, but the Government was too dependent upon his popularity to accept it. The rumour of it spread through Versailles; and 'the streets,' writes his daughter, 'were immediately filled with the people shouting his name.' The King and the Queen sent for him the same evening, and both entreated him, for the 'safety of the State,' to resume his place. The Queen added that the security of the King's person depended on his return; she promised solemnly to follow no other counsels than his. This was then her intention, for the popular demonstrations had alarmed her; but, as 'she always believed that any limitation of the royal power would be a misfortune, she necessarily fell again under the influence of those who thought as she did.'

Necker returned, but with little or no other hope than to mitigate rather than avert the coming doom. The deputies, on hearing of the fact—all the 'Third Estate,' the majority of the clergy, the minority of the nobles—crowded his house to thank him. 'I heard my father conjure the deputies of the Third Estate,' writes his daughter, 'not to press their claims too urgently. "You are now the most powerful," he said, "therefore you can afford to be cautious." They wept as he pointed out to them the condition of France and the good they might do.'

But the reconciliation was transient. The Government only apparently favoured him till it could make preparations by which it vainly supposed it could repel the popular opposition and dispense with his services. It adopted a measure which at last proved its ruin. It concentrated its *foreign* troops at hand, and 'on the 11th of July,' writes his daughter, 'just as my father was sitting down to dinner with a numerous company, the Minister of Marine came to him, and calling him aside, gave him a letter from the King, who ordered him to leave Paris, and to do so without noise. He was exiled for the popular cause; had he been factious, the slightest indication of his feelings would have roused the people and prevented his departure. Two hundred thousand armed men would have shouted his name in the streets of Paris and led him back in triumph. His brother, myself, his most intimate friends, were not apprised of his resolution. My mother, who was in very feeble health, took no maid, no travelling dress with her. They mounted their carriage under pretext of an evening drive, and travelled day and night to Brussels. When I rejoined them there, three days later, they still wore the same clothes in which they had departed after a dinner, the numerous guests of which had no suspicion that they were agitated in the slightest degree, and had now quietly separated themselves from France, from their home, their friends, and power. My father's clothes were all covered with dust; he bore an assumed name, that he might not be recognised in France, and be retained by the love of the people. All these circumstances touched me to the quick; I was penetrated with a sentiment of respect which made me prostrate myself before him, as I entered the inn where I found him. Indeed, I have never ceased to experience this sentiment, in the smallest circumstances of his domestic life as in the greatest events of his public career.'[5]

Necker, accompanied by Baron de Staël, left Brussels for Basle, followed soon after by his wife and daughter; but at Frankfort a messenger overtook them with surprising news and urgent orders from the King. Paris had received some intimation of his departure, on the day that it occurred. An insurrection broke out the very next day; on the following day the National Assembly voted that he bore with him its esteem and regrets; on the next, the Bastile fell before the enraged people; and the trembling Court recalled the Swiss heretic. But, though he returned, it was too late; the hurricane

[5] *Du Caractère de Necker* &c.

of the Revolution was rising, and its murmurs were in all the air.

Allusion has already been made to the popular enthusiasm with which he was escorted back to Paris. There is a letter in Grimm's Correspondence which details the splendid ovation, 'the most beautiful spectacle,' he says, 'that I have ever seen,' the happiest witness of which was Necker's daughter, as she rode in the procession with her father. 'A host of cavalry, infantry, and citizens marched out to meet him and conduct him to the Hôtel de Ville. It was one of those triumphal marches that we read of in ancient history.' Several carriages bore Necker and his family and friends—troops before, troops behind, all carrying bouquets and branches of laurel. The drums beat, the bands played; the flags of the overthrown Bastile, the banners of the city guards and of the districts, were displayed in the procession. They marched singing, and throwing flowers in the air. The streets were crowded; all the windows were thronged with applauding women. '*Vive* the great Minister! God preserve him!' resounded everywhere. 'It was one continual acclamation, a universal intoxication.' At the city hall, Lafayette his faithful friend, and Bailly the mayor, received him in the grand hall; the wife of Lafayette accompanying Madame Necker and Madame de Staël thither. Congratulatory speeches were made, and the great throng wept like children at Necker's words. For an hour and a half he was detained in the excited assembly, and meanwhile a countless multitude thronged the neighbouring streets, and greeted him, when he appeared at the window, with the wildest acclamations. 'They wept, and he seemed to them as a god.' Such is popular enthusiasm. Like the multitude which cried on one day, ' Hosannah in the highest!' to the Son of God, and on another, ' Crucify him!' this fickle people were soon to curse the man whom they now hailed as their only political saviour. But again the innumerable host —cavalry, infantry, citizens, with flowers, laurel branches, flags, and music—take up their march, and conduct him onward; for he goes with his family in his *cortége*, to resume, amidst the mortified courtiers, his high functions in the Government. The Assembly vote, as he passes, that ' the day on which this Minister, so beloved, so necessary, has been restored to France, shall be a *fête* day,' and declares ' an amnesty to its enemies.' This very clemency, at which Necker gratefully wept, provoked in a few hours the furious resentment of the people, for it liberated prisoners for whose blood they thirsted. France was morally as well as financially ruined, and the atrocious horrors of the Revolution became inevitable.

But his daughter brushed aside all discomforting anticipations amidst the grateful excitements of this proud day. She saw only the triumph of her beloved father. 'What an interval of felicity,' she exclaims, 'was this journey back from Basle to Paris, such as we made it after my father decided to return. No one but a sovereign of a nation ever made a similar passage... Alas! it was I, above all, who enjoyed it. It was I that it intoxicated. I cannot be ungrateful for those days, whatever has since been the bitterness of my life.... Fifteen years have passed since that time, and nothing has been able to efface this impression, the most vivid of my life... There are few women who have the happiness of hearing the name dearest to their affection thus repeated in the acclamations of a nation, but they will not contradict me when I say that nothing can equal the emotion excited by such circumstances. All those faces which seem kindled by the same love that animates your own heart; those numberless voices which resound through your soul; the beloved name which rises on the air, and seems to echo from the heavens after having swept through the applause of the earth; the enthusiasm, the indescribable electricity that multitudes communicate to one another when excited by a common passion—these all appealing to one's love—love filial or maternal—thrill the soul, and it succumbs to emotions more powerful than itself.'[6] Describing the festal pomps of the journey, she entreats permission to 'dwell upon this day;' and in concluding her account of the transports of the people, writes,

[6] *Du Caractère de M. Necker &c.*

'I saw nothing else at this time, for my consciousness was overpowered by my joy.' 'But,' she sadly adds, 'it was the last day of the prosperity of my life.'[7]

Her present happiness was, however, too great for painful apprehensions about the future. There remains an unpublished letter, written with familiar freedom after the restoration of Necker, by Mlle. Huber to her family in Geneva, which shows that the young authoress had lost little if any of the vivacity and *abandon* of her nature, by the trying scenes through which she had passed since their idyllic life in the woods of St. Ouen. 'My sister asks,' she says, 'if I never see Madame de Staël, as I never speak of her. I speak of her no more than of eating or drinking, because the one is as well understood as the other. During the eleven years of my intimate acquaintance with her there has never been an hour's coolness between us, although we have often differed in opinion, and, in consequence, disputed. Since her father's return to the Ministry, I see her, if possible, more frequently than ever, as we have more to talk about. She does not write a line which I do not see—concerning which she does not consult me; and there is nothing which I am not accustomed to blame, to praise, or correct. For my part, I have all the confidence in her which I ought to have. If Madame de Staël had less levity of head, she would

[7] *Considérations*, i. 23.

be, with the astonishing *esprit* which she possesses, the most celestial creature that one could find on the earth; for, with intelligence above all others, she has a perfect heart but often an erring head. I, who know her better than anyone else, and better than she knows herself, often find her unique, adorable—often blamable, always extravagant and charming. And this intimacy, through which I enjoy all the treasures of her mind and all the good qualities of her heart, is, I assure you, one of the charms of my life. She even spoils me for the other women whom I meet; none love me as she does, and no one pleases me as she.' [8]

She was to pass through farther and severer trials, which, if they were to give more sobriety to her 'head,' were never to break her will or subdue the romantic sensibility of her heart.

Her home was now in Paris, where the name of the Swedish Embassy, on its front, was a protection from the daily increasing tumults of the people. Her parents were at the château of Versailles, towards which the popular agitation constantly gravitated. She was anxious for her father's safety, notwithstanding his late popularity. On the 5th of October, she was alarmed by the report that the populace of the metropolis were thronging towards Versailles. A spectacle was then presented such

---

[8] Family manuscripts of her relative, Prof. Rilliet de Candolle, Geneva.

as had never been recorded in the history of the world. An army of thousands of women, headed by a drummer, and bearing with them, as their chief heroine and chief spokeswoman, a prostitute seated on a cannon, with a lighted torch in her hand, was marching out of the city through a rain storm. Madame de Staël, to avoid the riotous procession, hastened by another road, through the Bois de Boulogne. She reached her parents' apartments, which were connected with those of the King by a long corridor, but they were absent. 'M. Necker,' she says, 'had hastened to the King, and my mother, alarmed by the news which had reached her from Paris, had gone to the *salon* which is next to that of the King, in order to share the fate of my father, whatever it might be. I followed her, and found the *salon* crowded. The scene about the palace was frightful—women and children armed with pikes pressed on all sides. The lowest class of the people were there, imbruted by fury and drunkenness—an infernal host.' Lafayette led up the National Guard, and, 'traversing the *salon* where we were, entered the King's apartment, very calm—I have never seen him otherwise. He came forth from the King, reassuring us all.' They remained on the spot till after midnight, when they retired, hoping that the crisis was passed. Lafayette and his troops were supposed to be a sufficient protection for the palace; but a single passage had been inadvertently left unguarded, and the mob with its assassins found entrance there at five o'clock the next morning. 'At an early hour,' continues Madame de Staël, 'the mother of Count de Choiseul-Gauffier entered my chamber: she came, in her fright, to seek refuge with me, though I had never had the honour of seeing her. She informed me that the assassins had penetrated to the antechamber of the Queen, had massacred some of her guards at her door, and that, awakened by their cries, she had saved her own life only by flying to the chamber of the King, through a secret passage. I learned at the same time that my father had already gone to the King, and my mother was getting ready to follow him. I hastened to accompany her. As we approached the royal apartments we heard the discharge of fire-arms in the court-yard; and, in crossing the gallery, we saw on the floor recent traces of blood. In the next *salon* we met troops who shouted *Vive* Lafayette! for he had saved their lives. We passed through these brave men, but what a sight beyond! The clamorous multitude had demanded that the King should return to Paris with them: he consented, and they were shouting and firing their guns for joy, over their success. The Queen appeared in the *salon* with dishevelled hair and pallid features, but her whole bearing was dignified.' Marie Antoinette, though stricken with long-continued grief, was still beautiful, and her soul was naturally heroic; but she had been maliciously slandered. She had reason to fear their violence, for the court-yard bristled with their arms. Her countenance revealed her apprehensions; nevertheless, she courageously advanced upon the balcony, leading her two children. Lafayette, as generous as gallant, seized the moment to conciliate the ferocious multitude; he stepped to her side, and, kneeling, kissed her hand. The people, struck by the spectacle of their desolate Queen and her children, and the gallantry of their favourite General—'the hero of two worlds'—'shouted her name,' continues Madame de Staël, 'to the very clouds. In returning from the balcony the Queen approached my mother, and with suppressed sobs said, "they force the King and myself to go to Paris, with the heads of our body-guard borne on their pikes." They were thus led into the capital. We returned to Paris by another route, by which we escaped the frightful spectacle. We crossed the Bois de Boulogne: the day was one of rare beauty; the sun irradiated the scenery, not leaving one sombre hue; no external object responded to our sadness. How often this contrast, between the beauty of nature and the sufferings inflicted by man, is renewed in the course of life!' They were then passing over the same road on which she had accompanied her father in the serene moonlight, and with inexpressible joy, at his return to office, in 1788. How prophetically had he then said to her, 'It is too late!'

I shall not discuss here the brief, final administration of Necker. That he was inadequate to the exigency of the crisis need not be denied; for where on the earth could a man have been found adequate to it? There was now no practicable salvation for France. It required the appropriation of the church property, the confiscation of the estates of the nobles, and the spoliation of all Europe by the armies of Napoleon, to restore her finances. If Necker was not a great statesman, he was at least a great financier, and he did what no other man in France could have done to save the nation. But it was 'too late.' His enemies were too mighty for him. Some of the revolutionary leaders, particularly Mirabeau (whose character he justly despised, but whose talents he did not appreciate), turned against him.[9] The popular enthusiasm for him subsided, or rather became demoniacal for slaughter at home and war abroad. Necker's admirable wife saw better than he the coming catastrophe. They had tasted the bitter fruits of ambition; he had, as Gibbon wrote, attained the most conspicuous position in Europe. She urged

---

[9] Mirabeau's hostility arose more from a moral than a political antipathy. It began before he had ever seen Necker, but he knew his character well. He commenced a refutation of Necker's answer to Calonne, on the Finances, but gave it up because he found Necker's figures to be irrefutable; he never acknowledged this reason, but his most confidential friend, Dumont, knew it. Calonne had sustained Mirabeau at Berlin. Clavière, the intimate associate and coadjutor of Mirabeau, and the originator of the *assignats*, aspired to the place of Necker, and stimulated the opposition of Mirabeau. Comp. chaps. i. iii. and xx. of Dumont's *Souvenirs sur Mirabeau*. Paris, 1832.

him to retire, and he had the good sense to follow her advice. In but little more than a year after his last recall to power, he was fleeing before the storm to his native country. Twice was his carriage arrested on the highway, by the mob, which was now ready to sacrifice him among the hecatombs of victims whose blood was about to drench the land. He reached the frontier, and the remainder of his life was spent in his beautiful Swiss retreat, where he wrote numerous works, and found consolation in the ever-increasing fame of his daughter, whom Napoleon himself soon recognised as a rival in the attention of Europe.

We have thus followed her somewhat particularly into the tragic arena of the Revolution, because she is about to reveal to us, amidst its sanguinary scenes, some of the best traits of a truly heroic character.

CHAPTER VII.

MADAME DE STAËL'S HEROISM IN THE REVOLUTION.

Necker at Coppet—His Daughter's Correspondence with him—Parisian Society at this epoch—Influence of Woman—Madame de Staël in the Perils of the Revolution—Heroic Efforts for her Friends—She is arrested—Terrorism in Paris—Her Escape to Coppet.

NECKER left France in September 1790. Madame de Staël was too ill at the time to accompany him. She had given birth, about a week before, to her first child, Augustus Baron de Staël (born August 31, 1790), who was to survive her, and to become the defender of the memory of his grandfather and the editor of his works.[1] As soon as she was able, the young mother hastened to her father. 'I found him,' she says, ' on his estate at Coppet, sad, thoughtful, but without bitterness. In this retreat he developed a soul divine, a character every day more pure, more noble, more sensible.'[2] Her intense affection for him could not detain her at Coppet; her family at Paris required her attention, and she never felt at home in any other place than her native city. Solitude especially was insupportable

[1] *Œuvres complètes,* 15 vols. 8vo. Paris, 1820-21.
[2] *Du Caractère de Necker.*

to her. 'He lived,' she writes, 'in a land which is not my country; where the sciences are much more cultivated than literature. He felt keenly the unhappiness that I experienced, in the struggle between my tastes and the pain of leaving him, even for a few months. He had always taken my part against others; he now took it against myself. When I accused myself of not knowing how to endure the loss of that emulation of thought and of fame which doubles life and all one's forces, he encouraged my predilection for France.'

On returning to Paris, she continued her intercourse with him by correspondence. 'He often told me,' she says, 'that my letters and conversation were all that now kept up his connection with the world. His active and penetrating mind excited me to think, for the sake of the pleasure of talking with him. If I observed, it was to communicate my impressions to him. If I listened, it was to repeat to him.' She wrote to him constantly. It was the task and felicity of her daily life. He burned these letters, fearing that, if discovered by the Government, they might compromise her. Madame Necker de Saussure regrets their loss, and says they excelled any of her published productions; they were full of anecdotes, brilliant passages, and profound reflections.

The charm of Parisian society, a fascination with her down to the last day of her life, was unabated, notwithstanding the popular tumults which now agitated the city. Contrary to what is generally supposed, the intellectual activity of the metropolis was unusually brilliant, amidst the fermentation of these times. It did not display itself in literary productiveness, as in the immediately preceding period, when it was led by the Encyclopædists—by Voltaire, Rousseau, and a host of others; but it prevailed, with all the intensity of the times, in the social circles, the *salons*. She wrote, years later, that 'foreigners who have seen it only since the downfall of Napoleon cannot conceive of the attractions, the *éclat* of the society of Paris. It can be affirmed with truth, that it has never been so brilliant, nor so serious, as during the first three or four years of the Revolution—from 1788 to the end of 1791. Political affairs were still mostly in the hands of the higher classes; all the vigour of liberty and all the grace of the old politeness were combined in their persons. The men of the *tiers état*, distinguished by their culture and their talents, joined themselves to these gentlemen, who were prouder of their merit than of the privileges of their rank; and the greatest social and political questions ever agitated were treated by minds the most capable of understanding and discussing them.'[3] She found, in the freedom with which her sex was allowed to share these discussions, a special attraction for her own superior faculties; for, notwithstanding the restriction

---

[3] *Considérations*, ii. 17.

which the French Salic traditions impose on women in the actual affairs of government, in no other nation has the sex had more effective influence in politics. Woman has, in France, avenged her privation of direct political power by a tenfold greater indirect power. 'In England,' continues Madame de Staël, 'women are accustomed to be silent before men, when political questions are discussed; in France they direct all conversation, and their minds readily acquire the facility and talent which this privilege requires.' She herself had already wielded this indirect influence in the administration of her father. The guests of the Necker *salon* had felt her power. Lafayette, Siéyès, Lally-Tollendal, Narbonne, Talleyrand, and other popular leaders, were her intimate friends, and sought her counsel. She wrote 'the most important part' of Talleyrand's Report on Public Instruction in 1790, and had procured the appointment of Narbonne to the Ministry. She is hereafter to procure the recall of Talleyrand from exile and his appointment to the department of Foreign Affairs; to gather in her *salon*, and become the oracle of, the opposition to the usurpations of Napoleon; and, through Benjamin Constant and others, to influence parties more or less down to the end of her life.

On returning to the capital she plunged into its social and political discussions. But events followed one another swiftly and appallingly; the mob triumphed; and enormities at which the world still shudders were of almost daily occurrence. Her character, as wife of the ambassador of Sweden, was still her protection; and she witnessed, not without a painful sort of fascination, the rapid and frightful progress of the Revolution—the dissolution of the Constituent Assembly; the session and failure of the Legislative Assembly—the pompous ratification and royal acceptance of the Constitution; the utter failure of the Constitution; the march of the Marseillais upon Paris; the attack on the Tuileries; the assassination of the Swiss Guard; the downfall of the monarchy and the imprisonment of the royal family in the Temple; the beginning of the atrocities of the guillotine; the September massacres—the infatuation and the madness of the metropolis, the outburst of general war in Europe, 'drilled Europe against mad undrilled France' [4] —the reign of terror, and the cry, throughout the land, *Aux armes! Marchons!*

Meanwhile the daily increasing tumults of the capital admonished her to provide for her own safety. The Government of Sweden suspended its embassy in 1792; her husband was in Holland; it was again necessary for her to fly, but she delayed in order to save her friends. Before midnight of the 9th of August, the forty-eight tocsins of Paris began to sound, and continued their alarms from steeple to steeple, without a moment's intermission,

[4] Carlyle's *Revolution*, iii. 1.

till after the dawn. 'I was,' she writes, 'at my window, and every quarter of an hour the volunteer patrols of the constitutional party sent us news. They said that the faubourgs were advancing, led by Santerre and Westermann. No one could foresee what might happen the next day, and no one could be sure of living beyond a day. There were, nevertheless, some moments of hope during this frightful night. We flattered ourselves with it. I know not why; perhaps because we had exhausted fear. Suddenly, at seven o'clock, the noise of the cannon was heard.' They were attacking the Tuileries, and butchering the Swiss Guards. 'News was brought me that all my friends who had been guarding the palace were seized and massacred. I went forth immediately to learn more of their fate. The coachman who conducted me was stopped on the bridge by men who assured him that our throats would be cut on the other side. After two hours spent in useless efforts to pass, I learned that those who most interested me still lived, but that most of them had to conceal themselves in order to escape the proscription with which they were menaced.' Notwithstanding the terror which prevailed in all the streets, she went forth in the evening, on foot, to visit them, at the obscure houses where they were hidden. She found armed men and women, asleep with drunkenness, before the doors, half-waking at times only to utter execrations and obscenities.

Orderly people were everywhere fleeing at the approach of the patrols, for the latter were but the servants of the assassins, seeking new victims. She drops her pen over the terrible recital, 'for one cannot have the resolution to continue such pictures.'[5]

From 10th August to 2nd September new arrests were made almost every instant. The seven prisons of Paris are all crowded. Danton and Marat have full sway. The victims are examined by a sort of mock trial, and, under pretext of being sent to the prison of the Abbaye, are confronted at the gates by piles of ghastly dead bodies, and by crowds of infuriated men and women, armed with axes, knives, swords, and pikes, who strike them down and cast them on the reeking heaps. Well might anyone, especially a sensitive woman, flee appalled from these scenes of peril and horror; but Madame de Staël stayed to rescue her friends, though alone, with her servants, in her house. Among these friends, Narbonne, Montmorency, and Baumets, were particularly in danger. They had to conceal themselves in separate private houses, and it was necessary to change their hiding places daily. She offered them asylum in her own mansion, but they declined it, fearing the danger to which it would expose her. At last two of them were compelled to take refuge with her, as no citizen would farther risk his life and that

---

[5] *Considérations*, iii. 9, 10.

of his family by receiving them. She shut them up in the least exposed chamber of the house, revealed the secret to but one of her servants, and passed the night watching at her front window, expecting every moment the 'domiciliary visit' of the patrols. One morning a servant reported to her that a placard at the nearest corner showed the assassins were seeking M. de Narbonne, one of the two friends under her roof. In a few moments the dreaded domiciliary visit was made. Narbonne, if discovered, must have perished the same day; and, whatever precautions she had taken, she knew he could not escape if the search should be thoroughly made. 'It was necessary, therefore,' she writes, ' to prevent the search. I collected all my forces, and I felt in these circumstances that we can always control our emotions, however violent they may be, when we know that they expose the life of another. In seeking the proscribed in all the houses of Paris, the authorities employed men of the lowest, the most ignorant class; military guards were stationed at each extremity of the street, while these ruffians searched the dwellings. I began by alarming them with the consequences of violating an ambassador's house. The common people must be subdued at once, or not at all; there are no gradations in their sentiments or their ideas. Perceiving that my arguments impressed them, I had the courage, with death in my heart, to treat them with pleasantries. Nothing is more agreeable to men of this class than humour, because, in spite of their fury against the higher classes, they are delighted to be treated by the latter as equals. I thus conducted them to the door, and thanked God for the extraordinary strength which He had given me at this critical moment. Nevertheless, this situation could not be prolonged; for the least hazard might ruin a proscribed man, like Narbonne, who was well known by his recent connection with the Ministry.'

She did not rest till she had saved him. A generous Hanoverian, Dr. Bollmann, known later by his endeavours to rescue Lafayette from his Austrian prison, offered, from no other motive than his enthusiastic humanity, to conduct Narbonne to England with the passport of a friend. It was at the risk of his own life that the brave Hanoverian undertook this difficult task; for it was death to any foreigner to be detected in helping away a proscribed Frenchman. In four days Narbonne was safe in London.

Madame de Staël had obtained the necessary passport for her passage, with her family, into Switzerland, where her parents anxiously expected her; but more of her friends were in danger, and she courageously delayed from day to day in order to save them. On the last day of August, M. de Jaucourt, a deputy to the Legislative Assembly, and M. de Lally-Tollendal, were sent to the Abbaye. To be sent to that prison meant assassination. Lally escaped this fate by his generosity and his talents. He pleaded the cause of one of his fellow prisoners before the tribunal with so much skill and eloquence, as not only to obtain his acquittal, but to interest the Court in his own behalf, and, by the aid of Condorcet and the British ambassador, he was saved. But Jaucourt had no other help than that of Madame de Staël. She looked over the list of the members of the Commune of Paris, then its masters. 'I knew them,' she says, 'only by their terrible reputation, and I sought, at hazard, a motive to determine my choice. I at once recollected Manuel among them, a man who made some pretensions to literature, for he had published "Letters of Mirabeau," with a preface, poor enough indeed, but showing some literary vanity.' She hoped to be able to touch this susceptibility, and requested, by letter, an interview with him. He appointed the next morning at eleven o'clock. She was punctual to the time, but had to wait an hour for him, in his study. Observing his portrait hanging over his desk, she indulged still stronger hope of making an impression upon him. 'He entered,' she writes, 'and I ought to do him the justice to say that it was by his good sentiments alone that I was able to move him. I painted to him the frightful uncertainties of popularity, proofs of which were of daily occurrence. "In six months," I said, "you may no longer have power. Save Lally and Jaucourt. Reserve for yourself a sweet and consoling recollection for the time when you may be proscribed."' She hardly needed prescience, in these terrible times, to be able to make such a prediction; in less than six months Manuel perished on the scaffold. 'He was,' she adds, 'a susceptible man, led by his passions, but sensitive to honourable motives.' He could not resist the pathetic appeal of Necker's daughter. He knew her reputation; she stood before him with the charms of her talents and her young womanhood, for she was now only about twenty-six years old. She was to him not only a woman, a genius, but a heroine. He yielded, and the next day wrote to her that Condorcet had obtained the liberation of Lally, and he himself had released Jaucourt, in answer to her entreaties.

It was now high time that she should make her own escape, for the delirium of the city was hourly rising and spreading. It was on the next day that the frightful massacre of September took place: the murder of the prisoners, in which two thousand and eighty-nine, including two hundred and two priests, were butchered. It required the more than manly, the superhuman moral courage, which sometimes reveals itself in woman, to face the horrors of that day. But the heroic young matron, though suffering again from the premonitory debility and anxieties of maternity, confronted the universal madness to save another life. She had made preparations to depart that morning. The tocsins were resounding over the city from the forty-eight spires. 'Terror,' says the historian, 'terror in the streets, terror and rage, tears and frenzy; tocsin *miserere* pealing through the air.'[6]

She had promised to take the proscribed Abbé de Montesquiou, disguised as one of her servants, from beyond the barrier to Switzerland, though the penalty for her generosity was death. She had given him the passport of one of her domestics, and they had agreed on the place where she was to meet him on the road. Were she to fail, the patrols, everywhere guarding the roads, would probably detect him. She committed a grave error in the outset. Supposing that her rank as wife of a foreign ambassador could protect her, she started in a carriage with six horses, and with her servants in livery. 'It was,' she says, ' a misfortune, for at such a time it is necessary not to strike the imagination of the people: the poorest postchaise would have been safer. Hardly had my horses made four steps, when we were surrounded by a crowd of haggard women. They threw themselves against the horses, crying that we ought to be arrested, as bearing away the gold of the nation to aid its enemies. Their clamours drew the mob around us, men of ferocious aspect, who seized the postilions, and ordered them to conduct us to the Assembly of the quarter in which we resided—the Faubourg Saint Germain. In

[6] Carlyle, *French Revolution*, iii. 1.

descending from the carriage, I seized the opportunity of whispering to the servant of the Abbé Montesquiou to report to him our misfortune.'

She entered the Assembly, and found it a scene of the utmost confusion. Its president declared that she was denounced as attempting to carry away proscribed enemies of the Government, and that her people must be examined. He perceived that one of them, mentioned in her passport, was not among them,—the one she had sent to the Abbé de Montesquiou. In consequence of this fact she was sent to the Hôtel de Ville. 'Nothing,' she says, 'could be more frightful than this order. It was necessary to traverse half of Paris to reach the Hôtel de Ville; and on the steps of this building many persons had been massacred, on the 10th of August.' She came near being the first feminine victim of the Revolution, in Paris, for no woman had yet perished there in the horrors of these times; but on the very next day the beautiful Princesse de Lamballe was assassinated. Led forth from her mock trial by two ruffians, she recoiled from the opening door, at the sight of heaps of dead and lacerated bodies. Her conductors pressed her forward. A drunken brute struck her with his sabre above her eyes; the blood flowed down her face, and her long hair fell upon her shoulders; she was fainting, but her supporters dragged her onward among the bleeding victims. She was struck again, with a bludgeon, on the back of her head, and fell, happily insensible, upon a pile of corpses. The mob tore off her clothes and dismembered her body with diabolical jeers and obscenities. They cut off her head, and bore it on a pike through the streets. For two hours her mutilated corpse lay exposed amidst their brutal revelry. It was hewed into pieces, which were borne about as reeking trophies. One of her legs was fired from a cannon. Her heart was cut out and carried on the point of a sabre, along with her head, in what has been called an 'infernal promenade,' under the prison window of Marie Antoinette, at the Temple. Such was the demoniacal madness of this day; such the possible fate that the daughter of Necker escaped by less than twenty-four hours. Womanly virtue and beauty have, perhaps, never suffered baser, more hideous insult, than in the person of the Princesse de Lamballe; at least, history has never dared to record an equally atrocious example.

Madame de Staël says of the common people who thronged her passage to the Hôtel de Ville, that their 'fury was now such that all eyes seemed to demand blood.' It required three hours for her carriage to make its way through the tumultuous streets. The armed mob assailed her with cries of 'Death.' Her aristocratic equipage excited their vengeance. She appealed to the *gendarmes* in the throng for protection, but they responded in derisive and menacing language. 'I was pregnant,' she says, 'but this did not cause them to relent; on the contrary, they were the more irritated as they felt themselves to be the more culpable.' The *gendarme* who had been placed in her carriage was, however, touched with sympathy for her, and promised to defend her at the peril of his life. Arriving at the Place de Grève, in front of the Hôtel de Ville, she passed under an arch of pikes and ascended the stairs, which were lined on each side with lancers. A ruffian thrust his weapon at her, but her *gendarme* averted it with his sabre. 'Had I fallen at this moment,' she writes, 'I should have been killed, for it is the nature of the mob to finish a fallen victim.' She stood at last in the hall before Robespierre. It was full of men women, and children, infuriated and shouting *Vive la Nation!* She pleaded her right to depart as 'Ambassadress of Sweden.' Such a plea might have availed her little, but, fortunately, Manuel appeared at this moment in the hall. Surprised to find her there, he pledged himself to be responsible for her till the Commune should decide her fate, and led her and her women out of this miserable place into his own office, where she remained six hours, suffering from hunger and thirst, and seeing, from the windows, the assassins return from the prisons with bare and bloody arms. They converted the Place into a hell by their horrible yells and orgies. The mob attempted to pillage her carriage, but a stout man in the dress of the National Guard mounted to the coachman's box, and there spent two hours in defending her luggage. She could not imagine who he could be; but in the evening he accompanied Manuel to his apartment, when she perceived that he was Santerre, the brewer, so noted in the tumults of the times, and later and for ever infamous as superintending the execution of Louis XVI. and ordering his drummers to drown, by their noise, the last words of the unfortunate monarch. Santerre had witnessed the distribution of corn provided by Necker for the poor of the Faubourg Saint Antoine, in a time of famine; and now remembered the generosity of the father in favour of the daughter.

Manuel, unwilling to expose himself, or her, to the mob during the day, conducted her to her home in the night. The street lamps were not lighted, but men bearing torches cast a weird *chiaroscuro* upon the scene, and frequently stopped him, demanding who he was? 'The Procureur of the Commune' was his answer; and he was permitted to pass on.

Manuel prepared for her a new passport, but it permitted no one to accompany her besides a single female servant. A *gendarme* was promised to conduct her to the frontier. The next day Tallien, who afterwards delivered France from Robespierre, called to see her safely beyond the barrier. 'At every step we learned,' she writes, 'of new massacres. Many persons thoroughly compromised were still concealed in my house. I entreated Tallien not to expose them; he promised that he would not, and kept his promise. I entered my carriage with him; and, separated from my friends, without our being able mutually to express our thoughts, the circumstances froze the words on our lips. I encountered yet, in the environs of Paris, difficulties of which I will not speak; but, as I hastened on my route, the fury of the tempest gradually abated, and in the mountains of the Jura nothing recalled the frightful agitation of Paris.' From their heights she beheld, below her, a picture which could not fail to restore serenity to her soul, the picture which she first saw in her travels in 1784—Lake Leman, placidly glittering in the early autumn sun, and shut in by the 'everlasting hills' which guard it in their tranquil majesty; and, amidst the quiet homes of vintagers, the spacious walls of the château of Coppet, where affectionate hearts, after long and anxious waiting, were about to welcome her to their own safety and peace. The change was to her as a transition from hell to heaven.

She thus escaped out of the very vortex of the Revolution. During the dismal four years since the publication of her Letters on Rousseau she had no time nor disposition to attempt any literary work. It would have been sacrilege, she says, to have thought of literary ambition. The disasters of her country, and the perils of her friends, absorbed her entire attention. They were years, however, of important mental and moral growth to her. She had studied humanity in some of its worst and best revelations. She had witnessed its basest crimes and its noblest heroism, and she had herself become heroic.

CHAPTER VIII.

AT COPPET.

Coppet—Madame de Staël rescues Achille du Chayala—Mathieu de Montmorency—Fate of his Family—Scenery of Lake Leman—Lacretelle on the Heroism of Madame de Staël.

PEACEFULLY sheltered in the château at Coppet, Madame de Staël immediately became its *châtelaine*, the priestess of its abundant hospitalities. Her mother was sinking under infirmities which the anxieties of her Parisian life had aggravated beyond hope of relief. For a long time she had suffered from a nervous malady which seriously incommoded her in the society of her *salon*, and which was to end her days in about four years after the arrival of her daughter.

Though Madame de Staël was herself in delicate health, she forgot herself in her interest for her imperilled friends. She could bear any affliction of her own better than her painful sympathy with the sufferings of others. The latter was unendurable to her sensitive nature. Excepting an interval of a few months which she spent in England, she made the Coppet mansion, during the

'Reign of Terror,' an asylum for Frenchmen who were fleeing from the guillotine. They were 'friends of liberty,' as she calls them, who had favoured the Revolution, but who now, in its atrocious excesses, were, like the 'emigrant' nobles, under its relentless proscription. Her husband had aided her generous efforts to save them, by giving them Swedish names, which were inserted in their passports, and were strictly used in their familiar intercourse at Coppet. 'Scaffolds,' she says, 'were prepared for them on the frontiers of their own country, and persecution of every kind awaited them in foreign lands.'

An example will show her devoted sympathy for these sufferers. Achille du Chayala, a nephew of Count Jaucourt to save whom we have seen her risking her life at Paris, was endeavouring to escape to Switzerland. She sent him a Swiss passport bearing an assumed name, with which he had nearly reached the frontier, but he was arrested in the village of Moret, at the foot of the Jura mountains, the authorities suspecting that his real name was not on the passport. He was imprisoned until they could ascertain, from a magistrate in Nyon, whether he was a citizen of Switzerland or not. M. de Jaucourt was then at Coppet, bearing a Swedish name; on hearing of the danger of his nephew he was in despair, for the young man not only bore a false passport, but was of a well-known aristocratic family, and a son of one of the chiefs of the emigrant army of Condé. Were his real name discovered, he would be immediately executed. Jaucourt appealed to his hostess to rescue the youth. She saw but one hope for him: could she induce M. de Reverdil, a functionary of Nyon, to claim him as a native of the Canton de Vaud, he might be saved. She hastened to Reverdil. 'He was,' she remarks, 'an old friend of my parents, and was one of the best cultivated and best esteemed men of this part of Switzerland. He refused my plea at first, making the gravest objections. He scrupled to disguise the truth for any reason whatever; and, moreover, he was afraid of compromising his country by a false official act. "If the truth should be discovered in this case," he said, "I could no longer have the right to reclaim our own countrymen who might be arrested in France. I should thus expose those who are confided to my official care for a man who has no legal claim on us." This was a very plausible argument, but I pleaded for an innocent man over whose head was suspended the murderous axe. I remained two hours with M. de Reverdil, endeavouring to conquer his scruples by his humanity; he long resisted me, but, when I repeated to him many times, "If you say no, an only son, a man without reproach, will be assassinated within twenty hours, and your own word slays him," my emotion, or rather his, triumphed over every other consideration, and the young

Chayala was saved. It was the first time in my life that two apparent duties were opposed to each other; but I think still, as I thought then, that the present and certain danger of the victim ought to have more force, as an argument, than the uncertain dangers of the future. There is not in the brief space of existence a greater chance of good than that of saving the life of an innocent man.'[1] She believed that, in a case like this, deception is as admissible as it would be in war, or in the treatment of a highway assassin, or lunatic. Du Chayala, being claimed by the Swiss official, was liberated, and found shelter among the numerous exiles of Coppet.

Among these refugees was Mathieu de Montmorency, of one of the most distinguished families of France. He had fought for the colonies in the American War of Independence, and had actively and early favoured the Revolution in his own country, but, like Lafayette and many other patriots, he had turned away from its horrors, and was now under its proscription. Sympathising with the political opinions of Madame de Staël, he was attached to her by a friendship which was to survive important changes in his own politics, and to be shared, through many years, with her dearest female friend, Madame Récamier, in scenes of common sufferings and common happiness. His subsequent public services to his country, his literary

---

[1] *Considérations*, iii. 18.

culture, his profoundly religious spirit, and the long life in which he outlived most of his associates of these troubled times, render him one of the most interesting characters in the Coppet portrait gallery. 'Alas!' exclaims Madame de Staël, 'I was not always so happy in my relations with my friends as in the case of Du Chayala. It was necessary for me to announce, about a month after, to a man the most capable of affection, and, therefore, of profound suffering, Mathieu de Montmorency, the sentence of death pronounced against his young brother, the Abbé de Montmorency, whose only crime was the illustrious name he received from his ancestors. At the same time the wife and mother-in-law of M. de Montmorency were equally menaced with death, for in a few days all prisoners were, at this frightful period, sent to the scaffold.' All these members of the illustrious family of Montmorency perished immediately by the guillotine. Mathieu de Montmorency was saved only by his timely escape to his friend at Coppet.

Though the numerous guests of the château were beyond immediate danger, they suffered incessant anxiety for their absent kindred, and were saddened by daily reports of new executions. Madame de Staël could not but feel the contrast between these horrors and the serene beauty of the scenes around her. 'One of the reflections which struck us most,' she remarks, 'in our long promenades on the shores of Lake Leman, was the contrast between the enchanting scenery, radiant with the splendid sun of the last days of June, and the despair of man, who would wish the very sun itself to sympathise with his sufferings and share his mourning. We were in utter discouragement. The younger we were, the less were we resigned; for in youth, above all, one expects happiness, and, claiming it as a right, revolts at the idea of failing to attain it. It was nevertheless in these moments while we looked in vain to the sky and the flowers, inwardly reproaching them for illuminating and perfuming the air in presence of so much misery, that the time of our deliverance was preparing.' The ninth of Thermidor was approaching, when Robespierre and his fellow assassins were to fall, and 'inexpressible joy thrill the heart of France:' the joy of deliverance from almost universal murder—'for poor human nature,' she adds, 'knows no higher happiness than that of the cessation of suffering.'

Lacretelle, the historian, in an eloquent chapter on ' The Heroism of Women during the Reign of Terror,' exclaims: ' While blood flowed in torrents in Paris and other cities, who dared to gather and conceal for long periods the innumerable proscribed persons of the 10th of August, and associated themselves with their fate?—Never is woman more beautiful than when she accomplishes a good and great action. Behold Madame de Staël watching, from the 10th of August even to the days of September, over the illustrious men, conquered on the 10th—

Narbonne, Montmorency, Jaucourt, and many others. Both her genius and her fortune are consecrated to friendship and pity. Even in the château at Coppet, crowded by the friends whom she has saved, she watches still over those who remain in the gulf. She knows certain asylums for them, and sends guides to lead them across France, through the continuous lines of the revolutionary committees. She, who had elevated herself to an intellectual height known to few men, studied now but one art—that of achieving, against crime, the most noble and most salutary of contraband acts. Coppet becomes a common asylum for *émigrés*, voluntary and involuntary. Neither she nor her father cares for opinions in the presence of misfortune. Ah! history is not large enough for the full commemoration of such hospitable devotion.'[2] Lacretelle himself had been in peril of the guillotine, and, after two years of imprisonment, owed his deliverance to Madame de Staël.

Jacques Treboux was her heroic agent in these merciful services. He was familiar with the mountain passes. He made many voyages from Coppet to Paris, charged with missions from the refugees of the château. He conducted across the Juras, to Coppet, many a compromised person. Mallet d'Hauteville has made him a character in a novel founded on the memories of Coppet.[3]

[2] *Testament Philosophique et Littéraire*, ii. 26. 2 vols. Paris, 1840.
[3] Gaullieur's *Etrennes Nationales*. Lausanne, 1845.

CHAPTER IX.

IN ENGLAND—THE ROYAL EXECUTIONS.

The French Mickleham Colony—Fanny Burney—Life at Mickleham—The Burney Letters—Necker and the King's Death—Madame de Staël pleads for the Queen—Execution of the Queen—Madame de Staël writes for Peace—Her Politics.

EARLY in 1793 Madame de Staël made her first visit to England. Most of the French *émigrés* had gone beyond the Rhine, and were in arms against the Government; not a few had taken refuge in England. They had hitherto been chiefly of the aristocratic classes: nobles, clergy, Government functionaries—original opponents of the Revolution. For some time, however, another class of refugees had been thronging to every accessible foreign asylum: men who had been active in the inception of the Revolution, but had now incurred its proscription. The two classes were nearly as mutually hostile abroad as they had been at home; and in England, especially, their respective circles were rigorously exclusive of each other, and rife with reciprocal accusations and slanders.

Madame de Staël was too conspicuous a character to escape disparagement from the aristocrats who had opposed her father as the principal instigator of the Revolution. She did not court their society, but gathered around her some congenial friends in an elegant home called Juniper Hall, at Mickleham, Surrey. Norbury Park, the seat of Mr. Phillips, son-in-law of Dr. Burney, the well-known historian of music, was not far from Juniper Hall; and the two households maintained cordial terms of good neighbourhood and hospitality. We may well thank God that, from the confusion of society, the delirium of the human world, we can find refuge in the solitudes of nature, in her quiet beauty and her tranquil stability, and in literature and the social amenities. These refugees from the most frightful scenes the nations have ever witnessed enjoyed among the natural beauties of Surrey an interval of serene, of even joyous life. Kindly nature gave them at least a temporary relief from the tumults and atrocities which had appalled them in their Continental homes.

Miss Fanny Burney, the sister of Mrs. Phillips, and the 'dear little Burney' of Dr. Johnson—now one of the waiting women of Queen Charlotte, and still better known as the author of 'Evelina,' 'Cecilia,' 'Cornelia,' &c.—was rusticating at Norbury Park, and has left us, in her published 'Diary and Letters,' some entertaining glimpses of her French neighbours.[1] They formed a considerable colony. Among them was, occasionally at least, Talleyrand, the ex-ecclesiastic, the statesman, and the wit; Guibert, whose eulogistic rhapsody on Madame de Staël has been previously cited, and whose memory she generously commemorated, as we have seen, in an eloquent 'Eloge;' Narbonne, who had been a familiar guest in the *salon* of her mother, whose appointment as Minister of War had been procured by her influence, whose life she had lately saved in Paris, and who, perhaps, was too dear to her; General d'Arblay, who gave lessons in French to Fanny Burney, won her affections, and married her, 'though she was more than forty years old;' a daughter of Montmorin, the Minister of Foreign Affairs, whose wife had forewarned Madame de Staël, in sight of the procession of the States-General at Versailles, that 'out of this day will spring frightful disasters to France and to us'—the father, mother, and one of their sons had already perished by violent deaths; Lally-Tollendal, whose pleading for one of his proscribed friends saved his own life, and who lived to vindicate the memory of Necker; Montmorency, the faithful counsellor of Madame de Staël; Jaucourt, whom she had saved from death; Girardin, late member of the Legislative Assembly, son of the Marquis Girardin of Ermenonville, and pupil of Rousseau,

---

[1] *Diary of Madame d'Arblay* &c., vol. v. part viii. (5 vols. 8vo.). London, 1842.

who died on his estate there; Sicard, one of Lafayette's officers; the Duke de Guignes, who had been the French Minister at London; the Princesse d'Henin, the Princesse de Poix, and others. They formed a circle distinguished by culture as well as by social rank, and contrived to alleviate their exile by dramatic readings and other literary entertainments, by their brilliant conversations, by rides among the scenery of the vicinity, and visits to and from the neighbouring gentry.

Fanny Burney was fascinated by this novel and elegant little society. 'She was forced,' says Macaulay, 'to own that she had never heard conversation before. The most animated eloquence, the keenest observation, the most sparkling wit, the most courtly grace, were united to charm her. She listened with rapture to Talleyrand and Madame de Staël; joined with D'Arblay in execrating the Jacobins and in weeping for the unhappy Bourbons; took French lessons from him, fell in love with him, and married him with no better provision than a precarious annuity of one hundred pounds.'[2]

Talleyrand is the wit of the circle. Madame de Châtre is described as 'about thirty-two years old, of an elegant figure; well read, full of *esprit*, very charming;' Narbonne as 'about forty, rather fat, but he would be handsome were it not for a squint in one eye.' M. de Jaucourt 'is far from

[2] Macaulay's *Essays*, v. 1.

handsome, but has a very intelligent countenance, fine teeth, and is very expressive.' He tells the English guests the story of Madame de Staël's heroism in rescuing him and others from the guillotine in Paris. 'This lady,' he says, 'who was seven months gone with child, was indefatigable in her efforts to save everyone she knew from the dreadful massacres. She walked daily (for carriages were not then allowed in the streets) to the Hôtel de Ville, and was frequently shut up for five hours with the horrible wretches who composed the committee of *surveillance* by whom these murders were directed; and, by her eloquence and the consideration demanded by her rank and talents, she obtained the deliverance of above twenty unfortunate prisoners, some of whom she knew but slightly.'[3]

Madame de Staël is the cynosure of these *conversazioni*. If Talleyrand excels all in *bons mots* and epigrams, she dazzles all by the splendid variety and happy pertinence of her ideas, the richness of her style, and the generous enthusiasm of her sentiments. At one time she thrills the company by her passionate recitation of a tragedy; at another she entertains them, and particularly commands the applause of Talleyrand, by reading the first chapter of her work on the 'Influence of the Passions on the Happiness of Individuals and of Nations,' one of her most elaborate productions,

[3] The D'Arblay *Diary* &c.

to which she now devoted occasional hours, but which was not published till 1796. 'She read,' writes Mrs. Phillips, 'the noble tragedy of "Tancrède," till she blinded us all around. She is the most charming person, to use her own phrase, that never I saw.' Though usually a very effective reader, she could not escape occasional criticism from Talleyrand. 'Madame de Staël was very gay and Talleyrand very comic this evening; he criticised, among other things, her reading of prose, with great *sang froid.* " You read prose very badly," he said; " you have a sing-song tone in reading—a cadence, and also a monotony which is not good at all; one always believes that you are reading verse, and that has a very bad effect." They talked over a number of their friends and acquaintances with the utmost unreserve, and sometimes with the most comic humour imaginable—Lally, Lafayette, the Princesse d'Henin, the Princesse de Poix, and Guibert, who was, Madame de Staël told me, passionately in love with her before she married—and innumerable others.' D'Arblay employs his leisure in copying, for her, her essay on the Passions. Lally reads to them his own tragedy on the 'Death of Strafford;' but the company, though they have come from actual scenes the most tragic in the history of the world, are not predisposed to melancholy sentimentality; they amuse themselves at the contrast between the lachrymose style of the drama and the violent gesticulation and Falstaffian corpulence of its author. French gaiety predominates in their circle. Poverty itself cannot damp their national vivacity.

They are compelled to economise; most of them have lost their all in the wreck of their country; and those who, like Narbonne and Madame de Staël, retain ample resources, are embarrassed by the difficulties which attend the remittance of their funds. The few that have any means share them with the many who have none. They are content with one small carriage, which they have bought for their drives in the beautiful scenery of Surrey. It can hold but two persons. Talleyrand and Narbonne gaily take their turns to ride behind as footmen; and, breaking the glass from the back of the vehicle, keep up the liveliest conversation with its inmates. Madame de Staël assures us that she never heard more brilliant talk than in these gay excursions. Penury had become honourable among the *émigrés*, not only at Mickleham, but in all their English resorts; for many of them who had been in the highest social positions of France were its victims abroad. Dutens, who, by his long connection with the diplomatic service of England, was more an Englishman than a Frenchman, witnessed their exemplary sufferings with admiration. 'They were not ashamed,' he says, 'to be poor, though they had to do their utmost to save themselves from want. I saw women of the highest condition and greatest name submit to their necessary work, and gentlemen devote themselves to various labours, and never thereby lose the elevation of their sentiments.'[4]

Madame d'Arblay's Diary and Letters, describing the life of the little colony at Mickleham, allude to the slanders which the aristocratic *émigrés* in London were jealously circulating against its chief members.

On the 4th of February 1793, she writes to her father: 'Madame de Staël is now at the head of the little French colony in this neighbourhood. Monsieur de Staël is at present suspended in his embassy, but not recalled; it is uncertain yet whether the regent, Duke of Sudermania, will send him to Paris during the present horrible Convention, or order him home. He is now in Holland, waiting for commands. Madame de Staël was unsafe in Paris, though an ambassadress, from the resentment owed her by the Commune. She is a woman of the first abilities, I think, I have ever seen. She is more in the style of Mrs. Thrale than of any other celebrated character; but she has infinitely more depth, and seems even a profounder politician and metaphysician. She has suffered us to hear some of her works in manuscript, which are truly wonderful, for powers both of thinking and of expression. She adores her father, but is alarmed at having had no news of him since he has heard of the death of the martyred Louis. Ever

---

[1] *Mémoires d'un Voyageur qui se repose*, ii. 24. Paris, 1806.

since her arrival she has been pressing me to spend some time with her before I return to town. She exactly resembles Mrs. Thrale in the ardour and warmth of her partialities. I find her impossible to resist. She is only a short walk from here, at Juniper Hall. There can be nothing imagined more charming, more fascinating, than this little colony; between their sufferings and their *agrémens*, they occupy us almost wholly. Monsieur Narbonne bears the highest character for goodness, parts, sweetness of temper, and ready wit. He has been affected by the King's death; but relieved by hearing, through Monsieur de Malesherbes, that his master retained a regard for him to the last. Monsieur de Talleyrand insists on conveying this letter to you. He has been on a visit here, and returns again on Wednesday.'

On the 19th of February her father writes to her: 'I am not at all surprised at your account of the captivating powers of Madame de Staël. It corresponds with all I have heard about her, and with the opinion I formed of her intellectual and literary powers, in reading her charming little "Apologie de Rousseau." But, as nothing human is allowed to be perfect, she has not escaped censure. Her house was the centre of the Revolutionists, previous to the 10th of August; and she has been accused of partiality to Monsieur de Narbonne. But perhaps all may be Jacobinical malignity. However, unfavourable stories have been brought hither, and the Burks and Mrs. Ord have repeated them to me. But you know that Monsieur Necker's administration, and the conduct of the nobles who first joined in the violent measures that subverted the ancient establishments, by the abolition of nobility and the ruin of the Church, during the first National Assembly, are held in greater horror by the aristocrats than even the members of the present Convention. If you are not absolutely in the house of Madame de Staël, perhaps it may be possible for you to waive the visit to her.'

In answer to her father she says: 'I am both hurt and astonished at the acrimony of malice; indeed, I believe all this party to merit nothing but honour, compassion, and praise. Madame de Staël, the daughter of Necker—the idolising daughter, of course, and from the best motives, those of filial reverence—entered into the opening of the Revolution just as her father entered into it; but as to her house having become the centre of the Revolutionists before the 10th of August, it was only so for the Constitutionalists who were at that time not only members of the then established Government, but friends of the King. The aristocrats were then already banished, or wanderers from fear, or silent from cowardice; as to the Jacobins, I need not, after what I have already related, tell you how utterly abhorrent to her must be that fiend-like set. The aristocrats, however, as you well observe, and as she has herself told me, hold the Constitutionalists in greater horror than the Convention itself. The malignant assertions which persecute her, all of which she has lamented to us, she imputes equally to the bad and virulent of both parties. The intimation concerning Monsieur de N. was, however, wholly new to us, and I do firmly believe it to be a gross calumny. Monsieur de N. was of her society, which contained ten or twelve of the first people, and occasionally all Paris; she loves him even tenderly, but so openly, so unaffectedly, so simply, and with such utter freedom from coquetry, that, were they two men or two women, the affection could not, I think, be more obviously undesigning. She is very plain, he is very handsome; her intellectual endowments must be, with him, her chief attractions. Monsieur de Talleyrand was another of her society, and she seems equally attached to him. In short, her whole *coterie* live together as brothers. Madame la Marquise de la Châtre, and a daughter of the unhappy Montmorin, are also with Madame de Staël. Indeed, I think you could not pass a day with them, and not see that their commerce is that of pure, exalted, and most elegant friendship. Nevertheless, I would give the world to avoid being even a guest under their roof, now I have heard the shadow of such a rumour.'

Madame de Staël attempted to correspond with Miss Burney in English. In one of her letters she tells how she studied the language, but in a style which shows that her method was not remarkably successful. 'When I learned to read English,' she says, 'I began by Milton to know all, or renounce at all in once.' She alludes with indignant emotion to the charges of the aristocratic *émigrés* who accused her of being in democratic sympathy with the Jacobins, and 'sought to embitter the security of friendship' by their reports respecting Narbonne.

Notwithstanding Miss Burney's opinion of the malicious character of the reports against the little colony, her own shallow character was revealed in her later treatment of Madame de Staël. She had occasion deeply to regret it, as we shall see. Her soul was essentially narrow and superficial. Some years afterwards, when she accompanied D'Arblay to Paris, as his wife, she evaded the proffered courtesies of Madame de Staël, who was then the object of Napoleon's paltry jealousy. The authoress of 'Corinne' and 'L'Allemagne' could not, however, be disparaged in being ignored by the authoress of 'Evelina' and 'Cornelia.'[5] Madame de Staël never knew envy or malice from her own heart—no human being was ever more sympathetic, more confiding; and it is affecting to observe with what sisterly tenderness she clings to the English authoress, notwithstanding the evident increasing coolness of the

---

[5] 'Miss Burney was a vulgar woman, and, if anyone doubts it, let him read her Diary and Letters.'—Wharton's *Queens of Society*, p. 367. London, 1867.

latter. When Fanny marries M. d'Arblay, she writes to her from Coppet: 'They tell me news which makes me extremely happy. Your heart is capable of appreciating the heroic conduct of our friend, and of justifying fate in giving you to him, as God's recompense of his virtues on this earth. As you are now, in a sense, of my family, I hope that if I return to England I shall see you as much as I wish—that is to say, without ceasing. All my regrets, as all my hopes, recall me to Surrey. It is the earthly paradise for me; I hope it will be for you. I do not know a better character than M. d'Arblay; and I have known for a long time how much he loves you. You ought to write to us very often at present. Please inform me of your projects; confide to me your happiness; and if I can ever serve you, in any manner, dispose of me as your own property. Adieu, adieu!'

The colony at Mickleham made the most of their resources of enjoyment, amidst scenery celebrated for its picturesque beauty, with occupations tending to their culture, and with the characteristic gaiety of their French temperament. Their want of means compelled them to sacrifice their jewels and laces. Dumont says of Talleyrand that 'he knew how to accustom himself in his exile to a simple life, to endure privations, and to share with his friends the single resource he had saved from France—the remnants of a superb library, sold at great loss; for the spirit of party even in London was unfavourable to competition of purchasers.'[6] Some of them had to give French lessons; others to undertake 'menial offices,' but they never failed to amuse themselves. Talleyrand was at last ordered out of the country by the Government, and sailed for America; Narbonne left; and Madame de Staël returned in the summer of 1793 to Coppet, and thence to Paris. Miss Burney was not with her at the time of her departure from Juniper Hall, but her sister, Mrs. Phillips, was there, and wrote soon after, that 'she could not rally her spirits at all; and seemed like one torn from all that is dear to her. I was truly concerned. After giving me a variety of charges, or rather entreaties, to watch and attend to the health, spirits and affairs of the friends she was leaving, she said to me, "And say to Miss Burney that I feel nothing against her—that I quit the country loving her very sincerely and without resentment." I assured her of your admiration, and chagrin at seeing no more of her. She seemed pleased, and said, "You are very good to say this to me," but in a low and faint voice, and dropped the subject. She actually sobbed on saying farewell to Mrs. Lock; and, halfway down the hill, her parting with me was likewise very tender. I determined to see her again, and met her near the school, on Wednesday. She could not speak to me; but kissed her hand, with a very speaking and touching expression of countenance.'

[6] Dumont's *Souvenirs sur Mirabeau* &c. chap. xvii.

Early in this year Louis XVI. was condemned to death. Necker had asked permission to return to Paris and defend his unfortunate King before the Convention. His prayer was refused; but he published a pamphlet in behalf of the royal prisoner, the only effect of which was the confiscation of all his own property in France. On January 21, the King, accompanied by a confessor, the Abbé Edgeworth, was conducted, in a close carriage, to the guillotine. The way was guarded by eighty thousand troops; all business was suspended, all shops were shut. Cannons bristled at points on the route, and the artillerymen stood ready with burning matches. The scaffold was surrounded by an immense crowd, impatient to witness the great crime. The drums were beating furiously. Louis, with a loud and indignant voice, bade the drummers be silent. They instinctively obeyed the last order of their King; but when he attempted to address the multitude, an officer (probably Santerre) commanded them to recommence their music, and they drowned the monarch's voice. Six executioners seized him, but he resisted them, and demanded the privilege of divesting his neck of its clothing. They bound him to the plank. 'Son of St. Louis, ascend to heaven!' cried his confessor, bending over him. The axe descended, and his severed head was held up to the view of the people, amidst resounding shouts and the waving of hats, and of the caps of the military lifted on their bayonets.

On the return of Madame de Staël to Coppet, it was manifest that the Queen was also doomed. The daughter of Necker had never been treated with much partiality by Marie Antoinette; on the contrary, both her father and herself had suffered deeply from her prejudices. But resentment was impossible to the generous and elevated nature of the young authoress. She hastened to appeal to her country in behalf of the menaced, the imprisoned Queen—now, perhaps, the most desolate woman on the earth. Her 'Reflections on the Trial of the Queen' is one of the best exponents of her own womanly heart.[7] It is passionate in its pathos, its entreaties, its arguments. She knew the atrocious judges to whom she appealed. 'She tries every tone,' says one of her critics; 'she uses every means to discover a tender place in the skin of the tiger, and to reach the heart of the man.'[8] She loses sight of the Queen and pleads for the woman, the beautiful, the tender mother, the devoted and courageous wife, the most wretched of her sex. But what could the plea of a woman, of even such a woman, avail in the sanguinary infatuation of these times? On September 16, 1793, the daughter

---

[7] *Réflexions sur le Procès de la Reine, par une Femme*, issued in August 1793, the same month in which the Queen was tried. 'Certainly the plea, at once ingenious and energetic, that she composed for the Queen's defence, would have had the honours of a triumph, if the latter had not been condemned in advance.'—*Encyc. des Gens du Monde*, xxi.

[8] Madame Necker de Saussure, *Notice* &c.

of Maria Theresa, the fairest Queen of Europe, for whom Burke's eloquence has commanded the tears of the world, was condemned to death, at four o'clock in the morning, after two days and two nights of horrors called a judicial trial. She cut off her own hair, prematurely grey from grief, to save it from the profanation of the executioner, and, dressing herself in white, courageously mounted the open cart, in which she was then bound and dragged through the streets to the place of execution, guarded by 30,000 troops, and an innumerable hooting rabble, who filled the air with clamours. She ascended the scaffold with perfect self-possession, and maintained the dignity of the Queen, and the fortitude of her race, to the bitter end. Her bleeding head was held up, by the executioner, to the gaze of the throng, and the politest capital of the world uttered a tempest of hilarious outcries at the pallid visage—still beautiful, though agonised by uttermost sorrow.

Not long after the publication of her *brochure* in behalf of the Queen, Madame de Staël again gave utterance to her profound anguish in her poetic 'Epitre au Malheur'—a production which is remarkable for its power and truthfulness of expression. The horrors of the Revolution and the interests of her country wholly absorbed her attention at this period. They had led her to commence, months before, her work on the 'Influence of the Passions,' but she dropped that more pretentious task for these briefer and more direct appeals to her countrymen. Soon after the fall of Robespierre she wrote her 'Réflexions sur la Paix, adressées à M. Pitt et aux Français,' and after a brief interval her 'Réflexions sur la Paix Intérieure.' The first was commended by Mr. Fox in the British Parliament; and both expressed all that she could then dare to say on the external and internal condition of France. They are important documents for the history of the period, and generous protests against the war-spirit which inflamed France against the rest of Europe, and the rest of Europe against France. Both these pamphlets show the masculine vigour, the strong common sense, of her intellect. Though she had never been averse to constitutional monarchy, such especially as is exemplified in the British constitution, she was not now favourable to the restoration of monarchy in France. She knew that the former political order could not be immediately re-established without a terrible reaction and probably a sanguinary revenge of the crimes of the Revolution; and any other monarchical order could only come through struggles and wars which must involve all Europe. One of her remarks has been cited as a striking example of her prescience. 'France,' she says, 'can never become a mixed monarchy without passing through a military despotism.' The young military despot who was to verify her prediction was already extant, but his character was not yet sufficiently known to foreshadow his career. She judged the future only by the instinct of her genius.

Meanwhile a dark shadow fell upon the home at Coppet, and Necker bowed his head under what he considered the greatest affliction of his life.

CHAPTER X.

DEATH OF HER MOTHER.

Madame Necker's Sufferings—Last Interview with Gibbon—Letter to him—Her Character—Posthumous Letters to her Husband—His Devotion to her—Moral Beauty of the Last Scene.

In 1794 Madame Necker died, almost in view of the picturesque scenes of her youth. What a career had she passed through since she went forth into the world from her mountain home of Crassier! She early saw the vanity of the ambition which had led her husband to so much distinction and so much suffering; and the hopelessness, at such a crisis, of the plans of reform and beneficence which had seemed to justify their joint aspirations. She prompted his resignation, in 1781, because she could not endure the distress which the public calumnies against him occasioned her. They shattered her health for life. When, in his second administration, he was exiled for a few days, she tried to deter him from accepting his recall. She instinctively apprehended the coming earthquake; and, in the magnificent ovation of his return, and throughout his ensuing administration, down to the hour of his final retirement, 'she had but a single thought—the fear of the dangers which menaced him.' In matters of duty she could brave any peril to herself, or even to him whom she so passionately loved; but for any other consideration, she could not consent that a life so inexpressibly dear to her should be hazarded. Her anxiety for him deepened into a species of terror, and it was an infinite relief for her to return to the quiet of her native country, to enjoy there the affections of her home, through a few years of declining health, and sleep at last in the perpetual rest of the family cemetery.

Notwithstanding her physical sufferings, during these few years of retirement, they were years of peace, of moral growth, and of serene and poetic reminiscences. Mementoes of her happy childhood were all around her, and she delighted to review them. The romance of her girlhood did not fail to recur in the retrospect, amidst the transcendant scenery which had charmed her early life, and was now, with its unchanging loveliness, beautifying her life's sunset. It was here that her young heart first awoke to the consciousness of love; and now that her life had grown weary and was closing, Gibbon the historian, the object of her first affection, reappeared by her side. They met for the last time in Geneva, and talked over the memories of their youth. Necker, the friend of Gibbon, respected and shared their sentiments, and soon after her death gave to the world her last letter to the historian. It was written on the 15th of June 1792, and says: 'We think frequently of the charming days which we have spent with you in Geneva. I experienced in those days a sentiment new to me, and perhaps to most people. By a rare favour of Providence, I combined in one place one of the sweetest and purest affections of my youth, with that which makes my lot in life and which renders it so enviable. This coincidence, joined to the charms of your unrivalled conversational power, formed a sort of enchantment; and the connection of the past and the present rendered the time similar to a dream coming forth from the Ivory Gate for the consolation of mortals. Do you not wish to prolong it? Coppet is in all its beauty; but I know that I ought not to insist, for we are now leading here a very solitary life; circumstances keep the Genevese in their homes, and these rural resorts are deserted.' She proceeds to advise him not to marry, now in his mature life—he was fifty-five years old—but, 'you are married to fame,' she adds, 'and your friends, who cherish you, are not jealous of this tie, the lustre of which is reflected upon them. I have thought a hundred times of the confidence you made me; I expect the execution of it with inexpressible interest. Your genius will make a new school of writers—you gather all the intellectual riches of your age. No one in the world has felt better than we, your unique association of the most brilliant and varied intellect with the sweetest and most equable character, and we can well say of you, what Cicero says of literature, " equally delightful in retirement and in the world,"—at Paris and at Coppet.'[1]

She died in May, a time of exceeding beauty in the scenery of Lake Leman. Her husband mitigated the sorrows of his bereavement by editing the five volumes of 'Mélanges'—fragments from her manuscripts. In his preface to the first volume, he says that 'her faculties ranged over an indefinite space, but her principles were immovable. With daily progress in knowledge, she preserved an innocence of heart which prolonged her moral youth, and shed an extreme grace over her person.' 'Singular contrast!' he exclaims, 'she witnessed all the developments of selfishness, the displays of vanity, the collisions of the passions, but never would believe in perfidious designs or in malicious ruses. This mixture of intellectual penetration and generous confidence formed a combination which was unique and full of charm. After passing much of her life among men of letters, at a time when "philosophy" was most reckless, it is remarkable that her religious opinions never underwent the slightest change. She had no bigotry in this respect; her reverence for God was great, noble, elevated, always worthy, if anything can be, of the worship of the Sovereign

[1] *Mélanges* &c. tome i. 360.

Master of the world. This reverence, mingled with a holy charity, had a character which I believe to be infinitely rare. In the extreme anguish of her last sufferings, she always turned her thoughts gratefully back to the blessings she had received, and lifted her hands in thanksgiving to God. I never witnessed a piety more simple, or more suitable to give a just idea of the relations of a virtuous and sensible heart to its Creator.'

' You see me,' she had said to her daughter, ' on the boundary which separates time from eternity; I place my hand on the one and on the other, and attest, by both, the existence of God and the blessedness of virtue.'

Her charities had been superabundant, both in Paris and in her rural retirement. 'If she is not in Paradise,' said a poor peasant woman to her mourning husband, ' then we are all lost.'

Thomas, almost the only *littérateur* of her *salon* who shared her moral sentiments, said, ' Her soul was a religious sanctuary to which few could have access without being moved to tenderness and reverence.'

All contemporary accounts of the family agree in representing its domestic concord as perfect. To the end, the relations of the husband and wife were regulated by a perfect love. Necker's allusions to her are passionately affectionate. She wrote a literary ' portrait ' of him, which fills more than thirty pages in her published writings, and every page glows with the ardour of her daughter's 'Corinne.' He was more than a human being to her fond admiration; she imagined in him something almost divine.

When Madame Necker perceived that her sickness was fatal, she wrote letters to her husband, to be read after her death. They are full of pathetic tenderness and religious trust. 'You weep, dear one of my heart,' she says, 'you fear that she whose existence was united at all points to your own, lives no more for you. You are wrong; that God who joined our hearts, and who has crowned us with blessings, has not annihilated my being. While I write this letter, a secret sentiment, or instinct which has never deceived me, sheds an inexpressible calm through my soul. I believe my spirit will still watch over your fate, and that, in the bosom of God, I shall still enjoy your tenderness for me.' She proceeds to give him directions about his subsequent life—not to give up his active pursuits, not to indulge in enervating grief over his bereavement and his official misfortunes. 'Employ still the talents which God has given you, for His glory and the good of humanity; seek, in sacred and sublime occupations, relief to your sorrows. Address to me your words: I will still be your judge, your tender judge.'

Madame de Staël has recorded the devotion of Necker to his dying wife. 'No language,' she says, 'can give any adequate idea of it. Exhausted by wakefulness at night, she slept often in the day-time, resting her head on his arm. I have seen him remain, immovable, for hours together, standing in the same position for fear of awakening her by the least movement. The cares that he lavished upon her were full of tenderness and emotion, animated by the love that pure hearts preserve through sufferings and years. Absent from her, during a few hours of sleep, he inquired, on his return, of her attendant, if she had asked for him? She could no longer speak, but made an effort to say "Yes, yes." She whispered to him "We shall see each other in Heaven."'

'She looked heavenward,' says Necker, 'in a most affecting manner, listening while I prayed; then, in dying, raised the finger of her left hand, which wore the ring I had given her, to remind me of the pledge engraved upon it, to love her for ever.'

'What calm,' he continues, 'what beauty at this death-bed! what resignation to the will of God! During her sufferings she opposed, to all expressions of pity for her, the thirty years of happiness she had received from God.'

These mournful pages of Necker fairly sob with emotion. 'Alas!' he exclaims, 'I have no longer this companion, who attended me in the pilgrimage of life. O my God, let her virtues serve to protect me near Thee. My beloved, if thou canst, help me, that, being purified, I may be judged worthy of a second companionship with thee.'

His daughter entered the death-chamber soon after her decease. The open window showed some of the most magnificent views of the Alps, illuminated by the brightness of the morning. 'Her soul perhaps is soaring yonder,' said Necker, pointing to a light cloud which was passing over their heads; 'and he was silent.'

Alluding to his reflections on her death, written immediately after the event, Madame de Staël says: 'I have not seen, in any history, any romance, a perfection of tenderness that can be compared to this. These pages reveal a love that is divine, agitated like that which is human; full of delicacy and passion, full of remorse without having committed a fault.'

Though it has sometimes been said that the daughter was too much absorbed by her affection for her father, to do full justice to her mother,— and she did, undoubtedly, entertain a less intense sympathy toward the latter than toward the former —yet she always venerated her character and deeply mourned her death. It was now that she declared to Madame Necker de Saussure, 'The more I see of life the better do I understand my mother, and the more does my heart feel the need of her.'

CHAPTER XI.

IN PARIS AGAIN.

Political Condition of France—M. de Staël—Social Reaction in Paris—Madame Tallien—The Salon again—Madame de Staël and Talleyrand—She rescues Dupont de Nemours and Narvins de Montbreton—Her Efforts for Lafayette—Her Womanly Sensibility—Education and Career of her Son, Auguste—Her Treatise on the Passions.

MADAME DE STAËL again returned to Paris. In spite of the agitations which still continued to be rife there, after the fall of Robespierre, the metropolis had irresistible attractions for her; and her husband had been reinstated in his official position, and could guarantee her safety.

Within six years three Constitutions had been provided by the revolutionary politicians. The one now about to be adopted by the reactionary party maintained the Republic and instituted a new Executive of five members. The epoch of the Directory was at hand. France began to breathe with some hope of personal safety. England and Austria were still in the field against her, and the French military spirit was still dominant, and rising daily; but Sweden recognised the new government as a pledge of better times, and the Baron de Staël had been sent back for the negotiation of a new treaty of alliance.

Madame de Staël, in reviewing this period,[1] regrets that Austria and England did not follow the example of Sweden. She believed that Europe might have thus been pacified, and the military career of Napoleon and the devastation of the Continent prevented. She deemed the Republic, as we have seen, the only practicable government for France at present, and dreaded the intermediate stage necessary for the restoration of royalty—the military despotism which she had predicted, and which was about to be developed by Napoleon, under the auspices of the Directory, and the belligerent provocations of England and Austria. Her good sense was displayed in her judgment of the situation. 'In the period from 1793 to 1795,' she says, 'England and her allies would have dishonoured themselves by treating with France—with Robespierre and Marat. But, when once the intention of inaugurating a regular government became manifest, nothing should have been neglected which could interrupt the military education of France. Eighteen months after the establishment of the Directory, England sent envoys to Lille for peace; but the success of the army of Italy had inspired with arrogance the chiefs of the Republic, and the Directory was already experi-

[1] *Considérations*, iii. 21.

enced in power, and believed itself secure. New governments naturally desire peace; hostile powers should wisely avail themselves of this fact: in politics, as in war, there are critical hours which should be hastily seized.' Pitt had eulogised the Constitution of 1795, but Burke's 'Thoughts on a Regicide Peace' renewed the popular indignation of England against France.

M. de Staël was still the only minister from a Monarchy to the Republic. The Republican leaders had received him with acclamations. They devised a solemn ceremony for his reception in the National Convention, where he was favoured with an elevated seat in face of the President, and, on April 22, 1795, delivered his address, sitting. 'I come,' he said, 'on the part of the kingdom of Sweden, to the bosom of the National Representation of France, to render a demonstrative homage to the natural, imprescriptible rights of nations.' He had evidently learned the political dialect of the Revolutionists. Amidst the shouts of the Assembly, the President gave him the 'accolade,'— the fraternal kiss. He was assigned a 'loge' in the Convention, where he daily witnessed its proceedings and was the object of general interest.

Manners are more powerful than laws; the old tendencies of French society began immediately to struggle for the ascendency, now that the revolutionary terrorism was giving way. Madame de Staël is surprised, on her return to the capital, by the *bizarre* contrasts and confusion of tastes and manners which characterise the reaction. The staunch Republicans change slowly, but their 'Spartanism' cannot withstand their innate French passion for gaiety and dress. In 1793 men wore 'red night-caps;' 'the municipality themselves went in *sabots*,' or wooden shoes,[2] but now these are discarded as follies. The men propose, the women actually adopt, the classic Greek costume. The *salon*, once so powerful, afterwards so perilous under democratic surveillance, revives, and Paris throngs it, hungering and thirsting for the amenities of 'society,' the blandishments of elegant women, the converse of intelligent men. One of those remarkable characters which surprise us at almost every stage of the Revolution leads, partly by her very follies, the social reaction. Tallien, accompanied by the guillotine dripping with the blood of innumerable victims, was extirpating Girondism in the region of Bordeaux during the Reign of Terror, when he became enamoured of a young Spanish beauty, Madame de Fontenai (*née* Carabus), and saved her from the general murder. He took her to Paris, and his ferocious nature is reported to have been not a little softened by her influence. But she was again in peril of death, and, from her prison, appealed to him for deliverance, warning him that his own head was in danger. For her safety, as well as his own, this sanguinary Terrorist

[2] Carlyle, iii. 7, 2.

led the conspiracy against Robespierre and delivered France from the Jacobins. The Senhorina Cabarus, the Dame de Fontenai, or, as she is better known, and will be always, in French history, Madame Tallien, now opened a *salon*, and reigned supreme in the society of Paris, cautiously at first, but effectually, impelling the social reaction. 'Whatever remnants of the old grace survived,' says Carlyle, 'are rallied here. At her right hand, in this cause, labours the fair Josephine, the widow Beauharnais, though in straitened circumstances; both of them intent to blandish down the grimness of republican austerity and recivilise mankind.'

The morals of Madame Tallien were those of the time; but she wielded the power of extraordinary benevolence and of superb beauty; and many were her good and brave deeds amidst the worst atrocities of the Revolution. Madame Junot (Duchesse d'Abrantès) knew her well, and always alludes to her with the kindliest language. The literary Duchesse pourtrays her, with feminine particularity, as she appeared in the *salons* of this period, costumed *à la grecque*, a representative of the epoch. She was above middle height; with a perfect harmony in all her person. 'She was the Venus of the Capitol, but more beautiful than the work of Phidias, with the same purity of lines, the same perfection of the hands, the arms, the feet; and all this beauty animated by a benevolent expression, a reflection of the magic mirror of the soul, which showed all the generosity of her nature.' Her dress added not a little to her charms: she wore a simple robe of Indian muslin, draped according to the antique, attached on the shoulders by two cameos; a girdle of gold encircled her waist and was clasped by a cameo; large bracelets of gold held her sleeves much above her elbows; her hair, of velvet black, was short and *frisé* all around her head *à la Titus*, as this coiffure was then called. On her white and beautiful shoulders was a superb red cashmere shawl, which she draped around her in a manner so graceful and picturesque, as to form a charming tableau. All eyes concentrated upon her, all the crowd gathered around her.[3]

In spite of her moral antecedents, Madame Tallien's gay and genial influence led the new social reaction among a large class which otherwise might have been able to retard, if not defeat it.

Madame de Staël reappeared in the metropolis to exert a still higher influence. The reopening of her *salon* was a restoration of the best ante-revolutionary society. One of the highest authorities says that 'she reappeared in France and founded there anew the spirit of Society. After those times of rudeness and cruelty, when anarchy had almost become barbarism, she reintroduced the influence of woman. These facts are historical. We behold

---

[3] *Mém. de la Duchesse d'Abrantès*, ii. 5. 18 vols. Paris, 1831.

in her the restoration of the normal spirit of France after the storms of the Revolution.'[4]

The society of the city, as she found it, 'was,' she writes, 'indeed a curious spectacle. The influence of women, the ascendency of good company, the *salons dorés* (as they were called) excited the jealousy of those who were not admitted to them; their political colleagues who were invited were considered to be the victims of seduction.' This very jealousy served as a provocation to egotism and vanity, and promoted the triumphs of the *salons*. 'One saw,' continues Madame de Staël, ' on the Decade (for the Sunday had been abolished) all the elements of the old and new *régimes*, united in the *soirées*, but not yet reconciled. The elegant manners of well-educated persons contrasted strangely with the humble costume which many still retained—their protection during the Reign of Terror. Men, converted from the Jacobin party, entered for the first time into the society of the *grand monde*, and their self-love was more sensitive about the etiquette of the manners which they wished to imitate than on any other subject. The women of the old *régime* surrounded them, in order to obtain the restoration of their exiled brothers, sons, and husbands; and the gracious flatteries which they knew so well how to use struck these rude ears, and predisposed the most

---

[4] Villemain, *Cours de la Littérature Française*, iv. Paris, 1873.

factious to the changes which followed—to the reestablishment of a court with even its abuses, but not without the appropriation of them for their own advantage.' They became apologetic, at first, for the late atrocities; then emulated one another in condemning them.

Daily the reactionary spirit grows stronger. Hundreds wear crape on their left arm, in token of their bereavements by the guillotine, and call themselves 'victims.' They can now resent, thus far at least, the sufferings of their broken households. The *jeunesse dorée* (as Fréron named them), the gilded youth, appear in the *salons*, the *cafés*, the streets, with reactionary audacity—young coxcombs in dress and manners, but valorous at heart as only French coxcombs have been—and defy the *sans-culotte* heroes. They carry bludgeons loaded with metal, and do not hesitate to use them on the heads of unrelenting democrats. Duels are frequent, and desperately fatal. Evidently France is again in transition. The *Carmagnoles* are passing away; the old gallantry, both in society and war, is resuming its sway, and, with it, the gilded depravity—if less offensive, yet hardly less corrupt, than the vulgar depravity of the Revolution—the depravity which had ruined France, and which is still to render precarious her public order and her liberties.

'Many of us,' says Madame de Staël, 'had emigrant friends whose restoration we were busy in soliciting. I obtained at this epoch many recalls, and, in consequence, the Deputy Legendre, a man of the people, denounced me from the tribune.' Her husband, sitting in state in his 'loge,' had to hear in silence this tirade; but Barras defended her.

In the confused reactionary state of public opinion, her influence was felt by both parties; the Jacobins dreaded it, the reactionists courted it. The heroic generosity which had led her to face death for the safety of her friends, in the terrors of the Revolution, was unabated, and she was incessantly labouring for the restoration of proscribed exiles. When Talleyrand was still far away beyond the sea she did not forget him, but succeeded in opening the way for his return. Chenier, the poet, who had been active in the Revolution, yielded to at least a literary sympathy with her genius, and was induced by her to deliver a speech in the Convention in behalf of 'Citizen Talleyrand.' The ex-bishop and ex-statesman was permitted to return. Her management with Barras led to his appointment to the department of Foreign Affairs under the Directory, and he was thus enabled to resume that remarkable public career which identified him for so many years with the history of Europe.

Dupont de Nemours, whom she describes as 'the most chivalric champion of liberty in France,' was in peril. 'I heard,' she says, 'of the danger he was in, and sought Chenier, who at my instance had delivered the speech to which Talleyrand owed his recall. The poet was a man of tender susceptibility. He was moved at the picture of the situation of Dupont de Nemours and his family, and hastened to the tribune, where he saved him.'[5]

These benevolent efforts endangered her own safety. 'Some words of a General, who accused me publicly of sympathy for conspirators, compelled me to quit Paris. I went to the country house of one of my friends, where, by a singular chance, I discovered one of the most illustrious and most heroic of the royalists of La Vendée, the Prince de la Trémoille, for whose head a price had been offered. I wished to cede to him the asylum which he needed more than I. We were indeed astonished that the same danger had befallen us both, notwithstanding our very different antecedents.' There was a magnanimous contention between them, each claiming the honour of retiring for the safety of the other. The gallant royalist refused to accept her proposal, and hastened out of France. She remained in concealment till the peril had passed, when she returned to the capital, to resume her hazardous endeavours for her emigrant friends.

M. de Montbreton called upon her, entreating her to rescue his brother, Narvins, who had been arrested, and would doubtless be condemned to

[5] *Considérations* &c. iii. 25.

death by the military commission which was in session trying him. She could not hope to influence the Directory in such a case; nor could she consent to do nothing for a man whom she had known, and who would be shot in two hours if no one came to his succour. 'I recollected,' she writes, 'that I had seen, with Barras, a General Lemoine, and that he had appeared to converse cordially with me. He commanded the division of Paris, and had the right of suspending the judgments of the Military Commission established in the city. I thanked God for this idea, and went instantly, with the brother of the unhappy Narvins, to the General, who was astonished to see me. He commenced the conversation by making apologies for his morning toilet, and for his apartments. I supplicated him not to lose a moment on these matters, as that momentary loss might be irreparable. I hastily stated the purpose of my visit; at first he refused me absolutely. My heart trembled at the aspect of the brother, who might think that I had not used the right words for the emergency. I repeated my solicitations, and collected all my forces to give them effect. I was fearful of saying too much or too little, of delaying beyond what might be the fatal hour, of neglecting a single argument which might be available. I looked one moment at the clock, another at the General, to see which of the two powers, his mind or time, approached most quickly to its conclusion. Thrice he took up the pen to sign the reprieve, and thrice was he arrested by the fear of compromising himself. At last he could no longer resist. He signed the document, and Monsieur de Montbreton flew with it to the tribunal.' It broke up the session; the accused was saved, though he had confessed enough to ruin him.

At another period she exerted herself to the utmost in behalf of her old friend Lafayette, then in the prison of Olmutz. She wrote letters, full of urgency and eloquence, to Governeur Morris (representative of the Government of the United States of America), beseeching his intervention, and that of his country, for the illustrious prisoner. 'I am,' she said, 'more afflicted than any other person, I believe, by the situation of Lafayette. Open the doors of his prison! You have saved his wife from death; oh, be the saviour of all his family; pay the debt of your country!' Eleven days later she renews her appeal to him, with intenser feeling, if possible. A daughter could not plead more affectionately for a father.[6]

She gives a reason for her zeal in such cases: it is, however, purely a woman's reason. 'It is the duty of us women,' she says, ' to succour at all times individuals accused for political opinions, whatever they may be; for what are opinions in times of party violence? Can we be certain that,

---

[6] These letters may be found in the *Revue Retrospective*, p. 473. Paris, 1834.

in this or that change of situation, we should not change our view of the case?' Her woman's heart controlled her, in all such instances; her sentiments placed in abeyance her masculine judgment. In the presence of appeals to her sympathies she was ever Corinne, never the acute thinker of the 'Allemagne.' It has already been remarked that no sufferings of her own distressed her as much as the sufferings of others. Her sensitiveness in this respect was morbid and insupportable; but, instead of shrinking from scenes of distress, she plunged into them with the peculiar moral courage, the recklessness, of woman, resolute to relieve them, or perish in the attempt. This was the necessary relief to her own agonised heart. We have seen her risk her life for her friends amid horrors before which the stoutest will might have recoiled. In the introduction to her work on the 'Influence of the Passions' (which was prompted by the terrors of the Revolution), she says that 'her only object, in writing it, has been to show how we may diminish somewhat the intensity of the sufferings of the soul. The image of the unfortunate, under whatever aspect it presents itself, pursues and oppresses me. Alas! I have suffered so much myself, that an inexpressible sympathy, a painful inquietude, seizes me at the thought of the woes of all and of each; of the inevitable chagrins of life, the torments of the imagination, the reverses of the just man, and even the remorse of the guilty ; of the wounds of the heart, the most touching of all ; and the regrets for which we blush without suffering them less ;—in fine, of all for which our tears flow : tears which the ancients collected in a consecrated urn—so much did they respect the sorrows of man.'

This feminine sensibility, this predominance of her womanly heart over her manly intellect, is one of the most admirable charms of her character. In her hours of happiness it rendered her irresistibly fascinating. She gave herself up to her spontaneous sentiments ; she was overflowing with joy, with admiration for what was well said or done ; fond and caressing to all who enjoyed her confidence ; excessive in her commendations and encouragements ; addicted to an *abandon* which was sometimes maliciously criticised. In her hours of sadness (and they were frequent) it gave her a boundless sympathy. Her cousin, Madame Necker de Saussure, lingers, after her death, with emotion over this phase of her character. ' It was,' she writes, ' near her unfortunate friends that she displayed the greatest power of her nature. Carried away by profound and rapid feeling, it seemed that she would search through earth and heaven for some relief to their sufferings. Everything ingenious, everything good, that she could think of, was used to divert their attention ; to illuminate, were it but for a moment, the sombre clouds of distress. She seemed to dispose of the future; to create one expressly for the sufferer; in which, by the force of her friendship, she would restore all things. The evils of the imagination (well understood by her) were alleviated by means as singular as themselves. With what avidity she listened! An ardent curiosity for the impressions of sincere minds so evidently mingled with her tenderness, that they could never have fear of fatiguing her while confiding to her their sorrows. Her soul blended with that of the sufferer; and her large explanation of the case enabled the victim to feel that God was accomplishing His sanctifying work in the soul, by salutary though terrible trials. Ah! it is frightful to have to suffer without her! We know not what to do with the sentiments which she shared with us. There is something akin to remorse in the grief we experience in losing her; for our regrets seem not disinterested. We feel exiled from a delicious region, where we had enjoyments which can never again be ours. She was, herself, as charming as her gifts; and then, she was the medium through which one received all that was interesting, instructive, and worthy of attention on earth. One feels a curtailment, an impoverishment of one's own existence in the loss of her; we have lost a part of ourselves, and we weep alone.'

Only in hopeless, irremediable affliction, such as silence and time alone could mitigate, did she fail. Madame Necker de Saussure records a touching example. She had lost by death an 'angelic daughter,' and wrote to Madame de Staël for consolation, but no answer came. The afflicted mother supposed her letter had failed to reach Coppet. Months afterwards she alluded to it, in conversation. Madame de Staël abruptly ceased to speak, and became troubled and pallid. 'What is the matter with you?' exclaimed her cousin. 'I could not answer it,' was the reply; and, hesitating and sobbing, she added, 'Let us speak of it no more, let us never allude to it again,' and hastened from the room, 'all in tears.'[7] Many a woman has, we may believe, had equal sensibility; but add to it the exalted genius of the 'Corinne,' and the profound intellect of the 'Allemagne,' and we have the supreme woman of literary history, Madame de Staël—ever the genuine woman, though often the manly thinker. Benjamin Constant (whose relations with her were more intimate than those of any other man beyond the circle of her immediate kindred) says: 'Her two most predominant qualities were affection and pity. She had, like all superior minds, a strong passion for fame; she had, like all elevated souls, a strong love of liberty; but these two sentiments, imperious and irresistible when not combated by another, ceded instantly when the least circumstances placed them in opposition to the happiness of those that she loved, or whenever the sight of a

---

[7] *Notice* &c.

suffering being reminded her that there was in the world something much more sacred for her than the success of a cause, or the triumph of an opinion.'[8]

While devoting herself to beneficent and hazardous services for her friends in Paris, two important tasks occupied her leisure: one was the education of her son, the other the composition of her work on 'The Influence of the Passions.'

Her treatise on 'The Influence of the Passions on the Happiness of Individuals and Nations' was a premature, but not, as usually represented, a hasty production. She had begun it, as we have seen, before her first visit to England, for parts of it were read in the little colony of Mickleham; and Talleyrand, who, if no great authority in literature, was certainly an astute critic of human nature, said, while hearing those readings, that 'nothing was ever better conceived or more felicitously expressed.' She was certainly preparing this book through some three or four years, but amidst the worst possible distractions: much of the time a fugitive, and several times in imminent danger of death. The public disorders suggested its theme, and gave to the work its melancholy tone. Her faculties had not yet attained the philosophic self-command and vigour which a subject so purely didactic demands. Had she written it at the time of the production of her 'Germany,' it would have been a very different work. In excusing, at a

[8] Constant's *Mélanges*, viii. Paris, 1829.

later date, its defence of suicide, she herself speaks of it as a premature production of her youth.[9] It was published at Lausanne and Paris, in two duodecimo volumes. The second part, on the 'Influence of the Passions on Nations,' was never written, but her plan for it is detailed in the Introduction. In the completed part she discusses the influence, on individual happiness, of ambition, vanity, love, avarice, party spirit, friendship, the conjugal and parental affections, religion, philosophy, beneficence, &c. Her classification is defective, her definitions vague, and the general temper of the work is morbidly sad. It is an example of the epidemic melancholy of the age, as we see it beginning chiefly in the writings of Rousseau, pervading the Werther of Goethe, and culminating in the cynicism of Byron, —the 'Sturm und Drang' period of European literature. A sensitive woman, suffering amid the actual tragedies of the French Revolution, her pensive sentimentalism is more excusable than that of her more fortunate literary contemporaries, who were comparatively distant spectators of the harrowing scenes which surrounded her. With all its faults, the essay on 'The Influence of the Passions' is a notable book, as the production of a feminine pen. It abounds in profound reflections,

---

[9] In her *Reflections on Suicide* (1812), she says: 'I have praised the act of suicide, in my work on *The Influence of the Passions*, but I have ever since regretted that inconsiderate word. I was then in all the pride and vivacity of early youth, but we live to learn.'

in striking individual thoughts, in brilliant descriptions. Impartial critics will generally accept Chénier's judgment upon it—that 'it presents rich and varied pictures, the power to move the heart, traits of ingenuity, of originality, and above all of independence.'[1] One of the best of later critics, after commenting on the defects of the book, says, 'but I acknowledge that in reading these pages, so irresistible in their energy, so dazzling with thought, one hardly perceives their faults. Eloquence covers all, and we can say of the author, as of the hero in a certain modern tragedy, her faults are hid in the splendours of her glory.'[2] Its final lesson is of the highest ethical character. In sketching its scheme, in her Introduction, she says: 'Following this plan, I believe I have proved that there is no happiness without virtue; to have reached this result by so many routes, is a new proof of its verity.'

Auguste, afterwards Baron de Staël-Holstein, was now advancing through his promising childhood. His mother was, in her ever-varying circumstances, assiduous in his education. Necker had been, and was still later, devoted to his training at Coppet. He spent some years in study at the college of Geneva. Accompanying his mother to

---

[1] J. de Chénier, *Tableau de la Littérature Française depuis* 1789. *Œuvres*, tome iii. Paris, 1819. He places her among 'the great writers of her age.'

[2] Vinet's *Etudes sur la Littérature Française au* 19eme *Siècle*, tome i. Paris, 1857.

Germany, he came under the tuition of Schlegel. He afterwards studied in Paris, and returning to Coppet, was again under the care of Schlegel and of the Pastor Cellerier. From the latter he received the religious bias which characterised his useful but modest manhood. Madame de Staël attempted an experiment in his education—training him without corporal chastisement, without even the use of authority. She had been a victim, in her early childhood, of parental rigour; and it had left with her memories which rendered it abhorrent to her generous nature. She believed that the child who could not be governed and successfully reared by kindness and love, could not be by any other means; that his failure under such a regimen necessarily implied inherent vices, which severity could only aggravate, at last, though it might temporarily seem to repress them, or rather transmute them into dissimulation and hypocrisy—to her, the worst of vices. She was successful, and her son, though he did not inherit her genius, exemplified every moral excellence which adorned her own character. He clung to her through all the vicissitudes of her life of exile, with the fondest affection. At the Restoration (1813) he returned with her to Paris. Being a devoted Protestant, he took a conspicuous part in the religious and philanthropic societies of his Church; he was one of the founders of the French Bible Society, of the Mutual Aid Society, and the Society of Christian

Morals, of which he became President. He shared in nearly every important movement of the French Protestantism of his times. By repeated visits to England, he became a zealous coadjutor of the Christian philanthropists of that country. Sir Walter Scott said that he was the only Frenchman he had ever met who could speak English as correctly as a native. He maintained intimate relations with Wilberforce, and was a conspicuous representative of the anti-slavery cause in France, and effectively promoted it by his pen. His literary culture was large and varied. With his brother-in-law, the Duc de Broglie, he edited the posthumous works of his mother (18 vols. Paris, 1820-21), and a complete collection of the works of his grandfather (Necker), with an able introductory narrative of his life, and defence of his official conduct. He wrote several occasional pamphlets, mostly on public questions; and 'Lettres sur l'Angleterre,' a study of the religious and philanthropical aspects of English society. The latter years of his life were spent at Coppet, where he was distinguished by his devotion to philanthropy and to agricultural science, and where he died, November 11, 1827. He rests worthily among the illustrious dead in the family cemetery. His sister, the Duchesse de Broglie (who shared his intellectual and moral accomplishments), published in 1829 his 'Œuvres Diverses,' with a biographical introduction, in five vols. 8vo.

CHAPTER XII.

MADAME DE STAËL AND BONAPARTE.

A new Epoch in her Life—Her Relations to Napoleon—The Cause of his Hostility—His Character—Anecdotes—Sophie Gay—Invasion of Switzerland—Scenes at Coppet.

WE now approach a new and important epoch in this brave life-struggle—the period of the 'Dix Années d'Exil'—the ten years of exile—in which the almost solitary literary woman confronted, with unswerving steadfastness, the greatest of military men since the first of the Roman Cæsars: never compromising her opinions, ever maintaining her intellectual independence, with all Europe for the theatre of the extraordinary contest.

Most of the literary men of the time had either succumbed to the great conqueror, or were wandering, like Chateaubriand, in England, or America, or beyond the Rhine.[1] Madame de Staël constantly endeavoured to maintain her ground in France. Her dearest social predilections were sacrificed;

---

[1] Chateaubriand returned and accepted office under Napoleon. He properly enough served his master at Rome and in the Valais. The murder of the Duc d'Enghien could alone restore his loyalty to his principles.

her dearest personal friends were, one after another, involved in her proscription; the prospects of her children, especially of her eldest son, in the new public order, were blighted; her and their fortune was imperilled; the payment of the two millions, lent by her father to the Government, was proffered her by Napoleon, if she would be reconciled to him, but was refused. She had instinctively detected his supreme egotism and the despotism of his policy; she was loyal to the liberties of her country and the convictions of her conscience, and no bribery could shake the firmness of her soul.

That her womanly heart felt inexpressibly the anguish of these sufferings, only adds to the moral sublimity of her example. Whatever may be said of the frequent, the irrepressible outcries of that anguish, in her letters and other writings, the spectacle of her unyielding persistence—of this prolonged and unrelenting contest between the greatest soldier and greatest female author of the age,—is one for which the whole literary world may well be for ever proud. Hard and long as the struggle was, her genius, as well as her will, triumphantly maintained its ascendancy. Pursued by unremitting persecution, a wanderer over Europe, her faculties nevertheless strengthened and flowered amidst her desolation. It was the period in which she gave to the world her greatest works —her essay on 'Literature,' her 'Delphine,' her 'Corinne,' her 'Allemagne.' Her oppressor, years later, when she was emancipated and the idol of intellectual Europe, and he an exile himself on St. Helena, was to read there these immortal works; and, though affecting to depreciate them, and uttering self-refuting libels on her character, was compelled to acknowledge that 'No one can deny that she is a woman of grand talent, of extraordinary intellect; she will last.'[2]

She begins the record of her 'Ten Years of Exile,' by declaring that 'Napoleon has persecuted me with a minute care, with an ever-increasing activity, with an inflexible rudeness; and my relations with him served to make him known to me long before Europe comprehended him. The greatest grievance which he felt towards me was from that love of liberty which I have ever cherished, which has been transmitted to me as a heritage, and which has been nourished in me by reflection on the great principles in which it is founded, and the glorious deeds which it inspires. The cruel scenes of the French Revolution have not been able to impair with me the homage due to liberty. Its misfortunes in France should not proscribe it over the world. When the sun disappears from the horizon of the lands of the far North, their inhabitants do not accuse his rays which still shine on countries more favoured by heaven.'[3]

[2] Las Cases, *Mémorial de Sainte-Hélène*, t. vii. p. 124. Paris, 1840.
[3] *Dix Années d'Exil*, i. 1.

She at first shared the enthusiasm of her countrymen for the young hero, especially as he persistently avowed loyalty to the Republic. His extraordinary genius seemed a providential gift to the nation, for the promotion of its fame, and the protection of the great political improvements which it had gained through so many misfortunes. 'We were dazzled,' she writes, 'by his achievements at the head of the army of Italy. The superiority of his understanding in affairs, joined to the splendour of his talents as a general, gave to his name an importance never yet acquired by any individual since the commencement of the Revolution. But though he spoke constantly, in his proclamations, of the Republic, thoughtful men began to perceive that it was, in his eyes, a means, not an end. All things, all men, were thus only means for him. The report was spread that he wished to make himself King of Lombardy. One day I met General Augereau, who had just come from Italy, and who was then a zealous Republican. I asked him if it were true that Bonaparte wished to make himself King. "Assuredly not," he replied, " he is too elevated a young man for that." This reply was entirely in accord with the public opinion of the moment.'[4] Again, she writes : ' We were so tired of oppressors who borrowed the name of liberty, and of the oppressed who wished the restoration of arbitrary power, that our admiration

[4] *Considérations* &c. iii. 24.

knew no bounds. Bonaparte seemed to combine in himself all that ought to captivate us. It was with this sentiment that I, at least, first saw him at Paris. I could not find words to reply to him, when he came to me and said he had sought an interview with my father at Coppet, and regretted that he had to pass through Switzerland without seeing him.'

But his flattering attentions could not deceive her penetrating insight. Her genius was clairvoyant in reading character. She felt that she was conversing with a man great in talents, but who was destitute of the moral sense; whose ambition knew nothing of patriotism, and combined, contrary to most examples of real greatness, in an equal degree pride and vanity; whose supreme egotism, capricious by its conflicting pride and vanity, would endanger the safety of France as well as of all individuals who should have relations with him without abject self-abnegation. She thus certainly comprehended the true nature of the man, the enigma of his singular character. Its secret was not his consummate egotism, but the fact that his vanity was as consummate as his pride. A great man may be too proud to be vain. Great military men have usually been too self-reliant to be sensitive to individual opinion. Napoleon was morbidly sensitive to it. No man was ever more resentful of personal opposition; no one ever more highly prized public ovations or popular applause.[5] The proclamations or bulletins of no other great captain ever approached his in grandiloquent or melodramatic style. We look in vain for any similar example of vanity in the military papers of his own conqueror, Wellington; in those of the great Frederick; in those of the greater Washington; in the records of his own campaigns by Cæsar.

While all Europe was ringing with his praises, Napoleon was stung to the quick by the refusal of this solitary woman to recognise and applaud him. We shall see him destroying the whole first edition of her greatest book, ten thousand copies of her 'Allemagne,' not because it had a single sentence directed against him (for it had none whatever), but because it had not one for him. The strength of his vanity was the weakness of his character, and the ruin of his career. Its only redeeming fact was the involuntary homage it paid to the superb intellect which it persecuted, but could not vanquish. It was the means of giving to the world the most remarkable example of the triumph of the pen over the sword and sceptre, that history records.

'When I was a little relieved from the embarrassment of my admiration,' continues Madame de Staël, speaking of their first interview, 'a singular

---

[5] 'He was happy; and with what effusion he said to me one day, on returning from a parade, "Bourrienne, do you hear those acclamations which still continue? They are as sweet to me as the voice of Josephine."'—Bourrienne's *Mémoires*, iv. 14. Paris, 1830.

sentiment of fear seized me. The dread he inspired was caused entirely by the peculiar impression of his character on all who approached him. I had seen men very worthy of respect: I had seen also ferocious men; there was nothing in the impression that Bonaparte made on me, that recalled the one or the other. I perceived quickly, on the different occasions that I met him, during his stay in Paris, that his character could not be defined by the words which we are accustomed to use in characterising other men. It was neither good, nor violent, nor tender, nor cruel, as in other cases. Such a being, having no parallel, could neither feel nor inspire any sympathy; he was more or less than a man. His turn of mind, his spirit, his courage, were stamped with something strange.' Far from being reassured by frequent interviews with him, 'I only became,' she says, 'the more intimidated. I saw that no emotion of the heart could act on him. A human being was to him but a fact, like any other fact; important only so far as he could use it. The force of his will consisted in the imperturbable calculations of his egotism. Every time I heard him speak I was struck with his superiority. Meanwhile, nothing could lessen my repugnance to what I perceived in him. It was in the interval between his return from Italy and his departure for Egypt (towards the end of 1794), that I saw him often in Paris, and never could the difficulty of breathing in his presence be relieved. I was one day between him and Siéyès at dinner—a singular situation! I examined with attention the face of Bonaparte, but whenever he noticed that I observed his features, he had the power of dismissing from his eyes all expression, as if he were become marble. His manner in society was constrained, without being timid; it had something disdainful when reserved, and vulgar when at ease.'[6]

His vulgarity, 'when at ease,' was especially manifest in his conversation with women,—a maladroit effect of his vanity—the affectation of a superiority which should exempt him from the conventional demands of courtesy. He delighted to embarrass them by his abruptness; by peremptory remarks which admitted of no reply; and even by rudeness of language, which could not fail at once to perplex and to mortify them. Bourrienne tells us that this abruptness and vulgarity before ladies was not at all unusual with him; that he often addressed to them the exclamations, 'How red your elbows are!' 'What a strange head-dress you wear!' 'Pray tell me, do you ever change your gown?'[7] To one of the most beautiful and accomplished women of his court, Madame Reynault, then but twenty-eight years old, he said, in a moment of ill-humour, 'Do you know, Madame, that you are aging terribly?' and this in full court, with hundreds of women around

---

[6] *Considérations*, iii. 26. Prof. Jules Barni gives a severe but just review of Napoleon's treatment of Madame de Staël, in *Les Martyrs de la Libre Pensée*, chap. x. Geneva, 1862.

[7] *Mémoires sur Napoléon*, iii. 13.

her, jealous of her superior charms and talents. Her answer was a lesson of good manners to him: 'What your Majesty does me the honour to say to me would be very painful to hear, were I of an age to be afflicted by it.' Turning to the Duchesse d'Abrantès (the young and still more accomplished wife of Junot), he remarked, 'Well, Madame Junot, you do not dance. Is it because you are *too old* to dance?' 'A similar phrase,' says the Duchesse, 'was addressed to another young lady who was near me, the wife of Duroc, I think.' No woman has said more in defence of Napoleon than Madame Junot, but she describes his Court as often 'trembling' at his entrance, especially women. She remarks that 'when he said a painful word to a woman, he never persisted if she answered him with respect and spirit.'[8] He recoiled before men, and even women, of intellect, as Milton's devil at the touch of Ithuriel's spear. Meneval, his secretary, says that his favourite caress, particularly for women, was to pinch their shoulders, ears, or noses, sometimes making the blood flow. Madame Junot often records her sufferings from these Bruinian manners. Without one drop of French blood in his veins, he knew nothing of the *politesse*, the sentiment, without which gallantry itself is disgusting to a Frenchman, and especially to a French woman. Even the wife of Scarron, and (still worse) of Louis XIV. —Madame de Maintenon—could say that 'delicacy

---

[8] *Mémoires de la Duchesse d'Abrantès*, ix. 10.

is to love what grace is to beauty.' Napoleon was Corsican in heart as well as in blood.

Madame de Staël soon became aware of the paltry weaknesses of the great man, and feared, she says, 'that he might address to me some of those rude expressions which he often took pleasure in addressing to ladies, even when they paid court to him.' 'For this reason,' she adds, 'when invited to a party at General Berthier's, where the First Consul was to be, I wrote down a number of tart and poignant replies to what he might have to say. Had he chosen to insult me, it would have shown a want both of character and understanding to have been taken by surprise; and as no one could be sure of being unembarrassed in the presence of such a man, I prepared myself to brave him. Fortunately the precaution was unnecessary; he only addressed the most common questions to me.'[9]

She was less fortunate on another occasion, if we may believe Napoleon himself, whose word was always doubtful in such cases. In attempting, at St. Helena, to make her ridiculous to Las Cases, he told him that, prompted by her vanity, and expecting a flattering answer, she once asked him, 'whom he considered the greatest woman in the world, living or dead?' 'Her, madame,' I replied, 'who has borne the most children.' She was disconcerted, and remarked that he was 'reported not to be a great admirer of the fair sex.' 'I am very fond of

[9] *Dix Années* &c.

my wife,' he replied, and abruptly turned away.[1] He insists, in this conversation with Las Cases, that she was in love with him. The whole conversation appears more than doubtful. This piquant story, so often cited, but originally from Napoleon himself, bears on its face the marks of its falsehood. He tells Las Cases that the conversation took place in the brilliant company at the fête given him by Talleyrand, on his return from Italy. At this time Madame de Staël, though well known by her conversational powers, had no important literary reputation. She had published only some minor works—her diminutive volume on Rousseau, her hardly known 'Morceaux,' or Novellettes, her unfinished essay on the 'Passions' which was considered a failure, and a few pamphlets. Her essay on 'Literature,' her 'Delphine,' 'Corinne,' 'Germany,' were all still unwritten. That such a woman, in such circumstances, should have had the immense

[1] The celebrated Sophie Gay, a friend and defender of Madame de Staël, was less timid before him, and repelled his cynicism by her ready repartee. She was intimate with his sister Pauline, and met him at her house, in Aix-la-Chapelle. In passing near the young authoress, he addressed her roughly, and with the eagle glance before which most women cowered:—'Madame, my sister has told you that I do not like intellectual women.' 'Yes, Sire,' she responded, not at all disconcerted, 'Yes, Sire; but I did not believe her.' The Emperor was surprised, and tried again. 'You write—do you not? What have you produced since you have been in this country?' 'Three children, Sire,' was her proud reply. He passed on, affecting a smile. The woman's *esprit* was too much for his own. One of these children was Delphine, well known in our day as the accomplished authoress, Madame Girardin. *Biographie Universelle*, xvi.

vanity to desire to be acknowledged as the 'greatest' of her sex, 'dead or living,' is a supposition too ridiculous to be admitted. If she asked the question, it could have been with no such egotism. Literary vanity, even when associated with real talent, has often been foolishly exacting, but such folly as this is utterly incredible. In a woman of Madame de Staël's good sense it would seem impossible. Napoleon's vanity overshot its mark in attempting, by this fiction, to make out a good case for himself. A high authority justly describes Las Cases' book as a work 'written under the dictation of a hero who too frequently has wished to lie (*mentir*) to posterity.'[2] Las Cases himself was an *émigré*, and prejudiced against all who, like Necker and his daughter, had promoted the Revolution.

Bourrienne wrote with Las Cases' 'Mémorial' under his eyes, and probably exaggerated his own recollections by the aid of its statements; yet he acknowledges its lack of truthfulness in important instances. He speaks of her letters as 'full of en-

---

[2] *Biographie Universelle*, vii. 112. Madame Récamier complained of its false statements regarding herself. *Souvenirs et Correspondance* &c. i. The book is full of such falsehoods—not accidental inaccuracies, but deliberate falsifications. We may attribute them not only to Las Cases, but to Napoleon himself; for they abound also in O'Meara's record of St. Helena. See the slanderous example respecting Madame Campan and the Queen Marie Antoinette. Courier says of it, that Napoleon *a menti à Madame Campan* (*Livret de Paul-Louis*; Courier's *Œuvres complètes*, vol. i. Paris, 1834). Junot's wife (the Duchesse d'Abrantès) corrects many similar misstatements and slanders respecting herself and her family. See first three volumes of her *Mémoires*, passim.

thusiasm' and 'extravagances,'[3] when Napoleon was yet only known to her as the 'Conqueror of Italy.' It is not improbable that she might have written enthusiastic letters at this period, when he was still supposed to be loyal to the Republic, and when all France was intoxicated with enthusiasm for him; the question concerns not the style of the letters, but their contents. She never saw him till after his return from Italy, and then still trusted him for some time.

Bourrienne says Napoleon would not answer her letters, but threw them into the fire, and called her 'a fool,' 'disgusted to an inexpressible degree;' and yet, after his return, they met on the most amicable terms, dined together, and complimented each other; and he indisputably endeavoured to conciliate her.

Bourrienne adds that these sentimental extravagances were accompanied by solicitations for the repayment of the two millions 'believed still to be due to Necker for his good and loyal services,' but Bonaparte, 'whatever price he might attach to Madame de Staël's approval, could not believe it a duty to pay so dearly for it out of the money of the State.' Now Napoleon well knew, though Bourrienne apparently did not, that these millions were not a reward due for 'good and loyal services,' but an actual debt, on account of a loan from Necker: a debt which the government had formally acknow-

[3] *Mémoires*, vi. 217.

ledged, and which the Bourbon government afterwards not only acknowledged, but paid. And further, what power had Napoleon, at this time, over the money of the State, that it could be a question with him whether he should repay this claim or not? Bourrienne's allusion to this debt is sufficiently falsified by a statement [4] which Madame de Staël herself made; and which was afterwards published while Napoleon's brother, Joseph Bonaparte, whose name it involves, was still living. 'Joseph Bonaparte, whose understanding and conversation I admire,' she writes, 'came to me shortly after the 18 Brumaire (November 19, 1799), and said, "My brother complains of you. 'Why,' he asked me yesterday, ' why does not Madame de Staël attach herself to my government? What does she wish? Is it the payment of her father's deposit? I will order it. To reside in Paris? I will permit it. In short, what is it she wishes?'" My reply was, "It is not what *I wish*, but what *I think*." If my answer were reported to him, I am sure he could attach no sense to it. He believed in the sincerity of the opinions of no one; he considered morality, in any case, only a formula. To say that you loved liberty, believed in God, or preferred your conscience to your interest, meant to him only that you followed usage in disguising the pretensions of your ambition,

---

[4] Bourrienne, like Las Cases, was one of the *émigrés*, and, like him, heartily disliked the friends of the Revolution. For abundant misstatements, not to say falsifications, in his *Mémoires*, see *Mémoires de la Duchesse d'Abrantès*, passim.

or your egotism.'[5] This statement was published nearly a quarter of a century before the death of Joseph, and was never denied by him. With him she maintained, through her life, an intimate and even confidential friendship. He was her only protector near the throne; and the sentiment of gratitude was always intense with her. With his collusion she sometimes ventured over the proscribed boundary line of her exile, to visit his family at Morfontaine. She acknowledged to him sometimes, with regret, the violence of her language against Napoleon, and never hesitated to express her admiration of his talents. She did not demand the right to attack him publicly, and never did so attack him, except in her posthumous historical works. What she asked was, not to be required to sacrifice her liberal sentiments and conscientious convictions, by sanctioning his usurpations, in her publications. When this was denied her, she was still silent before the public, however freely she used her right of private speech. In this guarded manner, and this alone, she 'never,' as we have said, 'compromised her opinions, and always maintained her intellectual independence.'

At a time when the new Napoleonic order appeared to be irreversibly established, she was not indisposed to recognise what seemed to be invincible fate—especially for the sake of her children, who were doomed to share her persecutions; but

[5] *Dix Années*, i. 1.

even then she would not prostitute her pen by publicly favouring Napoleon's ambition. When his dynasty was apparently rendered permanent by the birth of the King of Rome, a Prefect of Geneva, his obsequious servant, and sent from Paris to supersede a functionary who was deemed too kind to her, urged her to seize the propitious moment to conciliate the Emperor by writing something which might please him—' something in the brilliant, enthusiastic style of Corinne.' Her genius, he argued, 'was given for the celebration of such a man; he was a subject worthy of it.' 'I responded,' she writes, 'that persecuted as I was, all praise from me addressed to him would have the air of a solicitation, and that the Emperor himself could only consider my eulogies ridiculous in such circumstances. He strongly combated this opinion, and came often to pray me, in the name of my interests, to accede to his wishes, were it only to write four pages; this he assured me would suffice to terminate all my troubles. He made similar declarations to my friends. He entreated me, at last, to write on the birth of the King of Rome. I replied, smiling, that I had no ideas on the subject, and must limit my compliments to the wish that he might have a good nurse. This pleasantry ended the negotiations of the Prefect with me.'[6]

Nevertheless, that womanly sympathy for the

[6] *Dix Années.*

sufferings or perils of others, which we have seen in so many instances, was not withheld from her greatest enemy. When he himself was an exile on the island of Elba, she learned from a guest at Coppet, that conspirators were about to go thither to assassinate him. Such a secret, it was supposed, could be confided to her, his uncompromising opponent. She saw that it was important he should be forewarned. She made the facts known to Joseph Bonaparte, who resided not far from Coppet, and immediately offered to bear the warning to Napoleon; as a woman, especially one whom he had persecuted, could do so with the least suspicion from the conspirators or the Government. Talma, the distinguished actor, was a guest of Joseph at the time, and disputed with her the honour of bearing the warning to Elba. Joseph declined the offers of both, and sent a confidential friend of Napoleon, who had voted against the Empire, and had a passport by which he could reach the island.[7]

[7] *Mémoires et Correspondance du Roi Joseph, par A. du Casse*, tome x. p. 226. Paris, 1853-4. Napoleon's life was saved by this timely intervention of Madame de Staël. One of the conspirators had embarked, but was arrested. M. de Casse errs in saying the messenger sent was an old servant of the family. He was Boinod d'Aubonne, usually called 'the American,' as he had fought for the colonies in the War of Independence. His probity had procured him also the title of 'the Quaker.' He served in Napoleon's first Italian campaign, and rose to high rank. Though too honest a Republican to vote for the Empire, the Emperor left him a legacy of a hundred thousand francs, with the remark, 'He is the most honest man I have known.' *Joseph Bonaparte et Madame de Staël*, in Gaullieur's *Étrennes Nationales*. Lausanne, 1845.

In these comments we have somewhat anticipated important facts of our narrative, but only to render them more intelligible hereafter.

On his return from Italy in 1797, Napoleon saw clearly the fate of the Directory: but events were not yet sufficiently ripe for his intended usurpation of the Government. Some delay and, meantime, some dazzling enterprise, far enough away to separate him from the complications of parties in Paris, till the favourable hour should arrive, were expedient. The expedition to Egypt was planned; but he needed funds for it. The invasion of Switzerland, in order to seize the treasure which the Confederation had long and economically been accumulating at Berne, was proposed. Madame de Staël, interested for Switzerland, not only as the land of her family, but as the stronghold of freedom, remonstrated with him on such a crime against a sister Republic. 'I remained,' she says, ' nearly an hour in conversation with him. He heard me patiently, because he wished to learn all he could that might enlighten him on his own affairs; but Demosthenes and Cicero combined could not lead him to the least sacrifice of his personal interest.'[8]

The invasion of Switzerland being certain, she hastened, in January 1798, to join her father at Coppet. 'He was still inscribed,' she says,' on the list of the emigrants, and a positive law condemned to death an emigrant who remained in a country

[8] *Considérations* &c. iii. 27.

occupied by French troops. I did my best to induce him to flee from his home, but could not. "At my age," he said, "a man cannot be a wanderer over the earth." I believe his secret motive was his wish not to leave the tomb of my mother. He had, in this respect, a superstition of the heart, for which he could sacrifice not only the interests of his family, but his own.' His wife had lain in the family tomb, which was visible from his window, more than four years, but not a day passed without his going to walk and meditate near it. 'To desert his home,' says his daughter, 'would seem to him desertion of her.' 'When the French troops approached, we remained alone with my young children. On the day appointed for the violation of the Swiss territory, our servants, eager to see the army, hastened from the château. My father and I stood on the balcony awaiting our fate, and saw the troops advance. Though it was midwinter, the weather was superb: the Alps were reflected in the lake, and the noise of the drums alone broke the tranquillity of the scene. My heart beat cruelly with fear of the danger which menaced my father. I knew that the Directory had spoken of him with respect, but I knew also the rigour of the Revolutionary laws, especially on those who had helped to make them. At the moment when the army passed the Helvetic frontier I saw an officer leave his corps, and hasten towards the château. A mortal fear seized me but his words reassured me. He was charged, by the Directory, to offer my father a safeguard. This officer, later well known as Marshal Suchet, treated us with the highest consideration, as did also his Etat-Major, introduced by him, the next day, to my father. Though Coppet is thirty leagues from Berne, we afterwards heard, in the silence of a closing day, the sound of the cannon echoing among the mountains from the first battlefield.'

The Swiss fought, but were overwhelmed; the treasure at Berne was seized, stolen; the freest and bravest commonwealth of Europe was humiliated; and the sublime Quixotism of the Egyptian expedition began.[9]

---

[9] The Memoirs of Madame de Rémusat have appeared since the completion of my work. I need not say, to any of her readers, that she confirms, and more than confirms, all that I have here said, or shall hereafter have to say, against Bonaparte. A member of his Court, she has given us the best account of his intimate life and character yet published. Thiers (as usual when his hero is impugned), hastily repels the motive alleged in the text for the invasion of Switzerland, though he admits that it has been affirmed by a 'host of writers' besides Madame de Staël. He estimates the treasure of Berne at only eight millions (*Hist. de la Rév.* tome ix.). The Swiss historians deny his statements (*Hist. de la Confédération Suisse*, par Müller, &c., tome iii. 1), and estimate, from official documents, the stolen funds at not less than twenty millions. Jomini (*Hist. des Guerres de la Rév.* x. 292), admits that the expedition was delayed several weeks for want of money, and estimates the Berne treasure at thirty millions. He had, soon after the invasion, personal and official means of knowing the amount. The Swiss continuators of Müller say that the Berne coins were in circulation on the shores of the Nile for a long time after Napoleon's expedition.

CHAPTER XIII.

LIFE IN PARIS—BENJAMIN CONSTANT.

Necker—Madame de Staël's Separation from her Husband—Her Daughter Albertine—Lacretelle—Benjamin Constant—Madame de Charrière—Madame de Staël's Salon—Constant's Speech against the Government—Its Consequences—Madame de Staël's work on Literature—It restores her Social Position in Paris.

MADAME DE STAËL had hitherto had no serious altercation with Napoleon, and could hardly have yet anticipated the relentless persecution which awaited her. During his absence in the East, other matters absorbed her attention.

By the invasion of Switzerland her father became legally a Frenchman. 'He had always been one,' she says, 'in his sentiments and career.' But his name was still on the list of the *émigrés*, and it was necessary that it should be formally erased, in order that he might live with safety in his native country, now occupied by the troops of the Directory. 'He committed to me,' she adds, 'a petition, a document of true dignity and logic, with which I hastened to Paris. The Directory, after reading it, was unanimous in his restoration; and though this act was evidently one of mere justice, it afforded me so much pleasure, that I shall ever be grateful for it. I then treated with the Government for the payment of the two millions which he had left on deposit in the public treasury. It recognised the debt, and offered to pay it in confiscated lands of the clergy. He refused the offer; not that he agreed with those who considered the sale of these properties illegitimate, but he did not wish to unite his interests with his opinions, and thereby occasion the least doubt of his perfect impartiality.'[1]

It was about this time that Madame de Staël's separation from her husband was deemed necessary for the protection of the interests of her children. Their last child (Albertine-Ida-Gustavine, the Duchesse de Broglie), was born about the beginning of 1797. Their marriage, as we have seen, had been one of *convenance*, still customary among the higher classes in France. The Baron, a man of many accomplishments, had one uncontrollable vice. 'Their union, though a little cold,' says Madame Necker de Saussure, 'would probably not have been interrupted, if the unforeseen generosity of Baron de Staël had not degenerated into prodigality.'[2] It is said that on the day of his wedding he transferred to his friend, Count Fersen, the whole of his ministerial salary, and that the large dowry of his bride was soon nearly dissipated

---

[1] *Considérations* &c. iii. 28.
[2] *Notice sur le Caractère et les Écrits de Madame de Staël.*

by his reckless habits. He had no capacity for the management of his finances, and 'Madame de Staël was compelled to save the fortune of her children,' by placing it under the protection of her father. The laws of France provided for such an arrangement, without the necessity of a divorce. This separation was, however, not only no divorce, it was not of long duration. Learning that the Baron was seriously ill, she hastened from Switzerland to attend him. She attempted to convey him to the shelter of Coppet, but he died at Poligny, on the road thither, May 2, 1802.

Her young Albertine, her only daughter, was the delight of her life, and it was of her that she uttered the paradoxical phrase, so happily verified, 'I will *force* her to make a marriage of *choice*,' alluding no doubt to her own unfortunate marriage. She lavished on this child the affection of her exuberant heart; she superintended her education with unremitting care, and saw her at last exalted, by a marriage of affection, to one of the highest positions of French society.

During these times Madame de Staël was deeply absorbed in the preparation of her elaborate work, on 'Literature considered in its relations to Social Institutions.' It was the subject of her studies at Coppet and of colloquial discussion in its brilliant circle. She spent her summers there, but returned to Paris for the winters. On the 9th of November 1799 (the memorable 18th Brumaire), she arrived in the capital at a moment when a new revolution began to prove that her anticipations of the policy of Napoleon were, as she says, 'prophetic.' While stopping to change horses, some leagues from the city, she was informed that the Director, Barras, who had been her friend in several emergencies, had passed, accompanied by gendarmes, on his way to his estate at Grosbois. The Directory was overthrown. Napoleon's name was on the lips of everybody. He had been in Paris five weeks, ready for the new revolution which was effectively prepared by his agents during his absence in the East. The legislative body was transferred to St. Cloud. On the day after her arrival his Grenadiers marched through the assembly of the deputies, compelling them to flee through the windows as well as the doorways. The Consular Government was established under an ingenious constitution from the fertile brain of Siéyès. The great soldier, having become 'First Consul,' had no serious difficulty in becoming Emperor of France and dominator of Europe.

Madame de Staël shared in the general unfavourable opinion of the Directory; but to her the ambitious policy of Napoleon was a greater evil. Her salon became the centre, and she the soul of a conservative republican party—the *Cercle Constitutionnel*. The design of the *Cercle Constitutionnel* was the maintenance of the 'cause of liberty,' by a parliamentary opposition against the new administration, similar to that of the English legislature. Lacretelle, the historian, speaks strongly of her influence over the statesmen who now met at her house; and records *in extenso* a remarkable example of her colloquial eloquence.[3] 'I had,' he says, 'for six months the happiness of receiving her encouragement, and, what was not less precious, her inspirations for my political writings. One lived in an atmosphere of enthusiasm, near her; so thoroughly did her eloquence irradiate the dullest subjects, and animate the most frigid interlocutors. It flashed forth in sallies, in lightnings; it was impossible successfully to resist her.'

A remarkable man, Benjamin Constant, who will often appear in our narrative, was the representative of the conservative party in the *Cercle* and in the legislature. The relations between him and Madame de Staël, which are so incessantly alluded to in the publications of the period, began in 1794. During a number of years he had lived in the greatest intimacy with Madame de Charrière, then a literary celebrity of Switzerland, authoress of 'Lettres Neuchateloises,' of 'Caliste,' and numerous other works. She had met Madame de Staël in her youth, at Paris, in the salons of Théllusson and Necker, and in later years received letters and visits from her at Colombier, near Neuchâtel. In their correspondence Madame de Staël commended her writings with characteristic heartiness: a courtesy

---

[3] See his *Dix Années d'Épreuves pendant la Révolution*, chap. xi. Paris, 1842.

which was never reciprocated by Madame Charrière.[4] Though the latter possessed genuine talents, and persistently endeavoured to develop Constant's higher capabilities, her influence upon him was not salutary; he was excessively morbid and cynical till he came under the more genial power of Madame de Staël.[5] Madame de Charrière, like Madame de Genlis, was either from literary jealousy or from unfavourable rumours, strongly prejudiced against Madame de Staël, and had infected Constant's mind with her prejudices; but he soon corrected them. In September 1794 he wrote: 'A proof that she is not merely a talking machine, is the lively interest she takes in those that suffer. She has just been successful, after three costly and useless attempts, in saving from prison, and getting out of France, a woman who was her enemy in Paris, and who had displayed her hatred in every possible manner. This is more than talking. I believe that her activity is a necessity as much as a merit: but she employs it in doing good.' Three weeks later he fully comprehends his new friend, and writes to the old one, with enthusiasm: 'Now that I know her better

---

[4] Gaullieur's *Études sur l'Histoire Littéraire de la Suisse Française*, ix. Paris, 1856.

[5] Sainte-Beuve notices the favourable change, *Revue des Deux Mondes*, April 15, 1844. The *Revue Suisse* for April 1844 gives some of the letters of Madame de Charrière to Benjamin Constant. In the edition of her *Caliste* for 1845 (Paris), are given Sainte-Beuve's articles with these letters, and also letters of Madame de Staël to Madame de Charrière.

it is hardly possible for me to restrain my eulogies, and not to give, to all with whom I speak, the proofs of my interest and admiration. I have seldom seen an equal union of qualities so astonishing and attractive; so much brilliancy and accuracy; benevolence so expansive and so refined; so much generosity; politeness so sweet and so abundantly bestowed in society; so much charm, simplicity, *abandon*, among familiar friends. She is the second woman that I have found who could hold the place of all the universe for me; who could be all the world to me—she alone. You know who was the first. Madame de Staël has infinitely more spirit in intimate conversation than in society; she knows perfectly how to listen, as well as to speak; she enjoys the talents of others, as well as her own; she makes those whom she loves value themselves by her constant and ingenuous attentions—a proof as much of kindness as of sense. In fine, she is a being apart, a superior being, such as is met, perhaps, only once in an age; such that all who approach her, and know her as a friend, will demand no greater happiness.' Madame Charrière must have been more than woman not to have been piqued by such a triumph of her rival. Her letters to other correspondents show that she felt it bitterly. She criticises Madame de Staël's works (as yet few and unimportant) with severity, and insists that either Constant had abandoned the first principles of taste which she had 'nourished and caressed in him to her utmost,' or 'at least he criticises without regarding them.' 'In this case,' she adds, 'it is downright and vile slavery—this of Constantinus. In such a *liaison*, or any *liaison* whatever, they should mutually control one another, and alternatively be the soul one of another.' She had herself been noted for her beauty as well as her talents; her successful rival had superseded her without this advantage—a fact hard to bear. 'They met at Lausanne,' she continues, 'and admired one another. She showed an extreme interest in him, and he has written me his admiration of her. In fact, the rapidity of her mind and her eloquence are remarkable. They make one imagine her beautiful while you see she is ugly—I wish you had seen them.'[6]

Madame de Staël speaks of him in the highest terms; he is 'a friend of liberty,' she says, 'and is endowed with the most remarkable intellect that nature has given to any man.' Chateaubriand says, 'he had more *esprit* than any other man in France since Voltaire.'

Though a Swiss by birth, this eminent thinker and parliamentary orator had studied at Oxford, at Edinburgh, and in Germany; had early become intimately allied with Marmontel, La Harpe, and the other *littérateurs* and *philosophes* of Paris; had travelled in Germany, and knew personally Kant, Goethe, Schiller, Wieland. He became

[6] Gaullieur's *Études* &c. ix.

distinguished in authorship by his reproduction of Schiller's 'Wallenstein,' by his 'Adolphe,' by able articles in the 'Mercure,' the 'Minerve,' the 'Renommée,' and the 'Courrier,' leading journals of his times; by his elaborate essay on 'Religion considered in its Sources, its Forms, and its Developments,' in five volumes; his posthumous treatise on 'Roman Polytheism considered in its relations to the Greek Philosophy and the Christian Religion,' in two volumes octavo, and numerous other works.

Benjamin Constant was, in spite of the prevailing scepticism, and some unfortunate habits, ever addicted to the highest moral contemplations, and profoundly interested in the highest destinies of humanity. His politics were always 'humanitarian.'[7]

But a certain inherent moral weakness rendered him uncertain in his opinions, cynical in his temper, and bitterly, though brilliantly, sarcastic in his speech. He was to survive most of his compeers of these troubled times, and to share in the political vicissitudes of France down to the Revolution of 1830. When his remains were carried, in that year, from the Protestant church in Paris, the patriotic youth of the capital made a 'political demonstration' around his coffin, wishing to bear him

---

[7] For an account of his politics see Laboulaye's *Benjamin Constant: Cours de Politique Constitutionnelle, ou Collection des Ouvrages publiés sur Gouvernement Représentatif par Benjamin Constant*, &c. 2 vols. Paris, 1872.

to the Pantheon, that he might rest among the great men who sleep in its crypt. He was one of the most vigorous minds of his times; one of the finest talkers in the Parisian *salons*; one of the greatest athletes in parliamentary debate; 'of vast intelligence, prodigious resources, acute perception, powerful argumentation, lucid elocution; bold in address, happy in replies, incisive with urbanity.'[8] His bust, by Bra, in the art gallery of Geneva, wears the lineaments of a careworn, saddened, but superior man.

For no man, save her father and Mathieu de Montmorency, did Madame de Staël entertain a warmer admiration than for Benjamin Constant. He left an affecting tribute to her memory. He witnessed her long and cruel exile; and speaks of her neglect by so many whom she rescued from a similar fate and from death itself, with something like wrathful resentment. 'They have remained,' he says, 'indifferent spectators of the exile of their benefactress, and of the profound sufferings which that exile caused her. I have seen them, in their ardour to justify a despotism that had no need of their servile apologies, accuse its victim of having inspired by her activity, her spirit, her generous impetuosity, the alarm of the government. Yes, her activity, without doubt, was indefatigable, her spirit was powerful, she was impetuous against all that was unjust or tyrannical. You ought well to know

[8] *Nouvelle Biographie* &c.

it, for this activity succoured you in your misery, protected you in your perils; this powerful spirit devoted itself to the pleading of your cause; this impetuosity, which hesitated for no calculation of self-interest, no fear of incurring for itself the persecution from which it tried to rescue you, placed itself between you and those who proscribed you. Ungrateful friends! Miserable courtiers! you have made criminal in her the virtues by which she has saved you.'[9]

The *salon* of Madame de Staël was soon thronged by the best intellects of Paris; by men of letters, by foreign diplomatists, by members of the legislature; even the brothers of Napoleon were among her habitual guests, for Lucien and Joseph were proud of her friendship. The brilliant Sophie Gay, her literary contemporary, but never her rival, has given the first place to her reunions, in a work on the 'Salons Célèbres,' devoting forty pages to her. 'Garat, Andrieux, Daunon, and Constant, inspired by her enthusiasm, endeavoured to save liberty in the legislature. The most eloquent of the Republican orators were those who borrowed from her most of their ideas and telling phrases. Most of them went forth from her door with speeches ready for the next day, and with resolution to pronounce them—a courage which was also derived from her.'

---

[9] *Mélanges de Littérature* &c. Coulmane (*Réminiscences*, iii. ch. 7–15. 3 vols. Paris, 1862) gives an ample sketch of his public life, including a minute account of his conduct at this period, from his own dictation.

'Her salon, at this period, was composed not only of the chiefs of the opposition, but one saw there many persons who were attached to the Government—the brothers of the First Consul, the ministers, &c. Journalists were there to find news; Talma and Gerard sought inspiration there; returned *émigrés* bore there the exquisite politeness of the *ancien régime*; the Duke Mathieu de Montmorency could utter there the religious sentiments which characterised his pure and charitable soul; the Duke Adrien de Laval could maintain there his fine *esprit*, the delicacy and grace of his noble and simple manners; the Count Louis de Narbonne, the courtly traditions and flatteries which, later, endeared him so much to Napoleon; the Chevalier de Boufflers enchanted the company by his piquant recitals, his fine sarcasm, seconded by the brilliant repartees of M. de Chauvelin; the Count de Sabran gave there proof of that eminent intellect and generous heart by which he afterwards consoled the exile of Madame de Staël. These remnants of the *ancien régime* mingled there freely with the best minds born of the Revolution—Ducis, Chenier, Lemercier, Arnaud, Legouvé, Talleyrand, Regnault de Saint Jean d'Angely, Camille Jordan, Andrieux, Constant, &c. Their differences of opinion gave way to the necessity felt for conversation and mutual sympathy.'[1]

Madame de Staël saw, however, that a disposi-

[1] *Salons Célèbres*, par Madame Sophie Gay. Paris, 1837.

tion prevailed, all around her, to yield to the new Government; or, if not to yield to it, yet not to offend it, for the future seemed at its command. Her own opinions were well known among her intimate friends, but she did not impose them on her guests. Those who shared them formed an interior, an esoteric circle around her. Benjamin Constant, now becoming a notable man, was their chief representative with the public. He consulted her on a speech which he proposed to make against the 'rising tyranny.' 'I encouraged him,' she says, 'with all the force of my conscience. Nevertheless, I could not but apprehend unfavourable consequences to myself. With Montaigne I have always felt that I am French, because I am Parisian. The phantom of *ennui* has ever pursued me. From the terror which it causes me, I should, perhaps, have been capable of bending before tyranny, if the example of my father, and his blood in my veins, had not sustained me above this feebleness. Bonaparte well knew this predisposition. He quickly discerned the weak side of all about him; for it was by their defects that he subjected them to his control. He joined to the power with which he menaced them, to the treasures that he allowed them to hope for, exemption from *ennui*—always a terror to the French. A residence at forty leagues from the capital, in contrast with all the attractions of the most agreeable city of the world, in time enfeebles the wills of most exiles accustomed from their infancy to the charms of Parisian life. In the evening before the day on which Constant was to deliver his speech, I had with me Lucien Bonaparte and many others, whose conversation afforded me the interest, always new, which arises from the force of ideas and the graces of style. Constant approached me and whispered, " You see your *salon* crowded with persons who please you ; if I speak to-morrow, it will be deserted. Think again." " It is necessary to follow our convictions," was my reply. The exaltation of my feelings prompted this answer ; but I confess that, had I foreseen what I have suffered from that date, I should hardly have had the strength to make it.'

Constant's apprehensions were well founded. He delivered his speech, signalising the incipient despotism of the Government. On the evening of that day a large company was to have assembled at her house ; by five o'clock she received ten letters of excuse. 'I bore the first and second sufficiently well,' she says ; ' but in proportion as these notes followed one another I became troubled. Vainly I appealed to my conscience, which had counselled me to renounce all the advantages of Napoleon's favour ; so many honourable people blamed me, that I hardly knew how to maintain my position with firmness.' Bonaparte reproved his brother Joseph for attending her *salon*, and for some weeks he dared not repeat his visits. His example was quickly followed by three-fourths of her acquaintances. They did not acknowledge that they feared the power and resentment of the First Consul, but 'invented,' she continues, 'each day, some new pretext which could hurt my feelings, exercising all the influence of their political opinions against a woman persecuted and without defence, and prostrating themselves at the feet of men who had been the vilest Jacobins from the moment that Napoleon had regenerated them by the baptism of his favour.' One of these, Fouché, minister of police, waited on her, and said that the First Consul suspected she had prompted the speech of Constant. 'Constant,' she replied, 'is too able a man not to have convictions of his own.' Fouché acknowledged this, but assured her that Napoleon was irritated by the opposition, and she was implicated in it. 'He counselled me,' she says, 'to retire into the country, and in a few days all would "pass over." But on my return, I found it quite the reverse.'[2]

She knew, however, that an invincible power remained in her otherwise feeble woman's hand—the pen. Without using it against Napoleon, she resolved to vindicate by it her claims to social and public recognition. In these days of desertion, and of the worst chagrins that a woman can suffer, she completed her Essay on Literature, disdaining, however, to insert in it a single word which might conciliate her persecutor.

[2] Compare the *Considérations* &c. iv. with *Dix Années*, i.

It produced an immediate and surprising impression, for, whatever defects the critics find in it, no woman had ever attempted so elaborate a literary work, and the traits of her genius are obvious in every chapter. 'Its success,' she writes, 'entirely restored my position in society; my *salon* was again filled, and I recovered that most exquisite pleasure of my life,—the pleasure of conversing in Paris.'

CHAPTER XIV.

HER WORK ON LITERATURE.

Its Scope—The Perfectibility of Man—Contemporary Criticism on the Book—Fontanes—Chateaubriand—Christianity—What she meant by Perfectibility—Vico's Theory—Noble Thoughts.

HER work on Literature was published in 1800, and reissued in the ensuing year.[1] The plan and scope of this treatise are bold and comprehensive. Its first part presents an analysis, 'moral and philosophic,' of Greek and Latin literature, with reflections on the consequences, 'to the human mind,' of the invasions of the Northern peoples, of the establishment of Christianity, and of the revival of letters; and a rapid review of modern literature, with detailed observations on the chief works of the Italian, English, German, and French languages, considered in reference to the general idea of the essay: that is to say, the relation of the social and political conditions of a country to the dominant spirit of its literature. The extent of research, the acuteness of criticism, the subtlety of speculation, displayed in this part would be remarkable in

[1] *De la Littérature considérée dans ses Rapports avec les Institutions Sociales.* 2 vols. Paris, 1800.

any writer of the times: in the writings of a woman, they were a marvel to Europe. The second part discusses the state of intelligence and literature in France since the Revolution, and, inquiring what they would be if France should possess the morality essential to Republicanism, it shows her actual degradation, and her possible amelioration as deducible from the examples treated in the first part.

The doctrine, or hypothesis, of the treatise is the perfectibility of the human race. 'I adopt with all my faculties,' she says, 'this philosophic belief. It is the conservative, the redeeming hope of the intellectual world; it imparts a grand elevation to the soul—its highest consolation. Before it, the actual baseness of men, the vileness of their ordinary calculations, disappear from our view. The future of truth, the future of virtue, the future of glory, inspire us with new force. The doctrine lifts the weight of life, and gladdens all our moral being with the happiness and nobleness of virtue. It is not a vain theory: we are conducted to it by the observation of facts.'

The learning, the brilliant passages of thought, the vigorous style of the treatise, can hardly be questioned; but its hypothesis of the perfectibility of the race was contested in France at least. In Germany it was eagerly approved, for it agreed with the prepossessions of German thinkers.[2] M.

---

[2] For the latest expression of German opinion on the subject, see Dr. E. Pfleiderer's *Die Idee eines Goldenen Zeitalters*, Berlin, 1877;

de Fontanes immediately attacked it in the 'Mercure de France' (1800).³ Madame de Staël replied to him in her second edition (1801). Chateaubriand, the intimate friend of Fontanes, addressed to him a long and rhetorical letter, endorsing some of his criticisms, and rejecting others.⁴ Fontanes had admitted the progressiveness of the physical and mathematical, but not of the moral and political sciences. 'The spirit of the human race,' he affirmed, 'resembles that of the individual man; it shines and is eclipsed by turns.' Chateaubriand admits, ambiguously, the doctrine of Madame de Staël. 'She gives,' he says, 'to philosophy what I attribute to religion.'

But Madame de Staël would not exclude religion from philosophy, whatever qualifications she might attach to the influence of given forms of religion. The intellectual enlightenment and emancipation of the world were to her the comprehensive condition of the perfectibility of man; religion, of course, must be an element in such a condition. Philosophy was her name for its *rationale*. For intelligence must be its basis—the knowledge of truth, of any and every kind of truth. She would have no compromise here.

and Dr. R. Rocholl's *Die Philosophie der Geschichte*. Göttingen, 1878. The latter has been 'crowned' by the Faculty of Philosophy at Göttingen.

³ Fontanes' two articles (brilliantly written, and full of learning) are given in his collected *Œuvres*, ii. Paris, 1839.

⁴ Chateaubriand's *Œuvres complètes*, iv. Paris, 1827.

With Lessing, as she later says, in the 'Allemagne,' she ceased not to attack, with all the force of her logic, 'that maxim, so commonly repeated, that *there are some truths which are dangerous*. It is an extreme presumption, in some individuals, to believe that they have the right to conceal the truth from their species, and claim for themselves the prerogative of placing themselves, as Alexander before Diogenes, in such manner as to intercept the rays of the sun, which belong to all equally. This pretended prudence is only a theory of charlatanism. It would juggle with ideas, the better to serve mankind! The truth is the work of God, falsehoods are the work of man. If we study those epochs of history in which the truth has been feared, we shall always find that they were periods in which individual interests warred, in some manner, against the universal tendency. Search for the truth is the noblest occupation of man; its publication a duty. There is nothing to fear, for religion or for society, in this pursuit, if it is sincere; and if it is not, it is then no longer the truth; it is mischievous falsehood. There is not a sentiment in man, the philosophic reason of which cannot be discovered; not an opinion, not even a prejudice generally spread, which has not its root in nature. It is necessary, therefore, to examine, not with the object of destroying belief, but of founding it on intimate conviction, and not on fallacious conviction. There is a pre-established harmony between truth and human reason which tends always to bring them together.'

She distinguishes 'admirably,' says Villemain, 'the great social differences between the spirit of antiquity and the modern spirit. She sees them, conceives them by a sort of intuition; she has above all understood, and expresses with a grand superiority, the character of the reform introduced by Christianity into the midst of the ancient world.'[5] Chateaubriand, reviewing, in 1826, his earlier opinions, 'became,' says Sainte-Beuve, 'liberal, and as much as Madame de Staël a partisan of Perfectibility. He assigned to the march of humanity a series of concentric circles, which enlarge, without ceasing, into infinite space.' At the Restoration, Madame de Staël celebrated with festive songs and wit, at a dinner in her house in the Rue Royale, her reconciliation with Fontanes and Chateaubriand, who, with Pasquier, Madame de Vintimille, Lally-Tollendal, and others, formed there a 'perpetual friendship.' Her book was published the year before Chateaubriand's 'Genius of Christianity' appeared. The latter, says Vinet, has 'led us a little to forget the sensation produced by the former; it was, nevertheless, vivid and universal. The work would make a sensation were it to appear for the first time to-day, if only by its literary beauties. But appearing immediately after the 18th Brumaire, we can imagine what

---

[5] *Cours de Littérature Française*, iv. Paris, 1873.

a passionate tumult must have been excited by
the propositions that literature has relations most
intimate and most essential to public virtue,
liberty, glory, and felicity; that a law of progression is imposed on human destiny, raising
the level of manners and of literature from epoch
to epoch; that this progression is indefinite, and
advances with the growth of institutions: that is
to say, with the tendency to republican government and republican manners, and will have for
its distinctive character the triumph of the serious
spirit of the North over the frivolous spirit of the
South.'[6]

This greatest of Swiss thinkers criticises freely
the defects of the work, especially its failure, as he
thinks, to appreciate the relation of Christianity to
its hypothesis, though she 'enumerates loyally,' he
admits, 'the benefits of religion.' Vinet's objection
is hardly relevant; her treatment of Christianity[7]
ought to satisfy the Christian critic. She not only
enumerates 'loyally the benefits' of Christianity, but
vindicates it against the sceptical criticism of the
day, and shows it to have been essential to the
progress of civilisation. Christianity was not, however, with her, any dogmatic formula of Rome,
of Wittenburg, of Geneva, or of Oxford. Vinet
exhorts his readers to respect her faith. 'At the

---

[6] Vinet's *Etudes sur la Littérature Française au XIXe Siècle*, i. Paris, 1857.

[7] *De la Littérature* &c. i. 8.

foundation it is yours,' he says: 'you believe in perfectibility if you believe in revelation.'

The severest criticism on these volumes deals with minor defects which might have been avoided by the author without impairing her argument. She seems to assume that Republican government is an essential condition of the perfectibility of man; she means Constitutional government, based upon the common interests of the people, recognising the co-ordinate rights of the governed and the governing; for we know that she approved the qualified monarchy of England.

She eliminates from her argument works of the imagination; for the superiority of the classic monuments of art and literature seemed formidable to her theory. The maximum advancement of special departments of culture may, however, be attained in a given age, and the race may still advance in other directions. The Romans could not surpass the Greeks in Art, but they went forward in their own direction, that of government and jurisprudence (supreme in the interests of the world), and modern civilisation borrows from both Greece and Rome.

Her generalisations were not sufficiently large; her perspective not sufficiently extended; she was too anxious to account for, or rather to explain away, apparent contradictions of her theory,—the decline of Greek art under the Romans; the decline of Rome itself; the decline of Europe, generally, for a thousand years (which, she acknowledges, presents an apparent difficulty to her logic), the retrogression of some important modern nations, &c.

But a great current may have its backward eddies: these must not be mistaken for the current itself; or, if the whole current seems at times to be arrested, and dammed up, its accumulated force may at last burst its obstructions, and sweep onward the more swiftly. Humanity always advances, says Goethe, but in a spiral line. The mediæval centuries, in which northern barbarism alone seemed to prevail, resulted in the civilisation of the North, and the development at last of that mighty Teutonic energy which has since been renovating the world.

The European invention of the mariner's compass, without apparently borrowing it from China; the discovery of America; the Renaissance in art and letters; the invention of printing; the Reformation; the outspread of colonisation; the subsequent birth of so many great ideas (still more potential than potent) such as popular government, popular education, religious toleration, freedom of speech, freedom of the press, freedom of trade,— the progress of the natural sciences, the introduction of the steam-engine, the steamboat, the railroad, the telegraph, the spectroscope, the telephone, and many more improvements, which are changing the face of the world—all prove the law of human progress, notwithstanding any temporary or local retrogressions. All are the results of advancing intelligence; and literature is the symbol, the exponent of intelligence.

The Greek architecture may be perfect in its kind, and may never, therefore, be surpassed; but the Gothic may also be perfect in its kind. Which is preferable, is not the question. The world has both: is the world richer with both than it would be with one, is the only question. Does the world grow richer, from age to age, in ideas, in truths?

Her critics were captious and played on words. Had she been more precise in her definitions, she would have forestalled them. In a note to her new preface, in the second edition, she defines more completely her theory of Perfectibility, not as a definite and final perfection, but a law of progression, tending towards perfection. 'This system,' she remarks, ' has given origin to so many absurdities, that I am obliged to indicate exactly the sense that I give it, in my work. First, in speaking of the perfectibility of the human mind, I do not pretend to say that the moderns have greater intellectual faculties than the ancients; but only that the mass of ideas, in every department, augments with the ages. Secondly, in speaking of the perfectibility of the human species, I do not allude to the dreams of some thinkers respecting an improbable future; but to the successive progress of civilisation in all classes and in all countries.'

She propounded, then, a sublime truth: she failed at many points, in its treatment; yet few hands, perhaps no feminine one, could have treated it better in her day. She applied to philosophy and literature substantially the same grand but still disputed generalisation which her great countrymen, Lamarck and La Place, afterwards applied, the one to natural history, the other to cosmical science,[8] and which a majority of the naturalists of our day apply to biological science generally.

For more than half a century before the publication of her treatise, eminent thinkers had affirmed the doctrine of Perfectibility—Ferguson in England, Kant in Germany, Turgot in France. Condorcet, at a time when he might well despair of the Republic, and when he himself was under its proscription, still argued for the perfectibility of the human race. It was one of the intuitions of the greatest genius of the middle ages, Roger Bacon. 'The high law of the sciences, of man—Indefinite Perfectibility—is read in the Opus Majus, five hundred years before Condorcet.'[9] More than three quarters of a century before Madame de Staël's treatise, the Italian philosopher, Vico, had created the 'Philosophy of

---

[8] Lamarck's *Philosophie Zoologique* appeared nearly twenty years later (1819); the last part of La Place's *Mécanique Céleste* was published in 1825.

[9] Michelet, *Hist. de France* ('La Renaissance,' Introd.), vol. vii. Paris, 1857.

History' (in his 'New Science' and in his 'Universal Law,'[1]); but though he asserted the leading principle of her theory, namely, that history is subject to law, yet his conclusions fall infinitely short of her sublime humanitarianism. He begins in barbarism and ends in the consolidation and forced order of monarchy; she begins in barbarism and ends in liberty—in the representative, not to say Republican, self-government of the race, under the reign of universal enlightenment. His doctrine of the *Ricorsi* implies ever-recurring cycles of growth and decay; she rejects the supposition of necessary decay. She justly claims to be the first to apply the hypothesis of perfectibility to literature.[2] Sir James Mackintosh, writing in 1813, says: 'The philosophy of literature is one of the most recently opened fields of speculation; a few fragments of it are among the most beautiful parts of Hume's Essays. The great work of Madame de Staël, on Literature, was the first attempt on a bold and extensive scale. In the neighbourhood of her late residence, and perhaps not uninfluenced by her spirit, two writers of great merit, Sismondi in his " History of the Literature of the South," and Barante in his essay on " French Literature during the Eighteenth Century," have treated various parts

---

[1] His *Nuova Scienza* first appeared in 1722. His *De Universi Juris* &c. still earlier, in 1720.

[2] See note to her preface in the second edition, *Œuvres complètes*, tome iv. p. 17. Paris, 1820.

of this wide subject.'[3] It will hereafter be seen that Sismondi and Barante were under her tutelage at Coppet.

An able French thinker of our day has shown how, almost universally, the new theory has affected French literature, especially the French historians: 'The phrase of Charles Nodier, attributed to Madame de Staël, has, by the studies of æsthetic critics, become the formula of this method, "Literature is the expression of society." Works of art and of literature are no longer considered as products of free, individual minds alone, as Plato, Aristotle, Horace, and Quintilian taught; but modern criticism sees in them the genius of the race, of the epoch. Thus has the criticism of antiquity been revolutionised, and literary history has become a science.'[4]

'Many opinions,' says Madame Necker de Saussure, 'which have since been subjects of discussion among critics, were propounded for the first time in this book. We find in it the origin of nearly all we have since read on its hypothesis, and later writers have evidently used it much more than they have cited it. One cannot but be singularly struck by its intellectual amplitude.' It shows that she was familiar with all the standard works of ancient and modern literature; but her use of them is not in the mere details which diligent research in a

---

[3] *Edinburgh Review*, Oct. 1813.
[4] Vacherot's *La Science et la Conscience*, iii. Paris, 1872.

well-stored library might afford, but in philosophic and profoundly meditated generalisations.

'Its style,' says Palisot, 'if we except here and there an obscure passage, is always proportioned to the grandeur of its subject. This is an observation which continually forces itself upon us in reading it. No work of the kind is richer in single great thoughts.'[5] 'Envy and revenge,' says Pougens, 'prompted the criticism which was hostile to the book. But posterity will avenge its author.'[6] Whether the critical reader accepts or rejects her theory, he cannot but wonder at the variety of learning and the virility of mind which the work displays; he will search in vain for any equal example among all the literary productions of women. Should he even deem that, as a whole, it has now little value, still there is hardly a page of it which he will not pronounce invaluable for its brilliant or profound individual thoughts. Her 'Allemagne,' though much better known, shows not richer or more vigorous faculties. Every page reminds us of her early studies of Montesquieu. Villemain accredits her as the first of French critics who appreciated Shakespeare. Voltaire's prejudiced opinions of the English dramatist had been canonical, in France, down to the publication of her treatise. She was the first of great French writers who struck an effectual blow against the mechanical rigour with

---

[5] Querard's *La France Littéraire*, ix. Paris, 1838.
[6] *Bibliothèque Française*. Nos. 6, 8 and 10. Paris, 1801.

which the genius of her country had been shackled by the classical 'unities,' and thereby opened the way for the Romantic school of writers. Her critical views of taste are especially profound and noble; to her, taste is the *morale* of literature. 'All that theory of taste,' says Villemain, 'which continually connects the study of letters with the dignity of the human soul, she expounds admirably. This is the great innovation which she bore into criticism; it is the noble originality of her treatise.'

Sainte-Beuve, admirable critic as he is, is not a good theoriser. He remarks that the theory of literature which Madame de Staël proposes, in this work, 'was already struck at the heart, by the prostration of the institutions which alone could favour and guarantee it.' She is rich, he admits, 'in ideas; much richer than Chateaubriand; but could not vivify her theory.'[7] Republicanism was dying in France: how then could a literature, founded in Republican conditions, live? The only just question is: Has she correctly defined the influence of Republican institutions, or rather of popular liberty, on literature? If so, then her theory is as secure as liberty itself. Sainte-Beuve did not perceive that, though the Revolution was passing away, yet the spirit of liberty which it had evoked was inextinguishable, and would reassert itself in spite of any political reactions. Had he

[7] *Chateaubriand et son Groupe,* i. 1.

survived to our day, he would have seen the Republic again erect in France, with better possibilities than ever for the theory of Madame de Staël. All sects or schools in literature, as in philosophy and theology, are, however, precarious; they at best afford but the germs of something better. The Romantic and the Classic schools are, for example, in contrast, but need not be in opposition; they may complement one another. Madame de Staël's theory of the literature of freedom is but one phase of the broader rationale of all literature, of all intellectual progress.

Though this book restored her social status in Paris, and, as she says, gathered Europe again around her, in the persons of its diplomatic representatives, it could only delay the resentment of Bonaparte. She had written in favour of Republicanism. The Republic still survived, nominally at least, under the First Consul; but it was not accordant with his designs that it should long survive. Villemain, familiar with the literary traditions of the times, and judging from the 'anecdotal and political point of view,' supposes that particular passages of the book offended Bonaparte—passages too noble for his express condemnation. In one of them she says: 'Behind Alexander still rises the shadow of Greece. It is necessary for the renown, even of illustrious warriors, that the countries which they subdue should be enriched with the gifts of the human mind. I know not but that the power of thought will some day extinguish the plague of war, but, before that day, it is this power, it is eloquence and imagination, it is philosophy, which must dignify the importance of military achievements. If you allow all nobleness to become effaced or degraded, force can dominate society, but no true glory can environ it. Men will be a thousand times more degraded by the loss of intellectual emulation than even by the jealous passions with which the pursuit of military glory may infuriate them.' Again: 'It is not true that a great man has more renown by being celebrated alone—without being surrounded by famous personages who cede to him the pre-eminence. It has been said, in politics, that a king cannot exist without nobles, without an aristocracy. In the court of public opinion it is also necessary that the supremacy of rank shall be guaranteed by gradations of rank. Of what importance is it that a Conqueror opposes barbarians to barbarians in the night of ignorance? Cæsar is famous in history because he decided the destiny of Rome, and that in Rome were Cicero, Sallust, Cato, &c.'

If Bonaparte was intellectually capable of appreciating such thoughts, he was, nevertheless, morally incapable of appreciating the moral attitude of the writer—the sublime integrity of her soul, maintained throughout the book. In its last and most eloquent chapter is a passage, worthy to live for ever, in which, after acknowledging the susceptibility of her temperament to the fears, the dangers which then beset independent thinkers, she says, 'But this feebleness of the heart ought never to affect our judgment of general ideas. To whatever suffering the expression of such ideas can expose us, it is necessary to brave it. We can develop usefully only the principles of which we are intimately convinced. Opinions that you would sustain against your own convictions, you can never profoundly analyse nor effectively express. The more the mind is true to nature, the more it is incapable of retaining any force, if the support of conviction fail it. We should, then, free ourselves, if possible, from the fears which can disturb the independence of our meditations; we should confide our life to the supports of the moral world, our happiness to those whom we love, our opinions to time, the faithful ally of conscience and truth.'

Napoleon saw that, in one way or another, he must check the influence of this formidable woman. He waited and watched for his opportunity.

CHAPTER XV.

DE GÉRANDO, THE PHILOSOPHER—MADAME DE KRÜDNER, THE MYSTIC.

Her Relations with De Gérando—Annette de Gérando—Spiritualism—Madame de Krüdner—Letter from De Gérando—Her Salon in Paris—Necker's 'Last Views'—Napoleon's Resentment—Conversation with Lacretelle—Kant—Return to Paris.

Soon after her return to Coppet for the summer, she was cheered by an article in a Paris journal, favourable to her book, which she recognised as from the hand of one of the greatest thinkers and best men of the age—her friend De Gérando, the philosopher and philanthropist. He was now rapidly rising in public consideration, and became her lifelong correspondent. He had barely escaped death in the horrors of the Revolution; he shared the exile of his and her friend, Camille Jordan; and, later, served in the armies of the Republic. Prompted by rare native genius, he pondered, in camps and barracks, the profoundest problems of humanity. While yet in military life, at a distance from Paris, he competed for a prize offered by the Institute, and surpassed all his rivals by his work on 'The Signs and Art of Thinking, in their Mutual

Relations,' which was published in the same year in which appeared Madame de Staël's essay on Literature. It was the first of four or five of his productions which were 'crowned' by the Institute, or the Academies of Lyons and Berlin, and the germ of those greater works which made him conspicuous among contemporary thinkers, on 'The Origin of Human Intelligence,' the 'Comparative History of Philosophic Systems,' &c. His moral qualities were as great as his intellectual faculties. Madame de Staël remarked that 'his thoughts always followed his sentiments, and he could write only for the practical good of his race.' His sympathy with her hopeful views of humanity and with her 'spiritualistic' philosophy drew him towards her; for though he received Locke's doctrine of the origin of ideas, yet, like Locke himself, he could reconcile it with the purest spiritualism and the highest ethics.

The success of his first essay produced a sensation in the literary circles of Paris. He was called from the army to the capital, and Madame de Staël, by letters to Lucien Bonaparte, then high in office, procured him an appointment under the Government, by which he could live with sufficient leisure for his favourite studies. He occupied, for some time, Necker's villa at St. Ouen, and letters, ardent with sentiment and on the loftiest themes, constantly passed between the old home, near the capital, and the château on Lake Leman. A greater charm than that of the genius of the philosopher attracted the interest of the authoress to the old home. Her highest ideal of woman's happiness was 'love in marriage,' and she found one of its most beautiful exemplifications now in St. Ouen. The philosopher's wife, Annette de Gérando (the 'sweet Annette,' as Madame de Staël called her), was a woman of perfect virtue and cultivated mind, but she aspired to no exterior distinction for herself. Her aspirations were identified with those of her husband; she was content to be the priestess of his home and to encourage there, in retirement, his great aims. The beautiful Juliette Récamier found in her a congenial friend for her own good heart. In a time of affliction she wrote to her: 'Dear Annette, I have need of consolation; my heart is lacerated. How I regret to be so far from you—you who are so good, and know so well how to understand all the sufferings of the soul. All that you say in your letters makes a profound impression on me and on Madame de Staël. Dear Annette, you take so much pains to do good! Your life appears to me the most touching example of all the virtues. It is my happiness to think that I am loved by such a being as you. I am very sad; I have need of passing some moments with you, to speak of my inmost feelings. You are the woman whom I wish to resemble, yet it seems to me that if I had all your qualities I should be tempted to be vain. Adieu! I love you.' 'You know well,' wrote

Madame de Staël to De Gérando, 'that in the home of Annette you have a centre of tender sentiments and elevated ideas, to be found in no other place.' She esteemed her one of the best critics of her works: 'I recognise her,' she writes, 'as the judge of vivid and delicate sentiments in whatever situations I can place them.' All that was attractive in the man was reflected and enhanced by his charming wife, to the eyes of Madame de Staël and her circle.

The noble character and great abilities of De Gérando raised him to high public positions, and retained him in them, through all political changes, down to his death in 1842. He became Secretary of the Ministry, Administrator in Tuscany, in the Roman States and Catalonia, a Councillor of State, a Baron of the Empire, and a Peer of France. His Napoleonism never seriously affected his relations with Madame de Staël, though she sometimes thought that he was unnecessarily cautious against compromising himself with Napoleon in her behalf. Differing in politics, the affinity of their souls, in the higher sphere of philosophy and letters, maintained their friendship tranquil above the storms of public opinion which raged around them. Lacretelle, the historian, as we shall hereafter see, recognised Madame de Staël as the leader of the reaction against the materialistic philosophy which the Revolution had spread over France; De Gérando became one of the principal characters in the circle of illustrious men who soon gathered around her in this reaction—Sismondi, Chateaubriand, Constant, Camille Jordan, Mathieu Montmorency, and a host of others. Most of them attached little importance to theological dogmas; some of them were far from being morally scrupulous in their lives; it was chiefly in behalf of the intellectual world—of philosophy and literature—that they waged this war of reaction, though the better minds among them saw that the social and political welfare of the race was involved in the issue. They agreed with De Gérando, who, at the publication of a materialistic work by Cabanis, wrote to Madame de Stael: 'Camille Jordan and I are thoroughly discontented with the book of Cabanis. It is a discredit to Philosophy, thus to make it considered the enemy of all consoling ideas. No! Men who believe only in fate and materialism cannot be sincere friends to liberty. We can agree with Cabanis in but one thing—in the good he says of you. I hope you will always share our indignation against the disastrous influence of his book. Thus to reduce all things to brute matter, is it not merely to invite us to mould ourselves to any character we may wish?'

The friendship of such a man was precious to the authoress, and his good opinion of her book was its most flattering commendation. 'I recognise your hand,' she wrote him, 'I can always recognise you. Here I am at the foot of those mountains which

you envy me. I find my father quite well, and eager to read your book; my eldest son already a brave little man, though but ten years old; my young daughter very graceful. Is my villa still agreeable? My thoughts rest there, as I know you are there; enjoy it as much as you can. Give us news: *solitaires* like us live on facts. My father and I are not in love with the country, like you; we long for anecdotes even in the presence of Mont Blanc. Talk with Annette of me; never cease to love me.'
He wrote her respecting the criticisms on her book: 'It is in some respects a sad profession, that of the man of letters; he must brave the disdain of those who are not of it, and the jealousy of those who are. The first are irritated if they have not his talent; the second, if his manner differs from theirs. Only one thing can console you: it is the desire of doing good; and I believe that, when this intention exists in all its purity, it renders one nearly impervious to contradictions. Form around you a circle in which friends shall be faithful, enemies generous, and all sincere; where you can live in security; where the accord of hearts shall produce harmony of minds; where philosophy shall be without scepticism, religion without intolerance, wit without causticity, learning without pedantry. You will still rediscover yourself, in this society; but you will discover yourself there honoured, cherished, surrounded by true friends. I beg for a place there, among those who are the most devoted to

you.'[1] She soon formed such a society—the most remarkable, perhaps, that ever gathered around a literary woman—a brilliant circle, of which she was always the more brilliant centre. We shall have occasion presently to enter it, and frequently to re-enter it, as we advance in our narrative.

Napoleon's next blow against the genius of the irrepressible authoress was to strike her tenderest sensibilities, for it was to be given through her father, the object of her idolatrous affection; and in such a manner as to smite both their souls—his with the self-suspicion that he had, unconsciously, brought perpetual misfortune upon his child; hers with the greater pain, if possible, of witnessing his grief and self-accusations. It was to be an example of that satanic sagacity which she attributes to the tyrant in her 'Ten Years of Exile'—his skill in defeating his personal adversaries by an almost intuitive knowledge of their personal weaknesses, and by playing off their mutual affections, or antipathies, against one another. To him extraordinary affection was extraordinary weakness; and nowhere could it be more readily found than in the family of Necker. But the fitting time was not yet; the book on Literature had produced a universal impression, and Europe was not prepared to see its now greatest woman crushed, without some more apparent provocation.

[1] *Lettres inédites et Souvenirs biographiques de Madame Récamier et de Madame de Staël,* by his son, Baron de Gérando. Paris, 1868.

She was allowed, therefore, to enjoy tranquilly for the time being, her restored salon, with the best society of the capital crowding it. Bonaparte, the same year (1800) in which her essay on Literature was published, passed through Geneva on his way to Italy, and had there an interview with Necker. 'The result,' she writes, ' of this conversation was my assurance, for some time yet, at least, of an abode in France. It was the last time that the protective hand of my father was extended over my life; for he was not to witness my severer persecutions, which would have afflicted him even more than me.'[2]

After spending the summer, as usual, with him at Coppet, she returned to Paris for the winter, 'where,' she says, 'I passed the time peacefully. I never called on the First Consul; never saw Talleyrand. I knew that Bonaparte did not like me, but his tyranny was still self-restrained. Foreigners treated me with distinction; the Diplomatic Corps spent their leisure with me; and this European atmosphere served me as a safeguard.' Even Joseph Bonaparte openly resumed his friendly relations to her, and she now spent some time at his charming estate of Morfontaine. Napoleon himself met her at General Berthier's, and did not disdain to address to her some indifferent words. Fouché, Napoleon's grand policeman, seemed mysteriously amiable, and 'sweetened,' she says, 'the

---

[2] *Dix Années d'Exil*, i. 4, *et seqq.*

winter of 1801 by the readiness with which he granted several requests I made for the restoration of *émigrés*. He thus gave me, in the midst of my disgrace, the pleasure of being useful; and I am grateful to him for it.'

It was about this time that she became acquainted with one of the most extraordinary women of the period, who will repeatedly appear in our pages. Madame de Krüdner was ambitious to be her rival in society, and afterwards in literature, but was won by her cordiality to an affectionate friendship; and, by a later and singular moral change, became too much absorbed in other aims to admit of an emulation which she considered culpable, and her best friends would have considered futile. Born in Russia, of noble lineage, she was married in her eighteenth year[3] to Baron de Krüdner, who, as ambassador of the Czar, introduced her into the highest—that is to say, the most corrupt, society of the age. She had personal attractions which, if not entitling her girlhood to the pretensions of beauty, matured in her womanhood, and became irresistibly fascinating. Surpassingly graceful in her manners, and endowed with an intellect which, if not really genius, was very like it, she was the centre of every circle she entered: the object of admiration to men, and of envy to

---

[3] Not in her fourteenth, as Sainte-Beuve says, *Revue des Deux Mondes*, 1837. Compare Eynard's *Vie de Madame de Krüdner*, i. 3. Paris, 1849.

women. She travelled extensively in Germany, France, Switzerland, and Italy, and everywhere made a remarkable impression. She had, withal a moral instinct, a native sensitiveness of conscience, which never allowed her to be content with the life she was leading, but which was temporarily overborne by the maxims and usages of the society in which she moved. She fell, not only into its frivolities, but its vices; and, though her marriage had been one of passionate affection, she acknowledged that its sanctity was violated. Her husband, who (an illustration of the morality of the times) had been twice married and divorced before, treated her, after her fall, with a forbearance hardly conceivable in our age, and refused her solicitation for a legal separation. She subsequently devoted her attention to literature and wrote 'Eliza,' 'Alexis,' and the 'Cabane des Lataniers.' Her style, simple yet rich and elegant, recalls that of her friend and correspondent, Bernardin de St. Pierre, the immortal author of 'Paul and Virginia.' In 1804 she published her 'Valérie,' a work of 'prodigious success in France and Germany,' says Sainte-Beuve, 'and which can be read thrice over in a lifetime '— in youth, in middle age, and in old age. It is a picture of the best part of her own early life, and has given her a permanent place in French literature.

She was at the height of her success in the fashionable world when she met Madame de Staël, at Coppet, in 1801. 'This interview, which,' says

Madame de Krüdner's biographer, 'had long been desired, was somewhat embarrassed, at first, by the remembrance of some social rivalries, but immediately became what it ought to be, thanks to the presence of Madame Rilliet-Huber and Madame Necker de Saussure. Madame de Staël made it agreeable by her amiable frankness, and the conversation became as easy as interesting. The asylum offered by Madame de Staël to numerous victims of proscription had preserved at Coppet all the traditions of French society, and the charming art of French conversation. The appearance of Madame de Krüdner, in the midst of this circle of *élite* minds from all countries, made a sensation; literature, art, philosophy—all subjects—were discussed in the reunion of these four women, so richly ornamented with the precious gifts of the mind and the heart. They occupied themselves chiefly with literary topics.' The 'Genius of Christianity' was discussed. ' It is absolutely necessary that you should see Chateaubriand at Paris,' said Madame de Staël; 'I will write you a letter of introduction to him, or I will present you to him, in person: one cannot comprehend a work without knowing the author.' She did present her, soon afterwards, in company with both the Montmorencys and Benjamin Constant, when Chateaubriand read to them two unpublished fragments of the 'Genius,'—'an event in her life.'

In this intellectual atmosphere Madame de

Krüdner 'felt herself,' continues her biographer, 'electrified, and re-inspired with the literary ambition which had been extinguished by the storms of her soul and the frivolities of her life.' She now devoted herself to the composition of the works above mentioned, without yet sacrificing her social ambition. She shone in the highest circles of Geneva. She excelled in the dance as well as in conversation; and Madame de Staël, who took a generous pleasure in representing her friends in her writings, gave, two years later, a graceful picture of her 'Shawl Dance,' in 'Delphine.' It is probable, indeed, that the character and story of Delphine were largely copied from Madame de Krüdner at this time. The latter, writing to a friend in Paris, after 'Delphine' appeared, says that the author has not only copied the dance but 'painted the appearance, the manner of speaking, the imagination of Sidonia.'[4]

The death of her husband, about a year before her visit to Coppet, had struck her conscience with remorse. 'In vain,' remarks her biographer, 'she remembered that her return and her avowals to him had surpassed all that his generous heart demanded. She heard, from the depth of his grave, sobbing reproaches.' But the habits of her life were still too strong for her good resolutions; she avoided, indeed, the sanctioned corruptions of the

---

[4] *Vie* &c. i. 7. Sidonia is the name of the heroine of her *Cabane des Latoniers*, a personation of herself.

fashionable world, but not its gaieties. The great success of her 'Valérie' intoxicated her; but in 1806, while the applause and flatteries which that work commanded were still greeting her everywhere, a surprising revolution transformed her whole being: she became mystically devout. She abandoned the dissipations of society, but not society itself, nor the graces with which she had fascinated it. She became to it a Sibyl, a prophetess. Her superior intelligence, her rare faculties, seemed intensified by a new moral force, a spiritual magnetism, which drew around her the highest minds; her *salon* in Paris was thronged by fashionable as well as by serious guests, attracted not only by the novelty but the ability of her discussions, now confined to the highest religious themes. She travelled among the scenes of her former social triumphs—in France, Switzerland, Italy, Germany. Russia—everywhere colloquially preaching against the corruptions of the age, and declaring her new religious convictions: in some places provoking persecution, and sometimes municipal opposition: but, in most, strangely interesting all classes, from kings to peasants. Her influence on the Emperor of Russia, the Queen of Prussia, Queen Hortense of Holland, and the Princess Galitzin, was remarkable. For some time she was Alexander's oracle on religious, if not political questions. She maintained intimate relations and correspondence with not a few noble, and some royal personages, especially of

Germany; and her intimacy with St. Pierre, Chateaubriand, La Harpe, Benjamin Constant, Madame de Genlis, Madame de Staël, and other eminent minds, has rendered her name familiar in the literary history of her times.

After nearly a score of years, spent in doing good among the poor and afflicted, as well as among the rich and noble—with a sincerity and purity which could never be doubted, but with some religious fantasies which impaired her usefulness—Madame de Krüdner died in the Crimea on Christmas-day, 1824, a death beautiful in its peace, its hope, and its humility. 'That which I have done well,' she said 'will remain; that which I have done wrong (for how often have I taken for the voice of God what was only the suggestion of my imagination or my pride!) the mercy of God will efface. I have nothing else to offer to God or to men, but my numerous sins; but the blood of Christ cleanses me from all sin.'

At the time of her visit to Coppet, Necker was preparing his 'Last Views of Politics and Finance,'[5] At Madame de Staël's next summer visit he consulted her about it. 'I found him,' she says, 'very indignant at the course of affairs in France. He had always so loved true liberty as to detest popular anarchy; he now felt that it was his duty to write against the tyranny of a single man, after so long combating that of multitudes. He was

[5] *Dernières Vues de Politique et de Finance.* Lausanne, 1802.

proud to expose himself to peril, if he thereby merit the public esteem. I saw the danger of his displeasing the First Consul, but I could not stifle the song of the dying swan which might yet be heard over the tomb of French liberty. I encouraged him to write.'

She postponed her return to Paris, in order not to witness the Napoleonic festivities there. 'I know of nothing more sad,' she continues, 'than these public rejoicings: the bewildered people celebrating the preparations of their own slavery; the deluded victims bowing before their sacrificer; the hypocrisy of courtiers casting a veil over the arrogance of their master—all inspired me with unsurmountable disgust.'

De Gérando endeavoured to relieve her discouragement—discouragement which arose from the treatment of her father, more than from her own, and especially from the prospects of Europe. 'The price which I attach to our friendship,' he wrote, 'increases daily. All those philanthropic ideas which at twenty years of age exalted my soul, and gave me entire nights of transporting study, are to-day more fixed, more profound than ever, and constantly fill my thoughts. It is necessary that all elevated minds should war with energy against that spirit of calculation and personal interest which has become so general; against that scepticism which is perverting all the elements of morality; against that moral enervation, that baseness, which threatens the national character. I would address to you the fine appeal of Socrates to Anaximandra (in Aristippus) : " You seem to me destined to become the priestess of moral truth on the earth, to show to men the sublime path to the beautiful and the good." You have with you one of the best men in the world ;[6] in him you can study a model of virtue. It seems to me that this sublime excellence can alone satisfy the immense activity of your soul; and I am persuaded that your generous devotion to the good of mankind will solve for you that problem of happiness which appears to you so unsolvable. It will be delightful to awaken and sustain in all hearts around you the love of virtue and of liberty ; to associate the hope of human progress with that of immortality ; to lead men to religion and to the sentiments of nature. If I could visit Coppet and pass some hours with you on the shore of your beautiful lake, it seems to me that I could convince you that you should banish the sad memories which discourage you, and give your life a new object, an object worthy of you. I am wrong in saying a new object, for it is towards this noble goal that your works are directed ; and their success is owing, in great part, to the generous emotions which they have inspired in all hearts.'

On returning to the capital she found Bernadotte, and a number of other generals and senators,

---

[6] Mathieu de Montmorency was now at Coppet.

her personal friends, secretly combining to forestall the usurpations of Bonaparte. They frequently met at her house. 'The detection of their designs,' she says, 'would have ruined me. Bonaparte affirmed that they always came forth from my *salon* less his friends than they were before they entered it. At last he looked upon me alone as culpable among all the disaffected.' Her *salon* was, meanwhile, a centre of polished, and especially of literary society. There were many similar resorts [7] about these times (1800-1803,) but none equal to hers. Madame Récamier gathered about her distinguished men of all classes. Around Madame Joseph Bonaparte assembled diplomats, military officers, and functionaries of the Government. In the *salons* of Madame d'Houdetot and of Madame Suard were still continued the traditions of the eighteenth century; the philosophers and *littérateurs* rallied there. In that of the Princesse de Poix, and there almost alone, were strictly maintained the sentiments and manners of the old *régime* by the returned *émigrés*. Madame de Beaumont (the daughter of Montmorin), whom we have met in the little colony of Mickleham, England, attracted a select society in the Rue Neuve du Luxembourg, where Fontanes introduced Chateaubriand, and where that tender friendship was formed between the latter and the accomplished hostess which ended only with her death at Rome—and of

---

[7] Sainte-Beuve's *Chateaubriand et son Groupe Littéraire.* i. 7.

which we shall hear again. Madame de Staël was
a frequent guest of most of these circles, and was
never present without being prominent; but her
own house was a court thronged by the most distinguished personages of all classes, except the
most exclusive adherents of Napoleon. Sainte-Beuve
found among the papers of Chênedollé a note on
her *salon*, as it appeared about this period. 'We
used to see there,' he says, ' Chateaubriand in all
the *éclat* of his first glory; Madame Récamier in
all the delicate flower of her grace and her youth;
Madame Viconti with her majestic Roman beauty;
the Chevalier de Boufflers in the *négligé* of a country
vicar, but smiling with the exquisite aspect and
finesse of a courtier, and scattering the most piquant
words with extreme good humour; the Comte de
Narbonne, one of the most agreeable talkers of the
old court, always in a vein of happy remarks, and
giving to the *salon* his inexhaustible treasures of
grace and gaiety and the charms of a conversation
which fascinated Napoleon himself; and, among
politicians Benjamin Constant, tall, erect, well-made,
blond, a little pale, with long hair falling in curls on
his neck. He had an extraordinary expression of
mockery and malice in his smile, and especially in
his eyes. Nothing could be more piquant than his
conversation. Always epigrammatic, he treated
the highest questions of politics with transparent,
concise, and powerful logic, sarcasm pervading
his argument. When, with admirable but dis-

guised address, he led his adversary into the snare which he had set for him, he left him there confounded and helpless, under the blow of an epigram from which there was no recovery. No one understood better how to surprise with unexpected overthrow an opponent in conversation. In a word, he was an interlocutor, a second, worthy of Madame de Staël.'[8]

Bonaparte's suspicion of her influence on Bernadotte, and other disaffected men in high positions, was soon known to her; it was expedient for her to escape. 'I left,' she writes, 'for Coppet again, and arrived with my father in a state of profound anxiety. Letters from Paris reported that the First Consul, after my departure, expressed himself passionately against my relations with Bernadotte. He had also rebuked the son of the Stadtholder, the Prince of Orange, for dining with me. He could not afford to lose Bernadotte, but he could crush me.'

Necker's 'Last Views &c.' appeared in 1802. He appreciated Napoleon's genius, and pronounced him the man for the actual exigencies of France —for her restoration to order and prosperity, but prophetically showed the tendencies of the Consular government to military despotism and hereditary monarchy; assuming, nevertheless, that the First Consul was still sincere in his avowals of loyalty to the Republic. Napoleon was extremely irritated

---

[8] *Chateaubriand et son Groupe,* i. 7.

by this tacit detection and premature exposure of his ambitious designs. At his dictation, the Consul Lebrun wrote to Necker, severely reproving his boldness, advising him to abandon politics and leave them to the First Consul, 'who was alone able to govern France,' and threatening his daughter with exile for having shared in the preparation of his book. She had indeed approved his design of writing it, but it was prepared while she was absent in Paris; and, at her return to Coppet in the spring, it had been sent to the press. The Government accused her of having, at least, conveyed to him false reports of the state of France.[9] 'I have since,' she writes, 'I trust, myself deserved this exile; but Bonaparte, who troubled himself to find out how to wound most effectually, wished to disturb the intimacy of our domestic life by representing to me my father as the author of my sufferings. This thought struck my father, who could never repel a scruple; but, thank God, he was always able to assure himself that it never entered my mind.'

It was in this summer that her friend Lacretelle went to Coppet to thank his 'eloquent benefactress,' as he calls her; for she had procured his liberation after two years of imprisonment and of still greater dangers. He had passed through nearly all the stirring events of the Revolution, in Paris; was proscribed on the 13th Vendémiaire (year IV.) as one

[9] *Considérations* &c. iv. 7.

of the chiefs of the movement against the Convention; was arrested, two years later, and not released till the end of the next two years. He became a member of the Academy and Professor of History to the Faculty of Letters. His public lectures were attended, for many years, by enthusiastic crowds. His writings are numerous, comprising more than thirty volumes, chiefly on the history of France during his own times, of which he is one of the best authorities—impartial, exact, judicious, and vividly eloquent. He has given us much of his own personal history in his 'Dix Années d'Épreuves pendant la Révolution;' and his maturest thoughts, on the highest subjects, in the two volumes of his 'Testament.' He now (1802) spent ten days with Madame de Staël, days of high converse on the sublimest topics—Christian spiritualism, optimism, &c., and has devoted a long chapter (nearly forty pages) to a record of his walks and talks with her on the picturesque shores of Lake Leman.[1] 'Nature,' he says, ' had denied her beauty, but had given her an enchanting voice, and charming eyes which reflected all the sky of her soul—a sky sometimes stormy. The man who should murmur against her lack of beauty would fall at her feet dazzled by her intellect. She was born an intellectual conqueror. As her friendship was full of devotion, she made

---

[1] *Testament Philosophique et Littéraire*, ii. 19. 2 vols. Paris, 1840.

devoted friends, who gave proof of their fidelity during her long persecutions. Her contest with Napoleon was a struggle between two conquerors, the one aspiring to the empire of the world, the other to the empire of opinion. Necker was still alive at the time of my visit, and had published a writing which could not fail to augment the resentment of the First Consul; for the old and illustrious Minister invited him to follow the example of Washington. His daughter saw clearly that such a publication would definitively fix her fate, and her exile at Coppet seemed imprisonment; but far from her was the thought of making her personal danger an obstacle to the glory of her father and the welfare of France. You can judge how such circumstances must have troubled the tranquillity of this retreat, this beautiful château, visited by most of the illustrious men of Europe, and which, in the days of horror, was consecrated by the most delicate and courageous hospitality. Necker showed the serenity of a man who had done his duty and satisfied his conscience; but you could see that joy had long been absent from his soul. He returned only with a smile the vivid sallies of his daughter, who affected to be tranquil, and for whom everything else disappeared in the presence of her father. Benjamin Constant entered into these conversations with his sharp pleasantries. Madame de Staël appeared to me now under new and touching aspects. I saw her translate Tacitus with her eldest son (laureate of the College of Geneva), and frequently her genius sparkled in her commentaries; but, too frequently carried away with passion, she seized the arrows, thrown by the historian against Tiberius, and directed them against the First Consul. She would amuse herself with the amiable extravagances of her second son slain some years later in a duel in Germany. She devoted herself to the education of her daughter, afterwards the Duchesse de Broglie, whom all have agreed to recognise as the model of her sex, and whose premature death has occasioned universal regrets.'

During a long walk in the park of the château, they talk of Napoleon's severities towards her. 'My courage bends,' she says, ' but not my will. I suffer, but wish no remedy which can degrade me. I have the fears of a woman, but they cannot make me a hypocrite or a slave.' They turn to more agreeable topics—the spiritual philosophy, final causes, and ultimate, universal good—when she suddenly arrests the discussion. 'Let us walk farther,' she whispers, 'it is the hour at which my father goes to my mother's tomb.' She pointed to a sort of chapel in which reposed the body of Madame Necker, and added, 'My father's limbs are so badly swollen, that he dreads to be seen tottering along: he can only take this short walk; he takes it regularly, but with extreme fatigue.' 'We went to the border of the lake to continue our conversation; the waters were tinged with the colours of the setting sun. She was in a reverie: I saw that her thoughts were with her father at the tomb. But her looks became animated when she raised them towards the resplendent sky. The serene lake, the balmy air, the dying murmurs of the evening, and, above all, the necessity she felt of seeking a refuge above against the sad thoughts that assailed her—all suggested to me that our conversation was about to take a new charm.'

It did take a new charm, and a sublime one; but the discussion was too long to be reproduced here. It was on Fontenelle's 'Plurality of Worlds,' the Theosophy of Saint-Martin, and the Theodicy of Leibnitz; on the moral system of the universe, and the reality of the spiritual world: chiefly on the hope that out of all evil—even such atrocious evil as they both had witnessed in the Revolution—final and immeasurable good will come. 'My optimism,' exclaimed Lacretelle, 'is but a complete spiritualism, an absolute faith in a beneficent God.' The discussion waxed dithyrambic. Madame de Staël's eloquence reminds us of the remark, often made by her friends, that her conversation far surpassed her writings. It is not without vivid sallies, and occasional traits of piquancy, not to say pleasantry; but it rises to the height of the subject. 'There is a charm, my friend,' she exclaims, 'in such a spiritualistic discussion which presents God in all the grandeur of his goodness. I experience intimately its sweetness even at this moment, when I am haunted by the fear of a long separation from all that pleases me, all whom I know, all whom I love; and I know not how to love moderately. This mysticism is in reality but the reverie of love and of hope, expanded into the infinite. It is the most precious treasure that Christianity has borne to our world. "God is great," says the law of Mohammed, and Mussulman fatalism bows, with the frozen submission of slavery, before its despot, who conducts whither he will, and strikes when he will. "God is love," says the law of Christ, and behold His grandeur, at once sublime and merciful! If human love draws together all souls, divine love draws together the creature and the Creator, the intelligent atom and the Intelligence which fills the universe. All worldly as I am, I have, at times, some of the experience of St. Theresa; and these are the best moments of my life. But they are rare with a mind as mobile as it is ardent. Oh, that I could enjoy them more frequently! Then, should I be chased even to the ice of the pole, and see all potentates, all nations, bow under the flaming sword of the European dictator, the pupil of Machiavelli transformed into a Cæsar, I would " still hold myself erect," as Montesquieu says, " backed against the limits of the globe," to repel the universal servitude; and in the horrors of the frozen deserts still commune with God. But I was not born for a contemplative life.'

'Such,' concludes Lacretelle's record, 'such was the ecstasy of Madame de Staël on this beautiful night. The bell recalled us to the château. It was the hour at which she received the good-night benediction of her father.'

Though she was now meditating her 'Delphine,' she found leisure to study the philosophy of Kant, which had been recently revealed to France by a young Frenchman, M. Villers, who became one of her favourite correspondents.[2] She wrote to De Gérando on the system of the great German; and, his son says, the correspondence shows that 'in appreciating the system of Kant she rises to the highest philosophic conceptions, and defends the cause of spiritualism with an ardent logic.' This was, probably, her first inclination towards that study of the German mind which at last culminated in her greatest work, the 'Allemagne.' She admired Villers as a man of 'extraordinary intellect, and remarkable for the flexibility and perspicacity of his thoughts.' She insists that there is in man a profounder faculty than that which takes cognisance of impressions received by the senses. 'The conscience,' she says, 'comes from no ideas received by the senses. If all men have called it an interior voice, another self, it is because they have felt that its impressions are not of the nature of other impressions. I consider all that Villers says on this subject very beautiful. In short, I think this system is grand, devout, and

[2] *Exposé de la Philosophie de Kant.* Metz, 1801.

worthy of both man and God. What I love in philosophy is, that it examines everything by reason; but I do not restrict myself to this or that system, as alone meriting the name of philosophy. The anti-philosophers are those who tell us that we have reason, but not to trust it; faculties, but not to use them; and who would introduce despotism even into our asylum—thought. I hold those to be intolerant who doubt my philosophy because I love, in what Villers has given us of the philosophy of Kant, that which is most favourable to the ennobling hopes of a future life. Show my letter to Mathieu, and let us hope to discuss the subject together; for such debates are always a pleasure to us. I congratulate you on the prize awarded you by the Academy of Berlin. I rejoice in it as if it were a success of my own. I have been reading with deep feeling your life of Caffarelli du Falga; it reveals your own mind and character, and will do you credit with all your readers.'

At the beginning of the winter (of 1802–1803) her thoughts turned longingly again towards Paris. 'When I read,' she says, 'in the papers of the many distinguished Englishmen and intellectual Frenchmen who were resorting to the capital, I felt, I confess, a vivid desire to join them. I will not dissemble that a residence in Paris has irresistible charms for me. I was born there; I passed my early life there; it is there only that I can find the generation which has known my father, the friends who have passed through the perils of the Revolution with us. That love of country which has inspired the strongest minds sways us most powerfully when it combines with the tastes of the mind, the affections of the heart and the habitudes of the imagination. French conversation exists only in Paris; and conversation has been, from my infancy, my greatest pleasure. The pain I experienced at the fear of being deprived of my home in the capital was uncontrollable by my reason. I was then in all the vivacity of my life, and it is precisely the need of animated enjoyments which most frequently leads to despair, because it renders resignation so difficult; and without this we cannot bear the vicissitudes of life.'[3] But she had still stronger motives for wishing to return: she desired to give her children, especially her sons, the educational advantages of the metropolis. The reported illness of her husband decided her wavering purpose; she hastened to attend him, but she soon perceived that it would be prudent to escape again. She was conveying him towards Coppet, when, as we have seen, he died on the route.[4] She hastened to her father and awaited better auspices for her return to Paris.

[3] *Dix Années*, i. 10.
[4] The allusions of French writers to his death are strangely confused. Geffroy (*Revue des Deux Mondes*, 1856) says: 'He departed in 1802 with her and her children, on a journey to Sweden, and died on the frontier of France.' Others say he died in Paris in 1798. I have followed Madame Necker de Saussure, *Notice*, ii.

CHAPTER XVI.

LITERATURE—'DELPHINE.'

Publication of 'Delphine'—Criticism on it—Madame de Genlis attacks it—Sophie Gay defends it—Madame de Staël's Defence of it—Talleyrand a Character in it—His *bon mot* respecting it—Madame de Krüdner's Criticism.

SHE had relieved her sufferings by the composition of her 'Delphine;' for she had learned by experience that the trials of life cannot, with elevated minds at least, be well borne without occupation, without a sustained and sustaining motive—that labour is the law of happiness. 'Delphine' was published in 1802,[1] and was therefore a child of her genius brought forth amidst troubles which would have disabled, for literary labour, most men, not to say women.

Baudrillart has expressed the purport of the

---

[1] The *Table Chronologique* &c. at the end of her *Œuvres complètes* (vol. xvii.), by her son, Baron de Staël, says 1803. This authority ought to be indisputable, but all others give 1802. See *Biographie Universelle*, *Nouvelle Biographie Générale*, Querard's *France Littéraire*, &c. I prefer Querard's authority. According to him, *Delphine* was first published at Geneva in 1802, but was re-issued at Paris in 1803. This difference of dates is not unimportant, as indicating the locality and circumstances in which the work was written.

book: 'the thought,' he says, 'which was always dear to its author marks it everywhere,—that of the happiness possible only in marriage; but incomplete and broken, sooner or later, in illegitimate unions.'[2] Her cousin more completely states its design: 'One melancholy thought had pursued her youth. Penetrated by a profound pity for the fate of woman, she sympathised, above all, with women endowed with superior faculties. And when the happiness of love in marriage—to her eyes, the highest of all—had not been accorded to them, it seemed to her equally difficult for them to enclose themselves within the narrow bounds of their fate, or to free those bounds without exposing themselves to the saddest sufferings. This thought, which could be presented in a romance under infinite forms, led her naturally to paint the picture of a woman, at once brilliant and unhappy, dominated by her affections, badly directed by her independent spirit, and suffering by her most amiable qualities.'[3]

Sainte-Beuve repels the charge that the book is an attack on marriage. 'It seems to me, on the contrary,' he says, 'that the chief idea is the desire of happiness in marriage; a profound conviction of the impossibility of being otherwise happy. This idea of happiness in marriage always pursued Madame de Staël, as the romantic situations of

---

[2] *Eloge de Madame de Staël.* Paris, 1850. 'Crowned' by the French Academy.
[3] *Notice* &c.

which they are deprived pursue and agitate other souls.' She had not known this happiness in her own experience. She had seen it in the life of her parents. Her mother had written about it, in her essay on 'Divorce,' her father in his 'Cours de Morale Religieuse.' In the chapter on 'Love,' in her own book on the 'Influence of the Passions,' she had spoken with emotion of an aged couple, still lovers in marriage, whom she had met in England. In her work on Literature she had cited from Thomson's 'Seasons' the concluding verses of 'Spring,' that describe the perfect union which, 'for her, was ideal and too absent.' In her 'Germany' she recurs to the subject in language full of moral significance, as interpreted by the secret circumstances which inspired it. In 'Delphine' she represents, by the picture of the happy family of Belmont, 'this domestic Eden, always desired by her in the storms of her life.' Incessant allusions to the subject occur in its pages. They are frequent also in her 'Corinne.' In the conversation after the scene of the Roman ball, Oswald scorns the Italian manners and poetry regarding love. 'Where,' he asks Corinne, 'do you discover the pathetic and tender sentiment which pervades our poetry? What can you compare with the scene of Belvidera and her husband in Otway; with Romeo in Shakespeare; above all, with the admirable verses of Thomson in his chant of the Springtime, in which he paints so nobly and touchingly

the happiness of love in marriage? Is there one
such marriage in Italy? And where there is no
domestic happiness, can there be love? Is not this
happiness the object of the passion of the heart,
as possession is that of the passion of the senses?
The qualities of the heart and the mind fix our
preferences. And what do these qualities make
us desire? Is it not marriage, that is to say, association with all the sentiments and all the thoughts
of another?'

'In recurring so frequently to this dream, she
had not,' remarks Sainte-Beuve, ' to seek for illus-
trations. Her thoughts, in going forth from herself, found always near her examples on which to
rest. In default of her own happiness she recalled that of her mother, and anticipated that of
her daughter.'[4] And she sought to realise her
dream in her own second marriage.

The Government controlled, at this time, the
press of France, if not by laws, yet by its influence
or its patronage, and a general attack was made on
the new romance. Its morality was questioned—a
remarkable criticism for the times. Madame de
Genlis, whose life had given her no authority as a
teacher of morality,[5] availed herself of its publication to gratify her rancorous jealousy of her literary
and unapproachable rival, though the latter had

---

[1] *Critiques et Portraits Littéraires*, iii.

[5] For her relations with the infamous ' Égalité,' see Ticknor's *Life
&c.* ii. 9.

paid her a generous but hardly merited compliment in the essay on Literature.[6] She published a novel in the Bibliothèque des Romans, in which, by mutilated citations and studied misconstructions, she tried to prove that Madame de Staël was a corrupter of public morality, especially as an apologist for suicide. The unguarded passages on this subject in 'Delphine,' and in the essay on the Passions, were afterwards amply explained, and suicide emphatically condemned in her 'Reflections on Suicide.' Sophie Gay (celebrated for her beauty, her wit, and her literary works) defended Madame de Staël and resented the attack of Madame de Genlis, in her 'Laure d'Estelle,' in which she paints the jealous critic (in the character of Madame de Gercourt) as pretentious, perfidious, pedantic, and suspected of 'placing the vices in action and the virtues in precept.' Madame de Staël gave a new *dénouement* to her story, in order to save it from such constructions—but not without the sacrifice of some of its finest artistic qualities. Her collected works include an able posthumous essay on the moral design of 'Delphine,'[7] in which she answers her critics, and vindicates the book from an artistic standpoint. Referring to its obnoxious features, she says: 'These are romantic sentiments which a severe morality ought to repress; these are sentiments for which it is just to suffer, but for which it

---

[6] *Littérature* &c. ii. 5. Note.
[7] *Œuvres complètes*, i. Paris, 1871.

is just also to be pitiful. Romances which paint life ought not to present perfect characters, but characters which show what is good and what is blamable in human conduct, and the natural consequences of such conduct. The character of Delphine, and the evils which result to her from that character, prove precisely what I develop. I never wished to present Delphine as a model to be copied.' She concludes with the just remark that 'Writers, like educators, can do more good by what they inspire than by what they teach. Delicate and pure thoughts, in life as in books, can animate each word; can paint themselves in every feature, without being formally declared or expressed in maxims; and the morality of a work of the imagination consists much more in the general impressions which it gives than in its narrative details.'

Just as these remarks may be, 'Delphine' is not a wholesome book, morally or intellectually. It is a too romantic romance. It is incomparably superior to similar productions in the French literature of its time, or of preceding times, and this is a consideration which should be accorded to its author. Vinet, after criticising the work from his own high moral standpoint, says, 'Delphine, with all her errors, is one of the most touching creations of genius; her character is as true as it is charming. It is impossible not to love this generous soul, which lives only for love and self-sacrifice. No fiction has ever been more vitally real. Need we be astonished at the fact? The author, in making Delphine speak, speaks herself; the events are fictitious, the character is not; here then the truth has cost nothing. No work of Madame de Staël has been written with more facile, more abundant power. If she had not yet the maturity of her opinions, she had, I believe, all the plenitude of her talents.'

Doudan, an excellent judge, writing to a friend, says, 'I have seen in no other book so profound a knowledge of the instincts of society; those instincts which are as unchangeable as the foundations of human nature. Neither La Rochefoucauld nor La Bruyère has excelled it in this kind of anatomy; still, you will discover the tone of enthusiasm, which pervades the book, too high by two or three notes. All this was and ought to be at the diapason of the end of the eighteenth century. The sentiments clothed themselves then in a manner more demonstrative. We are more reserved, more reticent, perhaps, because we have less vitality '[8]

Vinet remarks that there can hardly be a doubt that Madame de Staël gave her own character to Delphine; and in the supposition, so far as the character is concerned, 'there is nothing injurious to her.'[9] In the most original and thoroughly finished character of the book, that of Madame de

---

[8] *Mélanges et Lettres de Z. Doudan* &c. ii. (4 vols.). Paris, 1876.
[9] *Littérature Française au XIXe Siècle*, i.

Vernon, there can hardly be more doubt that she painted her old but treacherous friend Talleyrand. The 'feminine Machiavelism, the supreme yet indolent egotism, the cool systematic dissimulation, and passionless dissipation' of the character, have fastened it for ever on that unprincipled statesman. It was immediately recognised by himself, at least, and led to one of his notable *bons mots*. 'In her romance,' he said, alluding to the virile character of her mind, 'she has disguised us both as women—herself and me.'[1] Like most egotists, he disliked talent in women, as rendering them masculine and placing them too much on an equality with men—with himself. He could never forgive her for having proved herself his superior in conversation, and even in repartee. He had learned to appreciate her superb intellect, but could never appreciate her feminine heart.

Other real characters have been traced in her portraits with more or less probability. Madame de Cerlèbe is supposed to represent her accomplished cousin Madame Necker de Saussure; and Monsieur de Sebensei, Benjamin Constant; but in both cases, especially in the last, we must admit important qualifications.[2] Madame de Krüdner,

[1] *Univers Pittoresque*, xxvi. Paris, 1845. Sir James Mackintosh said that he heard from Madame de Staël herself the story of Talleyrand's *bon mot*. *Memoirs* &c. by his Son, ii. 5. London, 1836.

[2] Sainte-Beuve, *Critiques et Portraits*, iii. Paris, 1844. The author of the *Biographie de Haller*, chap. vii. (Paris, 1845), says that Madame de Cerlèbe was copied from the daughter of Haller, Madame

as we have noticed, is presented not only in the 'shawl dance' of the first volume, but in some of her personal traits. Delphine, if not an invented, is at least a composite character; the author has undoubtedly drawn much of the portrait from herself, but probably more of it from Madame de Krüdner. There are striking coincidences between both the characteristics and history of the latter and those of the heroine. Madame de Krüdner, intellectually reawakened by Madame de Staël, had nearly completed her 'Valérie,' and was now reading the manuscript in literary circles, where it was enthusiastically applauded. She 'suspected that the dear woman'—Madame de Staël—' was touched with the jealousy of success, above all now that some of the charms of Delphine were recognised in Sidonia,'[3] and that rumours were current respecting the extraordinary merits of 'Valérie;' yet she made, in a letter to M. Bérenger, of Lyons, a candid acknowledgment of the 'immense talent' of Madame de Staël, and a remarkably just criticism of 'Delphine,' excepting the general misapprehension, which she shared, of the teaching of the book regarding suicide. 'As to the rest,' she remarks, 'an inconsistency is not an intention; and why suspect that Madame de Staël has wished to make

---

de Zeerléber, and with but a slight change of name. The daughter of the 'grand Haller' inherited many of the excellences of her father and was worthy of the character.

[3] *Vie* &c. i. 7.

a dangerous book—she, who is so ethical in her studies, and who believes so firmly in perfectibility in this strange age? Let us render more justice to the beauties of the work. I see in Delphine only the sad victim of a strong and unhappy passion; and, in her last actions, the consequences of a mind which has ceased to reason. An upright woman, with an ardent soul, environed by the perfidy of the fashionable world, falls, with all her candour, into the snares of love and misfortune. And if Delphine is so terribly punished, has not the author, by her talent to appal us thus by the consequences of vice, divined the secret of moral teaching, and attained the aim of the romancer?'

She not only commemorated some of her associates in the characters of the book, but (writes one of her still surviving friends) 'the origin of its title is equally worthy of interest.' She was desirous of meeting the First Consul, for some urgent reason, and went to the villa of Madame de Montessan, whither he frequently resorted. 'She was alone in one of the *salles* when he arrived, accompanied by the consular court of brilliant young women. The latter knew the growing hostility of their master towards her, and passed, without noticing her, to the other end of the *salle*, leaving her entirely alone. She was thus placed in quarantine, and her position was becoming extremely painful, when a young lady, more courageous and more compassionate than her companions crossed the *salle* and took a seat by her side. Madame de Staël was touched by this kindness, and, in the course of the conversation, asked for her Christian name. 'Delphine,' she responded. 'Ah, I will try to immortalise it,' exclaimed Madame de Staël; and she kept her word. This sensible young lady was the Comtesse de Custine.'[4]

[4] Manuscript *Souvenirs* of Pictet de Sergy.

CHAPTER XVII.

COPPET AND ITS SOCIETY.

Glimpses of Coppet—Its Society—Madame Rilliet-Huber—Madame Necker de Saussure—Sismondi in Love—Madame de Staël initiates his Historical Studies—Bonstetten—Frederica Brun—Madame de Staël as a Mother—Daily Life at Coppet.

PUBLISHING her book at Geneva, Madame de Staël remained there, and at Coppet, through the winter (1802–1803), not without some gratification from the interest which 'Delphine' excited in the literary and fashionable worlds; and with still better enjoyment in the select but numerous society which always spontaneously gathered about her at her country asylum and in the neighbouring city. This society, comprising the best minds of Geneva and of the other communities on the shores of Lake Leman, was frequently enlarged by the presence of distinguished travellers from England, Germany and France; for Coppet was already becoming, like Ferney and Weimar, an intellectual centre of Europe. The associate of her childhood in the woods of St. Ouen, Madame Rilliet-Huber, now married and settled at Geneva, was often at the château. One of her intimate friends writes that 'she held, during thirty years, the sceptre of intellect in Geneva; with something, nevertheless, in her manners, a little *précieuse*. With less genius than Madame de Staël, Madame Rilliet-Huber was, like her, perfectly good; she loved conversation extremely, and shone very much in it; she wrote ably. She spent much of her time with her literary friend, M. de Chateauvieux, at the château of Choully.'[1]

Madame Necker de Saussure was a still more frequent guest at Coppet—one of the most cultivated women of her times, and now in the richest maturity of her faculties, the pride of Geneva, and to be later known throughout Europe by her treatise on Education. 'She had in her conversation,' says a visitor at Coppet, 'a sort of serious enthusiasm, exempt from acerbity, which strongly excited the interest of Madame de Staël's circle—a sustained and elegant firmness, relieved by sallies of amiable gaiety. Her features were grave but noble, her eyes penetrating but of extreme kindliness.'[2] A host of *littérateurs* and 'scientists,' already famous or rising to fame, gathered around the mistress of the château. One who knew them all enumerates: 'Candolle, the author of a new system of botany; Pictet, a professor of physics, who threw new light on his science; Chateauvieux, author of Letters on Italy, in which he studied

---

[1] Pictet de Sergy's unpublished *Souvenirs*.
[2] Secretan's *Galerie Suisse*, ii. Lausanne, 1876.

society with an exquisite judgment; Dumont, who, in reproducing the writings of Bentham, gave them new force; Prevost, who discovered the laws of radiant caloric and popularised the Scotch philosophy; Cellerier, who, in the pulpit, sustained morality by the persuasive authority of the Gospel; Sismondi, beginning his vast historical researches; Bonstetten, prodigious as a thinker—all these various lights borrowed, in some measure, their warmth and lustre from the brilliant centre of Coppet.'[3]

She was among the first to recognise the genius of Sismondi, and to determine his literary career. He had produced but one book and she had read only its introduction; but that was sufficient to reveal to her penetrating insight his capabilities. She sent him an invitation to dinner, and assured him that he could distinguish himself if he would persevere in his labours; that she considered him the most just and profound thinker in Geneva, the man most certain to rise. The young writer was, of course, charmed, not only by her encouragements, but by her frank and easy manners, which never failed to place at ease anyone who conversed with her. He was inspired with trustfulness, and immediately confided to her a passion which, at this time, swayed him infinitely more than his literary ambition. In short, Sismondi was in love; the only romance of his life, the sad brief episode of his Lucile, was now absorbing his thoughts,

[3] Pictet de Sergy's unpublished *Souvenirs*.

'and,' says his biographer, 'for the first time, he encountered from his mother the most ardent opposition.' Who could sympathise with him like the author of 'Delphine'? Lucile was poor; Geneva, though democratic, was preposterously aristocratic in the pretensions of wealth and family lineage. 'Madame de Staël responded to me,' he writes, 'that perhaps she might use the same language as my mother; that in "Delphine" she had taught firmness against public opinion, but not against that of parents; that the young girl might not only bring me no fortune, but might reduce me to dependence; that she herself regarded the Genevan distinctions of families as ridiculous, but nevertheless my choice might open or shut the doors of the best company for or against me; but that if Lucile were the best choice I could make, if she could not be replaced by a better in mind and character, then this consideration should outweigh all others.' They had later discussions of the subject, but fate solved the problem. His parent was unyielding. 'This painful opposition,' says his biographer, 'destroyed the health of the young girl, and she died of consumption in 1802.'[4] Madame de Staël fortified him with manly courage, and aroused the literary ambition which gave to the world the History of the Italian Republics, the History of the Literature of Southern Europe, the History of the French, and so many other great works. Sismondi was

[4] *Fragments de son Journal et Correspondance.* Geneva, 1857.

soon installed in the château at Coppet, and wrote there some of his most important volumes.

The sage Bonstetten, friend of her mother as well as of herself, became an oracle at Coppet. In 'seeing her, in hearing her, he felt himself electrified.' 'There is,' he remarked, 'more intellect displayed in one day at Coppet than in many whole countries in an entire year.' Madame de Staël's death was in the end an irreparable loss both for his mind and heart; the old man complained of being thenceforward intellectually maimed.[5] He delighted to read his works to her, for criticism, before their publication. 'She is so free from prejudices,' he says, 'so clear, that I see my pictures in her soul as in a mirror.'[6] A Bernese Swiss, his native language was German; but Madame de Staël insisted that French would serve better for his philosophic works. His friend Matthison, the poet, had urged him to write in German only; but Madame de Staël had stronger influence over him. Generously eager for the success of her literary associates, she inspired and directed his studies as she did those of Sismondi, Barrante, and others. She exerted herself to procure publishers for his books, and when his work on Latium appeared, she wrote notices of it for the French periodicals. He prized her friendship and yielded

[5] Secretan's *Galerie Suisse*, ii.
[6] Steinlen's *Charles Victor de Bonstetten: Étude Biographique et Littéraire*. Lausanne, 1860.

to her advice in favour of the use of the French language; but found it a formidable task. His German biographer gives a comical account of his difficulties, his despair, between the two languages. Born on the limit of both, and where neither was perfect, he was in danger of spoiling his style in either. During his residence at Yverdon and Geneva, and also in his youthful travels, he had used the French, and was familiar enough with it as a spoken, but not as a written language; meanwhile he was losing his German. In his sojourns with Müller, Matthison, and Frederica Brun, in Germany and the North, especially at Copenhagen, where he published six works in German, this language had again become habitual to him, at the risk of his French. 'Now,' says his biographer, 'Madame de Staël stormed upon him to force him back again to French. "You cannot conceive," he wrote, "what ox-work I am attempting; but I feel that it is necessary. My thoughts are in such conflict as to extort martyr-shrieks from me."'[7]. He resolutely persisted, however, in the vexatious task, but his readings at Coppet sometimes put some of the company to sleep, especially Necker. 'It is still a question,' he says, 'whether I can succeed in French. Nothing is more ludicrous than the history of my French book—what Necker blames, Sismondi thinks beautiful: it is with style as with the toilette. In the name of heaven, says one,

---

[7] Morell's *Karl von Bonstetten*, viii. Winterthur, 1864.

do not place this word here, or you will be lost; this term is best, this is the most French, says another. This French is a language for devils. The attention which the French give to style is exaggerated; it is more a matter of fashion than of reason. The Germans have the contrary fault.'

Bonstetten's friend and correspondent, the once well-known authoress, Frederica Brun, was with him at Geneva in 1802, and her letters,[8] give us some glimpses of Coppet. 'The family,' she writes, 'is perfectly interesting. The tall figure, the noble air, of Necker, are relieved by a kindliness which is irresistible. A great observer, intellectual like his daughter, he joins to these powers a delicacy and depth of sentiment, and a variety of thought, which fascinate me. I am deaf, but I have a sort of presentiment of his thoughts, and he divines mine. As for Madame de Staël—I have never seen anywhere a heart so superabundant in sentiment, a soul of fire like hers. The justness and celerity of her observations, the richness of her ideas, her eloquence, her intuition of truth, the energy of all her being, equally excite my admiration and attract my heart. With her I was under a serene sky; for she is so far from all that is limited, little, or half-true, that frank souls abandon themselves entirely to her, and find themselves in their true element. Nothing is more touching than the love of this father for his daughter, which is really

---

[8] *Lettres sur Genève.* Geneva. n.d.

passion itself, and the enthusiasm of the daughter for her father. Their eyes, which I think are the most beautiful in the world, express their mutual affection. She is his delight. Her vivacity kindles his old age, and he is perfection to her. She is as tender a mother as she is a good daughter. She devotes much of her time to her three children.'

Somewhat later, the enthusiastic Danish authoress writes, 'The centre of our society is, as you may well believe, our beloved Madame de Staël, who, with all her goodness and energy, gathers us in her heart. How attractive this creature is to my daughters! How they hang on her words! With what sweet sympathy her soul, full of love, abandons itself to the purest animation! It is necessary to see it, it is necessary to feel it: I cannot describe it. The quintessence of the best society is found in her mansion; it is there by the law of affinity. At her hearth one frequently sees, in a single evening, more intellectual brilliancy than in many cities in a whole year. Madame Necker de Saussure is there—the daughter of the great man who ascended Mont Blanc, and who is making scientific researches in the Alps. She is the bosom friend of Madame de Staël, and as worthy to be such as to bear the name of Saussure. This amiable Genevese joins to great force of mind, profound knowledge and clear reason, extreme tenderness of heart, and a purity of soul which paints itself on her beautiful and noble features. One is attracted to her, as to an image of the Good and Beautiful of Plato. Madame Rilliet-Huber is the friend of these two ladies. She is lovable, *spirituelle*, so interesting, so delicate and aërial, that one seems to see in her a Psyche with black eyes full of love, and wings ready for flight.[9] She is full of poetical and theatrical talent, and has a treasure of original manuscripts, which her modesty withholds from the public. . . . We assisted at Madame de Staël's in the representation of "Geneviève de Brabant," a drama in three acts, composed by her, and played by her, her children, and M. de Sabran. This piece, sentimental and religious, bears the character of its author; it has the energy and purity of style which characterise all her works. Every situation in it is a picture.' Private theatricals are a frequent entertainment of the brilliant society at the château. Its hostess herself composed for these occasions some six or seven dramas, which are given in her collected works.

Frederica Brun alludes to Madame de Staël's devotion to her children. Madame Necker de Saussure assures us that 'she was a very tender mother,' and gave much of her time to their education. Her daughter, the Duchess de Broglie, has left a record of her own recollections of her mother which illustrate particularly her maternal character. 'My mother,' she says 'attached great importance

---

[9] My friend, Prof. Albert Rilliet de Candolle, of Geneva, has a miniature portrait of her, taken in her youth, and of exquisite beauty.

to our happiness in infancy, and shared, with feeling, our early troubles. Some of her conversations with me, when I was but twelve years old, were adapted to me as if we were equals, and nothing can give you an idea of the joy I experienced in these confidential half-hour communings. I felt a new life; my soul was elevated, and received courage for all my studies. Her children always loved her passionately. From the age of six years we disputed who should be most loved by her; an intimate conversation with one of us excited the emulation of the others. It was a happiness to one's heart, a compliment to one's self-respect, to be near her. On Sundays she always read to us our grandfather's discourses, his Course of Christian Morals. She never wished to have a governess for me, and she gave me lessons daily, in her times of greatest trouble. The development of our minds was such a pleasure to her, that her happiness in it was our chief incentive to study. She endeavoured to place herself, as early as possible, in a relation of equality with her children; and she would say to them that she not only needed them for her affections, but that they could help her to support her trials; she often consulted us in the distresses of her exile. I have heard her say to Auguste, " I have need of your approbation." She would speak to me of my life, and all her projects regarding me, with perfect frankness. In certain circumstances she would remark that one of her children was superior to herself in courage or decision, and would show respect for his character; and yet we never ceased to respect her, and this respect was always mingled with reverential fear. Though she showed us the greatest confidence, yet, from the moment she entered upon our lessons, we felt this reverence, this fear. She showed great scruples about us, reproaching herself for our faults, and saying, "If you do wrong, not only shall I be unhappy, but I shall suffer remorse." When she blamed us, remarking that it was her own fault, that she had failed to set us a good example, it cut us to the heart. Nothing can give an idea of the impression produced by the union of dignity and confidence, of emotion and reserve, that there was in her intimate intercourse with her children. Her words, pronounced with restrained tears, were engraved on our souls; and the idea that we could cause her to suffer, to reproach herself, became one of the strongest barriers against wrong doing. No person has ever had more natural dignity than she; and therefore she could admit her children to the greatest familiarity, and inspire them with pity for her sufferings, without lessening their reverence. Never has a mother been at once more confiding and more imposing.'[1]

A writer who was a personal friend of Madame de Staël has given us some allusions to the interior

---

[1] In Madame Necker de Saussure's *Notice* &c.

of the château at this period.[2] 'Necker,' he says, 'after the death of his wife, devoted his entire affection to his daughter. The life of the family was, at first, somewhat grave. Its chief merit was in the prodigious intellectual activity which prevailed in the intercourse of Necker, Madame de Staël, and Benjamin Constant who sojourned there. They united for breakfast in the chamber of Madame de Staël. This meal frequently lasted two hours, for hardly had they met when she would start a question in literature or philosophy. She avoided politics out of deference to her father, whose political memories were so painful. But, whatever the subject, it was attacked with a vivacity and a profundity which rendered the place a school for Constant. Madame de Staël was always superior to her father in these intellectual contests; but, when about to conquer, she would, with an inimitable grace, yield the palm to him, her filial modesty crowning him with the glory. It was to him alone, however, that she ever accorded this advantage. From the breakfast each retired till dinner, which passed with no little ado between Necker and some old *maîtres d'hôtel*, deaf and grumbling remnants of the *régime* which he had overthrown, and who had followed his fortunes to Coppet in their embroidered costumes. After dinner commenced Necker's game of whist with his

---

[2] Frédéric de Chateauvieux in *Mém. de la Duchesse d'Abrantès*, xvii. 8. Paris, 1832.

daughter, always played with eagerness and tenacity, and then conversation for the rest of the evening. She thus devoted about eight years to the happiness of her father, excepting intervals spent in travelling. Meanwhile she educated her children, devoting to them all the force of her superior intellect. She wrote also, in this period, those works which I consider examples of her *second manner*—her Influence of the Passions, Literature, and "Delphine." She later entered into politics, and published her "Corinne" and her great work on Germany. Her most vivid taste during these times was for domestic theatrical representations. These were her chief amusement. She was seconded in them by Count Elzear de Sabran, Charles de Labédoyère, and Don Pedro de Souza, now Marquis de Palmella. She had an admirable voice and superior expression on the stage. She especially excelled in *soubrette rôles.*'

Sainte-Beuve says that what Ferney was to Voltaire, Coppet was to Madame de Staël, but 'with a much more poetic halo around it, and with a nobler life. Both reigned in their exile, but Coppet has counterbalanced Ferney and half dethroned it. We of the young age judge Ferney in descending from Coppet. The beauty of the site, the woods which shade it, the sex of the poet, the enthusiasm that we breathe there, the elegance of the company, the glory of their names, the promenades along the lake, the mornings in the park, the mysteries and the passions that we may suppose inevitable there, all combine to enchant us with the image of this abode.'[3] Its greatest days were yet to come; but it was already rising before the eyes of all Europe, not only as a refuge for the persecuted, but as an intellectual pharos. Its discussions, political, philosophic, literary, conducted with the highest conversational talent of the times, began usually before eleven o'clock in the morning, at the breakfast table, were resumed at dinner, were continued till supper at eleven o'clock at night, and often did not end till after midnight. Manuscript works were read, and the best poems of various languages recited, as well as dramas acted by the guests. The château became a little but a radiant world of its own. Nevertheless its *châtelaine* still longed for the greater world of Paris. Napoleon had been declared Consul for life; his peace with England had lasted but one year, and he was preparing to invade the island. She hoped to be forgotten by him in the universal agitations of France at this period, and she ventured again to cross its boundary.

[3] *Critiques et Portraits Littéraires*, iii.

CHAPTER XVIII.

EXILE—MADAME RÉCAMIER.

Madame de Staël returns to France—Her Persecution by Bonaparte—Madame Récamier—Her extraordinary Beauty and Character—Her first Interview with Madame de Staël—The latter seeks shelter with her—A Gendarme takes charge of Madame de Staël—Joseph Bonaparte—She departs for Germany—Madame de Beaumont—Letter of Madame de Staël to Chateaubriand.

MADAME DE STAËL approached the capital, in the autumn of 1803, with timid misgivings. Her Parisian friends had written to her that the First Consul was too much absorbed in his preparations against England to notice her movements; but she instinctively knew him better than they: she knew him to be as capable of personal revenge as of ambition for empire. The sun has its spots, and egotism is often the littleness of great men. If its vanity may be harmless, or even amusing, its resentments are nevertheless petulant and stinging. Napoleon was its very impersonation. Madame de Staël's father, who suffered intensely because he had caused her to suffer, wished to go to Paris to plead with him for her, and to take to himself the whole blame of his late book. She believed, at first, that his age, his public services, and his character, might render him successful, but at last declined his offer. 'When he saw me decided,' she says, 'not to accept it, I perceived how much it would have cost him. Fifteen months later I lost my father: had he made the journey to Paris, I should have attributed his sickness to this cause, and remorse would have envenomed my wound.'[1]

The Consul Lebrun's letter to him, against his book, had not pronounced her exile, but only threatened it. She determined therefore to venture back alone, 'hoping,' she writes, 'that I might be permitted to live some leagues from Paris, with the small number of friends who might be willing to visit, at a distance, a person in disgrace.' She took lodgings in a country house about ten leagues from the city. It was soon reported to Bonaparte that the roads were thronged by her visitors. There was no truth whatever in the report, but he seized it as a pretext for exiling her; and one of her friends conveyed to her warning that a *gendarme* would probably be sent to her in a few days. She was prostrated by anxiety. 'No one,' she says, 'who lives in a land where the laws guarantee at least the forms of justice, can conceive the alarm to which the apprehension of such sudden, arbitrary acts of the Government exposed the sufferer. I am easily shaken; my imagination has always been more fearful than hopeful; and though experience has taught

[1] *Dix Années,* i. 11.

me that most of our anxieties are readily dispelled by new circumstances, yet it always seems to me, when trouble is impending, that nothing can save me from it.' She appealed to her friend De Gérando, who, being in the service of the Government, might exert some influence for her, at least with Talleyrand, who owed, as we have seen, his own restoration to France and office to her instrumentality. 'I beseech you,' she wrote to the philosopher, ' come to me immediately. I have to pray you to speak a word for me to Talleyrand. My condition ought to touch your heart. In the name of Mathieu [de Montmorency], who suffers with me, come. I have need to see you before you see M. de Champayne.' De Gérando's efforts for her were unavailing; and Talleyrand was too shrewd and too selfish to compromise himself with his new master in behalf of a woman, whatever might be her merits or his obligations to her.

She addressed to Napoleon an imploring but indignant letter. 'I have lived in peace at Maffliers,' she said, ' under the assurance that you have been willing to give me that I could remain there, but am told that a *gendarme* is about to apprehend me with my children. Citizen Consul, I cannot believe it. You would thus give me a cruel proof that I shall have a line in your history. You will pierce the heart of my venerable father, who would, I am sure, in spite of his age, come to demand of you what crime his family has committed, to incur such barbarous treatment. If you wish that I should leave France, give me a passport for Germany, and grant me eight days at Paris, that I may obtain money, and consult a physician for my daughter, six years old, whose health has been impaired by travel. In no country on earth could such a request be refused. Citizen Consul, it cannot be in your heart to persecute a woman and her children. It is impossible that a hero should not be the protector of feebleness. I conjure you again, allow me to live in peace in my father's house at St. Ouen; it is sufficiently near Paris for my son to follow his studies at the Polytechnic School when the time shall come; and sufficiently distant for me not to be a resident of Paris. I will depart in the spring, when the season shall render travel possible for my children. In short, reflect, Citizen Consul, a moment before inflicting so great a suffering on a defenceless woman. You can, by a single act of justice, inspire me with true and lasting gratitude,' &c.[2]

A member of the Government (Régnault de Saint Jean d'Angely) who knew Napoleon's designs, risked his own interest by offering her an asylum, but she was not willing to involve him in her misfortunes; he then directed her to the house of Madame de la Tour—'a truly good and intellectual woman'—whom she had hardly known, but to whom she hastened, ' bearing,' she says, ' a heart

[2] *Coppet et Weimar,* i. 28.

lacerated with suffering. During the night, alone with a woman who for years had been devoted to my service, I listened for the approach of a mounted *gendarme*; during the day I laboured to control myself and to conceal from the company my wretchedness. I felt, with despair, that I was at last an exile, probably for a long time, possibly for ever.' She wrote to her friends, Joseph and Lucien Bonaparte; they made every effort to save her, but in vain.

Unable to bear this painful suspense, she recalled with hope the image of a friend, the loveliest woman, in soul as well as in person, then in Europe, of whom Mathieu de Montmorency had said that he ' loved her as an angel on earth,' one whose transcendent beauty produced a sensation in the streets wherever she passed; converged upon her the gaze of public assemblies, even when Napoleon himself was speaking; and was excelled only by the grace of her manners and the purity of her heart—a woman who subdued the jealousy of women as well as the passion of men, invincibly ' protected by the halo of virtue which always surrounded her;' whose ' presence anywhere was an event, and produced a tumult of admiration, of curiosity, of enthusiasm,' even the common people, in public places, calling upon her with shouts to rise, that they might pay their homage to beauty, in her person,—who, when it was understood that she was to be a collector for a public charity at St. Roche, found it impossible to make her way, without assistance, through the throng that crowded the aisles, stood upon chairs, hung upon the pillars, mounted even the altars of the side chapels, and gave twenty thousand francs, more for the sight of her than for the sacred design of the occasion,—who enchanted all men that beheld her, yet, by her moral fascination, compelled them to abandon lower hopes for her coveted esteem and her self-respectful friendship,[3]—who declined the proffered hearts of princes, and even the possibility of a throne, that she might maintain the obligations of a marriage of *convenance*, made when she was but fifteen years old, with a man who was forty-two; and who, when her opulent fortune was lost, and after the Restoration had re-established the factitious distinctions of society, and even in old age and blindness, could still hold spell-bound, around her, the *élite* society of Paris. 'She was,' says

[3] The younger Ampère was one among many examples: he but twenty, she forty-three years old. Three Montmorencys—Mathieu, the Duke de Laval, and his son—were his equally unsuccessful rivals. Lucien Bonaparte's ardent passion for her is fully attested by his letters in her memoirs. Chateaubriand's lifelong love for her, and his offer of marriage in her old age, are well known. 'I know nothing more beautiful or better than you,' he wrote her in her fifty-second year. In his *Mémoires d'Outre-Tombe*, tome viii., he says: 'Her beauty mingled its ideal existence with the material facts of our history—a serene light illuminating a picture of storms.' She managed with admirable tact the passion of the young Ampère, for the direction of his studies, and the development of his genius. See *André-Marie Ampère et Jean-Jacques Ampère: Correspondance et Souvenirs* &c. *passim*. 2 vols. Paris, 1875.

her niece and biographer, who knew her most intimate life, 'devoted, sympathetic, indulgent, self-respectful. You found with her consolation, strength, balm for suffering, guidance in the great resolutions of life; she had a passion for goodness.' 'She was,' says another authority, 'an incomparable being in all respects. Her charming qualities had something so peculiar that they can never be perfectly described. Only scattered traits of her supreme grace can be given.' Napoleon himself was smitten by her charms, and persecuted her, through Fouché, with his importunities to induce her to become a lady of his Court (*dame de palais*), but she disliked the man, and declined the brilliant offer. He seized the first opportunity of involving her in the exile of Madame de Staël, compelling her to leave her family and the charmed circle of her innumerable Parisian friends, and wander obscurely in the southern provinces and Italy for years. It was a remarkable coincidence that, in these degenerate times, two women, one the most beautiful, the other the most intellectual, in modern history, should appear in the same country, and should be united in an inseparable sisterhood.

'Madame Récamier,' says her biographer, 'gave her heart to Madame de Staël. It was in her nature to love passionately whatever she admired; and the premature death of the author of "Corinne" left with her an immense void.'[4] They had met,

---

[4] Madame Lenormand's *Souvenirs et Correspondance de Madame*

for the first time, some three or four years before our present date. 'That day,' remarks Madame Récamier, 'was an epoch in my life—I was struck by the beauty of her eyes. I cannot describe what I experienced. I was eager to divine who she was. Addressing me with a bright and penetrating grace, she uttered the name of Necker, her father: I recognised Madame de Staël. I could not understand the rest of her sentence; I blushed and was in extreme confusion; she intimidated and yet attracted me. My diffidence did not injure me. She fixed her great eyes on me, and with a curiosity full of kindliness praised my features in a manner irresistibly charming, especially as her compliments escaped her spontaneously. One saw in her, immediately, a being of a superior nature, but perfectly natural. It was a sudden apparition in my life; the impression was so strong that I no longer thought of anything but Madame de Staël, so profoundly had I felt the influence of her powerful and ardent nature.' Her admiration was more than reciprocated. Some years later, when her fortune was wrecked by her husband's bankruptcy, Madame de Staël wrote to her, 'Were it possible to envy one whom I love, I should be willing to give all that I am, to be you. Beauty unequalled in Europe, reputation without a spot, character proud and generous—what a happy fortune in this sad life!'

Récamier, passim, particularly the 'Avant-propos.' 2 vols. Paris, 1860.

Years later she spoke of her as 'an angel of beauty and purity.'

Madame Récamier was now living in a château at Sainte-Brice, about two leagues from Paris, and invited her friend to hasten thither for shelter. 'I accepted her invitation,' writes Madame de Staël, 'not supposing that my presence could injure a person so unconnected with politics. The most agreeable society was gathered under her roof, and I enjoyed for the last time all that I was about to lose.' After some days spent there, without a further intimation about her exile, she too readily persuaded herself that she was safe and returned to her country house, 'convinced that Napoleon had adjourned his resolutions' against her, and was content to have merely excited her fears. But, while at her table with some friends, she saw, through the open window, a man in grey, on horseback, stop at her gate and ring the bell. 'I was certain,' she says, 'of my fate. It was a fine day in September. I received him in my garden; the perfumes of the flowers, the beauty of the sun, struck me; the sensations which come to us from the combinations of society are so different from those which come from nature! This man told me that he was the commandant of the *gendarmerie* at Versailles, that he had been ordered not to wear his uniform, that he might not alarm me; he showed me a letter, signed by Bonaparte, which exiled me to forty leagues from Paris, and required me to depart within twenty-four hours.' A woman with her children could not leave so suddenly. The *gendarme*, a man of some politeness and literary tastes, consented to accompany her and her children in her carriage to Paris, and allow her three days for her preparations. They stopped on the way, a few moments, at the house of Madame Récamier, where she met General Junot (the Duc d'Abrantès), who promised to intercede with Napoleon for her. 'He did so with fervent urgency, but failed.' Napoleon so far yielded to the entreaties of Junot as to consent that she should reside at Dijon. Madame Récamier sent this permission, in a letter addressed to the care of Camille Jordan at Lyons; but it was never received by her, and could not have been acceptable if it had been received; for it insinuated conditions respecting her future course which would have compromised her intellectual independence.[5]

She had previously hired a small house in a quiet quarter of Paris, hoping to be able to retire there in peace. 'I now went into it,' she writes, 'with the certainty of soon leaving it; I passed the nights in running through its apartments, regretting, even more than I had hoped, the happiness I was losing. My *gendarme* returned each morning, as in the story of Blue Beard, urging me to depart the next day. My friends came to dine with me, and

---

[5] Sainte-Beuve discovered this letter, years after her death, among the papers of Camille Jordan. See *Nouveaux Lundis*, vol. xii.

sometimes we were gay, as if to exhaust the cup of sorrow, and be once more happy before parting. They said to me that this man, coming each day to summon me to depart, reminded them of the Reign of Terror, when the *gendarmes* came to the prisons to call out their victims. On the last evening that was accorded me, Joseph Bonaparte made yet one more effort for me; and his wife came to invite me to spend some days in their country house at Morfontaine. I went with gratitude, for I was touched with the kindness of Joseph, who was willing to receive me into his house while his brother was persecuting me. I spent three days there, but my situation was very painful. I was surrounded by officers of the Government. I knew not which way to turn. My father would receive at Coppet, with inexpressible affection, his poor bird beaten by the storms; but I did not wish to deepen his afflictions. I thought of Germany, and spent two hours in the garden, one of the most beautiful in Europe, considering what I should do. I at last entreated Joseph to obtain permission for me to go to Prussia without the liability of interference from the French minister there. He went to Saint Cloud for this purpose. I was obliged to await his answer at a country tavern, two leagues from Paris. I did not dare to return to my house in the city. A day passed without his answer. In order not to attract attention by remaining in the tavern, I made the tour of the wall of Paris, seeking another inn within the prescribed leagues, but on a different route. These wanderings, at a short distance from my city home and my friends, caused me anguish which I cannot describe. The chamber which I occupied now reappears to my mind: the window where I passed the whole day looking for the messenger; a thousand details which misery drags after it; the too great generosity of some friends, the selfish calculations of others. My soul was kept in a cruel agitation, such as I could not wish to be the lot of any enemy. At last the message arrived. Joseph had procured me liberty to depart for Berlin, and sent me excellent letters of introduction, accompanied by an adieu full of nobleness and tenderness. Benjamin Constant generously offered to accompany me, but I suffered from the sacrifice which he made for me. Every step of the horses sickened me; and when the postilion boasted of their high speed, I could not but sigh over the service he was rendering me.' She hastened to Châlons, Constant endeavouring to relieve her dejection, on the way, by his 'astonishing conversation;' for in all France he alone was second to herself in that talent.

They arrived at Metz, where she remained some days, awaiting letters from her father. 'He was indignant,' she says, 'at my treatment; he saw his family proscribed, and compelled to flee, as criminals, from a country which he had so faithfully served.' Even the debt which it owed him for a generous loan in the time of its utmost need, and which had been acknowledged by the Government, was still withheld by Napoleon. Necker advised her to spend the winter in Germany, and not return to Coppet till the next spring; for who could tell what severer measures might be taken by Bonaparte, were she still within his immediate reach?

Her reputation had preceded her at Metz, and she was received there with something like an ovation. Count Colchen, the prefect of the Moselle, hospitably entertained her; constant 'soirées and fêtes were given in her honour,' and the *élite* of a literary society of the city 'were pleased to award her, at the moment in which she was about to quit France with so much regret, the homage due to her genius and sufferings.'⁶ She found there Charles de Villers, her Kantian correspondent. She wrote to De Gérando, 'I am awaiting here, my dear De Gérando, letters from Strasbourg, before continuing my route. Send me, therefore, your letters for Germany; write me by every courier, for I wish to remain but six days. What most pleases me here is Villers, in whom I discover extraordinary intellect, and I advise you to draw advantage from this intellect, this winter; he has all the ideas of North Germany in his head. Without Benjamin, I should have succumbed to my griefs.

⁶ Baron de Gérando, *Lettres Inédites* &c.

I have been able to sleep but little, and my mind is full of painful apprehensions. Adieu! my excellent friend. Talk of me with Annette. I will write to Camille by the next courier. My address at Frankfort will be with the poor Maurice Bethman, about whom we have smiled so much, Camille and I, in my happy days.'

At Frankfort-on-the-Maine her sufferings were redoubled by the dangerous illness of her daughter. 'I knew no person in the city,' she writes. 'I did not know the language; and the physician to whom I confided my child could not speak French. But my father shared my trouble; he consulted physicians at Geneva, and sent me their prescriptions.' 'Oh,' she exclaimed at the sick bed of her daughter, 'what would become of a mother trembling for the life of her child, if it were not for prayer!'

At Frankfort her sorrows were further augmented by the news, from Chateaubriand, of the death, in Rome, of one of her dearest friends, whom we have met among her companions in the little French colony at Mickleham, England—Madame de Beaumont. She was a daughter of the lady who, while Madame de Staël stood at a window in Versailles, witnessing the procession of the States General, admonished her of the coming disasters of the Revolution, and of M. de Montmorin, associate of Necker in the ministry and a victim of the September massacres. The mother and one of her sons had perished, as we have seen, on the scaffold;

all the family, in short, had died prematurely except Madame de Beaumont. It was through her affectionate intimacy with this lady that Madame de Staël had become acquainted with Chateaubriand, then her only important literary rival in France. The author of the 'Genius of Christianity' had found in the daughter of Montmorin a congenial mind, a woman of culture and of vivid sensibility, whose cruel afflictions had not only saddened, but had ripened her soul. She suffered long from pulmonary disease as well as from grief, but 'whenever a loving voice appealed to this solitary soul,' says Chateaubriand, 'it responded in words from heaven.' Madame de Staël could not but cling tenaciously to such a woman. Chateaubriand's letter was addressed to her at Coppet. Necker answered it: 'Be not surprised,' he said, 'that you do not receive Madame de Staël's response as soon as you had a right to expect. You can be very sure of the pain with which my daughter will learn the loss of a friend of whom I have always heard her speak with profound feeling. I join in her sorrow, I join in yours, for I have a particular interest in it when I recall the unhappy fate of the family of my friend Montmorin.'

On receiving Chateaubriand's letter, Madame de Staël replied in one which was thoroughly characteristic of her ever overflowing heart, the *empressement*, the *abandon* of her grief and her affections. 'Alas! alas! my dear Francis,' she exclaimed, 'with what anguish am I seized on receiving your letter! Before it reached me, this frightful news reached me through the journals, and your agonizing recital now comes to engrave it for ever in letters of blood on my heart. Can you—can you speak to me of our differences of opinion about religion, about priests? What are two opinions, when there is only one sentiment? I have read your letter through saddest tears. My dear Francis, recall the time when you felt more friendship for me; forget not, above all, the days in which all my heart was drawn towards you; and assure yourself that those sentiments, more tender and more profound than ever, are still in the depth of my soul for you. I love, I admire the character of Madame de Beaumont. I have known no being more generous, more affectionate, more passionately tender. Since I entered into society I have never ceased to have relations with her, and have felt, notwithstanding some divergences of opinion, that I was bound to her by all the fibres of my being. My dear Francis, give me a place in your life; I admire you, I love you. I love her whom you mourn; I am a devoted friend, I will be to you a sister. I ought more than ever to respect your opinions; Mathieu,[7] who entertains them, has been an angel to me in my late sufferings. Give me a new reason to respect them; enable me to be useful or agreeable to you in some way. Have you

---

[7] Her Roman Catholic friend, Montmorency.

been informed that I am exiled to forty leagues from Paris? I am now making a tour in Germany; in the spring I shall return to Paris, perhaps, if my exile ends, or near Paris or Geneva. Manage that we may meet again. Do you not feel that my mind and my soul understand yours; and that, in spite of our differences, we resemble one another? M. de Humboldt writes me with admiration of your work; you ought to be flattered by the opinion of such a man. But how dare I speak of your success in such a moment? Nevertheless, our lost friend loved that success, and attached her own glory to it. Continue to render her illustrious who has been so affectionate. Adieu, dear Francis. I will write to you from Weimar. Alas, there is so much that is heart-rending in your letter! And that resolution of keeping the poor Saint-Germain;[8] you must bring her some day to my house. Adieu! tenderly, sorrowfully, adieu!'

Such a characteristic letter—in which the woman's heart placed her masculine mind in entire abeyance—could not fail to touch the soul of the enthusiastic Chateaubriand. 'This letter,' he says, in his old age, 'this eager, affectionate, rapid letter, written by a celebrated woman, caused in me redoubled tenderness. These, my comforters, have both passed away; and they now claim for themselves the regrets that they felt for one another!'[9]

---

[8] A woman in the service of Madame de Beaumont.
[9] *Mémoires d'Outre-Tombe*, iv.

Chateaubriand's sentimental relations with Madame Récamier, prolonged through so many years after the death of Madame de Staël and of nearly all their old friends, kept her memory ever fresh in their hearts and conversation.

She looked longingly towards Weimar, then the intellectual centre of Europe—more brilliant than Ferney had ever been, or Coppet was ever to be—and hoped to find rest and consolation in its tranquil little world of elect minds. On the recovery of her daughter she fled towards it, as to a city of refuge. Her persecutions had, however, but begun. 'Having exiled her,' says her son, ' first from Paris, then from France, after suppressing by an arbitrary caprice her " Allemagne," and making it impossible for her to publish anything whatever, however neutral in politics, the Government was at last to make even her home a prison, to interdict all travel, and to deprive her of the pleasures of social life and the consolations of friendship.'[1]

Talleyrand had written to her from America, that he should die if his exile were to continue another year. 'What then,' she wrote him, 'do you suppose must be my sufferings in my exile?' She had procured his restoration; he left her to her fate.

[1] Preface, by Baron de Staël, to the *Dix Années d'Exil*.

CHAPTER XIX.

MADAME DE STAËL AT WEIMAR.

Weimar—The Duchess Amelia—The Duke Charles Augustus—The Intellectual Circle of Weimar—Wieland, Goethe and Schiller—The Duchess Louise—Letters of Goethe and Schiller respecting Madame de Staël—Her Estimates of Goethe, Schiller and Wieland—Life at Weimar.

MADAME DE STAËL arrived at Weimar in December 1803. 'There I took courage,' she writes, 'in seeing what immense intellectual riches there were beyond the limit of French literature. I learned German; I heard Goethe and Wieland, who, happily for me, spoke good French. I understood the heart and genius of Schiller, notwithstanding the difficulty of expressing himself in a foreign language. The society of the Duke and Duchess pleased me extremely, and I passed three months there, during which the study of German literature gave my mind the occupation and interest which it needed to keep it from preying on itself.'[1]

No State in Germany was now better recognised throughout the literary world than the little Duchy of Saxe-Weimar with its two hundred thou-

[1] *Dix Années* &c. i. 12.

sand inhabitants, its capital Weimar with but ten thousand, and its university town of Jena with but five thousand. Weimar was, in fact, the capital of intellectual Europe. One of the most admirable of women, the Duchess Amelia, had secured for it this pre-eminence. Though a widow at nineteen years of age, she ruled her small dominion with rare wisdom. She saw that there was one, and but one, way of rendering it prominent among the larger states around it—she could make it intellectually great. She called Wieland to Weimar, as preceptor of her son, Charles Augustus; she gathered in her little court eminent writers, artists, and actors. Herder, one of the most vigorous and splendid minds of the German pulpit of the times, was appointed preacher of Weimar, and, under the faithful protection of the Duchess, became a commanding authority in the literary circle of the Court. Knobel, Seckendorf, Boettinger, and others were attracted to it by her patronage. Her son, to whom she surrendered the government in 1775, had been so imbued with her spirit as to follow spontaneously and even enthusiastically her policy of making his capital, otherwise so insignificant, powerful and for ever historical in the literary world. While travelling in Germany in the last year of his minority, he found Goethe in his parental home at Frankfort. The young poet was becoming famous by his 'Werther' and his recently published 'Goetz von Berlichingen.' Their friendship immediately became intimate, and, on assuming the government, the Duke claimed him for Weimar, where he was the reigning genius during the remainder of his long life. In 1787 Schiller entered the circle, and formed with Goethe a friendship which will be for ever memorable in literary history. They were destined to be the two most brilliant stars in the poetic firmament of Germany. By the marriage of the Duke to the Princess Louise of Hesse, a woman every way befitting her position was placed at the head of the Court by the side of the Duchess Amelia. She became the ardent friend and life-long correspondent of Madame de Staël.[2]

Before the arrival of the French authoress, her approach had been intimated by letters from Frankfort; and the Court circle, though curious to see the most eminent literary woman of the age, anticipated her coming with considerable anti-French prejudice; for German criticism and egotism had already begun to disparage alike French literature and French politics. Goethe was absent, at Jena, pursuing his favourite scientific researches. Schiller wrote to him that 'Madame de Staël is at Frankfort, and we may expect to see her soon. Provided she understands German, we may enjoy her visit; but to have to explain our religion, and contend with French volubility, may be a hard task. We may not be as successful as Schelling was with

[2] *Coppet et Weimar.* Paris, 1862.

Camille Jordan, who came armed *cap-à-pie* with the principles of Locke. "I despise Locke," said Schelling, and his adversary was smitten dumb.' Goethe rather dreaded her noted conversational powers, and made no haste from Jena. Schiller wrote to Körner (Jan. 4, 1804): 'The piece'—'William Tell'—'which I have promised to the Berlin theatre for the end of February, entirely absorbs me, and behold, Satan has led to me the female French Philosopher who of all creatures living is the most animated, the most ready for combat, and the most fertile in words. But she is also the most cultivated, the most *spirituelle* of women, and if she were not really interesting, I would not be disturbed by her. You can well suppose how such an apparition, such a spirit, placed on the summit of French culture—so entirely opposed to ours—and arriving here suddenly from the centre of another sort of world, must be in contrast with the German nature, and especially with mine. She dispels from me all poetry, and I am astonished that I am able to do anything. I see her frequently and as I speak French imperfectly I really have some hard hours to pass. One is obliged, nevertheless, to esteem and highly honour this woman, for her remarkable intelligence and her liberal spirit.' Goethe, hesitating at Jena, wrote to Schiller: 'I leave entirely to you to arrange in the best manner you can all that concerns Madame de Staël. If she wishes to come hither to see me, she shall be welcome, and, provided I am warned twenty-four hours in advance, she shall find an apartment well furnished, and good little dinners. In this manner we can readily see one another and talk together, and she can remain as long as she wishes. My occupations retain me only at brief intervals; the rest of my time shall be given to her. But travel to Weimar, make my toilet, go to Court and into society—this is impossible: I positively declare it.' Schiller replied: 'Madame de Staël will doubtless appear to you what you have *a priori* imagined her to be. All in her is of one piece. In spite, therefore, of the difference between her nature and ours, one feels at ease with her; we can bear anything from her, and feel at liberty to say anything in reply. She is the representative, as perfect as interesting, of the true French spirit. In all that we call philosophy—that is to say, on subjects of the very highest character—I am in opposition to her, and maintain this antagonism in spite of her eloquence. But with her nature and sentiment are paramount to all metaphysics, and elevate her spirit even to genius itself. Wishing to explain all, to comprehend all, to measure all, she admits nothing to be impenetrable, and whatever the light of reason cannot make clear does not exist for her. Hence her insurmountable aversion for the idealistic philosophy; she sees in it only the road to mysticism and superstition. The poetic spirit is wanting in her entirely; she can appreciate, in poetical works, only their passion and eloquence. She never approves what is false, but cannot always appreciate what is true. In spite of my poor French, we understand one another fairly; but, as you speak the language perfectly, I doubt not your conversation with her will have much interest for both of you.'

Candid and cordial as Schiller's judgment was, it was premature in some respects. She did not reject the Ideal Philosophy, but only its abuses. In the 'Allemagne' she defends it against Locke and the French materialists. Her remarkable analysis of Kant[2] (more remarkable, however, as a criticism than as an analysis) is a vindication of it; her next chapter, chiefly on Schelling and Fichte, is an exposure of its abuses. She believed in Christian spiritualism, and had, as we have seen, no little sympathy with Christian mysticism. Schiller's imperfect knowledge of the French language led him, probably, to misapprehensions of her opinions; and, as she was now only beginning her studies of the German mind, she may have dealt more in objections than in concessions, as the best means of eliciting the truth. As to her appreciation of poetry, had Schiller lived long enough to read the 'Allemagne,' he would have applauded with enthusiasm her splendid discussions on that subject, and wished no better criticisms on his own

---

[2] *Allemagne*, iii. 6.

works.[4] Not a few of her critics erred, in like manner, regarding her appreciation of the fine arts, till the publication of 'Corinne' conclusively refuted their opinion.

The Duke at last ordered Goethe to appear at Court, in order to meet her. She was impressed by the greatness of his genius, though she disliked his cool scepticism, and mistook his philosophic self-control for decay of the passionate ardour of his early works, especially of his 'Werther.' 'He is a man,' she writes,[5] 'of prodigious spirit in conversation. His eloquence is strong with thought, his pleasantries full of grace and philosophy. His imagination is struck by external objects, as was that of the classic artists, and nevertheless his reason has the maturity of modern times. Nothing disturbs the strength of his intellect.' 'But,' she adds, 'he no longer has the ardour which pervades his "Werther," though the warmth of his thoughts still somewhat animates him. One would say that he describes only as a painter—that he values more the pictures which he presents than the emotions he feels; time has rendered him a spectator. When he had an active part in the scenes of the passions, when he suffered in his own heart, his writings produced a more vivid impression. At first sight, one is astonished to perceive the coldness and even rigidity of Goethe, but as soon as he

---

[4] *Allemagne*, passim, particularly ch. x., xi., and xii.
[5] *Ibid*, ii. 7.

is at ease with you his imagination inspires him. His mind is universal, and impartial because it is universal; and there is no indifference in his impartiality. His is a double existence, a double force, a double light which illuminates at the same time both sides of a question. He represents in himself the principal traits of German genius—profundity of ideas; grace born of the imagination, and therefore more original than that which is inspired by the spirit of society; and finally sensibility, sometimes fantastic, but by this very fact the more interesting to readers who seek in books something to vary their monotonous being, and who would have poetry hold for them the place of real events.'

If she admired Goethe as greatest in genius, she admired Schiller more, for both his genius and character. 'I first saw him,' she says,[6] 'in the *salon* of the Duke and Duchess of Weimar, in presence of a company as cultivated as imposing. He could read French very well, but had never spoken it. I maintained, with warmth, the superiority of our dramatic system over all others; he did not decline the combat, and, without embarrassment from the difficulties and slowness with which he had to speak in French, without fearing the opinions of the auditors which were contrary to his own, his intimate convictions gave him utterance. To defeat him, I used at first the customary French arms, vivacity and pleasantry; but very soon I un-

[6] *Allemagne*, ii 8.

ravelled from the obstacles of his French sentences
so many ideas, I was so struck by the simplicity of
his character, I found him so modest, so impartially
indifferent about his own success in the contest, so
proud and animated in the defence of what he
believed the truth, that I felt for him, from this
moment, a friendship full of admiration. He was
a man of rare genius and of perfect good faith: two
qualities which ought to be inseparable in a man of
letters; for thought can be placed in equality with
action only when it awakens in us the image of the
truth, and falsehood is more disgusting in writings
than in conduct. Schiller was as admirable among
us for his virtues as for his talents. Conscience was
his muse. He loved poetry, the dramatic art,
history, literature, for themselves. Nothing could
make him alter his writings, because his writings
were himself; they expressed his soul, and he could
not conceive the possibility of changing an expression, if the interior sentiment which it conveyed
had not changed. It is a beautiful thing—this innocence in genius, this candour in strength. Schiller did himself wrong at his entrance into the
world by the errors of his imagination; but with
the force of age he attained that sublime purity
which is born of high thoughts. He was the best
of friends, of fathers, of husbands; no one good
quality failed in his sweet and serene character.
Attacked while yet young by a hopeless malady,
his children, his wife, who merited by a thousand

touching qualities the attachment that he had for her, consoled his last days.'

Wieland was especially agreeable to her: his French characteristics pleased her national prejudices, though they were critically objectionable; for she had the good sense to approve the aim of the Weimar *coterie* at originality—a purely national literature. 'Wieland,' she says, 'is the only German who has written in the French manner with real genius.' German writers had generally and servilely followed the French literature of the time of Louis XIV.; Wieland was the first to introduce that of the eighteenth century. In his prose works is traceable the influence of Voltaire; in his poetry, that of Ariosto; but his spirit is essentially German. He is infinitely better informed than Voltaire; he has studied the ancients more profoundly than any French poet has done. He lacks the lighter graces of the French, and this failure is attributable both to his talents and his faults. His conversation had for her 'great charms,' and precisely because his natural qualities were in opposition to his philosophy. This discordance might injure him as a writer, but rendered his conversation piquant; he was animated, enthusiastic, and, 'like all men of genius, still young in old age.' He is both a German poet and French philosopher, and the one character disagrees with the other. 'The new German writers, who would exclude foreign influence from their literature, have been unjust towards him. His works, even in translations, have excited the interest of all Europe; he has made antiquity contribute special charms to modern literature; he has given, in verse, to his fruitful but rude language a musical and graceful flexibility. It is nevertheless true that it has been unfortunate for his country that he has had so many imitators. National originality is preferable. Wieland is a great master, but he should be a master without disciples.'

Herder had died before her arrival at Weimar; Schiller and Goethe were now conspicuous in its intellectual constellation, with a radiance which streamed over Europe. The Duchess Louise, afterwards her faithful correspondent, presided in the learned *salon* with perfect grace. 'She is a true model of a woman destined by nature to the most illustrious rank. Without pretension as without feebleness, she inspires in the same degree confidence and respect: and the heroism of the days of chivalry has entered into her soul, without injuring the tenderness of her sex.' The Duke is described as a man of military talents, and of piquant and thoughtful conversation, which reminded the listener that he had been formed by the Great Frederick.

Her three months spent at Weimar were full of interest, and relieved, for the time, the sadness of her exile. She disliked small cities, as restrictive of talent, and as scenes of gossip and small talk; but 'Weimar,' she says, 'is not a little city; it is a grand château, where a chosen circle entertains itself with every new production of the arts; where women, amiable disciples of great men, are constantly occupied with literary works, as with important public events. They gather the whole world around them, by reading and study; they escape, by their range of thought, from the limitations of their circumstances. In reflecting together, habitually, on the general questions common to the destiny of all, they forget the particular facts or anecdotes of each. One sees there none of those petty tendencies which characterise provincial life and substitute affectation for elegance.'

Before leaving Weimar, she had conceived the design of her 'Allemagne,' and wrote to De Gérando: 'When we meet, you will have to aid me in a part of a work that I propose to write on Germany. I have studied, and shall still study, the new philosophic and æsthetic systems of Kant, Schelling, Schlegel, &c., and I wish to give an analysis of them. I must first, however, read what you have written on them. I do not pretend to write metaphysics; but, to give an estimate of the character of the Germans and of the spirit which distinguishes their literature, it will be requisite to give a simple and popular view of their philosophic theories. Apropos of this, what do you make of Villers? For two months I have had no news of him. He is a little like the Germans, whose enthusiasm is too exalted to endure. I find, however, no diminution in the extreme kindness and attentions of these good Germans towards me; and I have already letters from Berlin full of cordial interest. I have seen a great deal of Schiller and Goethe. Goethe is an extraordinary man in conversation. They tell me here that Camille Jordan never saw him in his best humour; in this case, he cannot know him. This Camille is, by the way, an unworthy idler—not a word from him for two months! I am going, in four days, to Berlin. By force of reflection I support life in spite of exile, but my heart is always oppressed. A thousand tender thoughts for Annette; and for Juliette,[7] who loves me still, I hope, and of whom I speak everywhere with love; I say everywhere, for she is very celebrated. As to Annette, she has concentrated her happiness in you and her son; neither calumny nor praise reach her.'

[7] Madame Récamier.

CHAPTER XX.

BERLIN—RETURN—DEATH OF NECKER.

Madame de Staël at Berlin— Her Reception at Court—Its Pageantries —Kotzebue—Augustus William Schlegel—Execution of the Duc d'Enghien—Death of Necker and Return of Madame de Staël— Effect of his Death on her—Her Publication of his 'Manuscripts' —Society at Coppet—She departs for Italy.

MADAME DE STAËL went from Weimar to Berlin, where letters from the Duke and Duchess procured her the most flattering reception at Court, especially from the Queen Louise, whose beauty and more charming qualities, as well as her subsequent misfortunes, have won for her the sympathies of the world. The contrast between the two Courts— the tranquil literary habits of the one, the gay and hardly intermitted pageantries of the other—was far from agreeable to her. She now wrote to the Duchess of Weimar the first letter of their long correspondence. 'It seems to me,' she says, ' that I owe you an account of my life at Berlin, since it is to your Highness and the Duke that I am indebted for the welcome I have received here. I was presented on the 10th of March (1804) to the Queen-mother [1] and to the reigning Queen. I find the

[1] Widow of Frederick William II.

former very affable. I had been told that she speaks in a confused manner, but I understand her perfectly; and her remarkable politeness, inspired by your letter, has rendered very delightful the moments she has graciously accorded me. She complains to me that your Highness never comes to Berlin, and she has planned a visit, for herself, to Weimar this summer. After my interview with her I visited the reigning Queen, and on this day the Court was truly imposing. At the moment the Queen entered, the band struck up. I was deeply moved. The Queen appeared in the full splendour of her beauty. She approached me and said, among many other gracious phrases, these words, which I cannot readily forget: "I hope, Madame, that you believe us to have sufficient good taste to be flattered by your visit to Berlin; I have been impatient to see you." All the Princesses whom I saw at Weimar, and who love me because you do, hastened to embrace me. The King spoke very graciously to me. I was surrounded with kind attentions and was deeply touched. But, above all, I heard them repeat that I was loved at Weimar, and I perceived by certain indications that it was Weimar which had given me importance here. The Princess of Orange has impressed me as very gracious. Her husband and the Prince Radziwill called on me the very next morning after my arrival. Everybody here has been thinking, for twenty days, only of the masquerade: rehearsals, costumes, ballets, fill all heads; and, by arriving a little late at Berlin, I have lost nothing but a more intimate knowledge of steps of the ballet, executed yesterday. We remained till three o'clock in the morning, to see the Queen dance in a pantomime which represented the return of Alexander to Babylon. There were two thousand spectators: the pomp of the costumes and the beauty of the figures were truly remarkable. Many quadrilles followed, and Kotzebue[2] entered as a priest of Mercury—or rather perhaps as Mercury himself—a crown of poppies on his head, a caduceus in his hand, and ugly and disgusting to such a degree, that, to use the words of Goethe, "it is inconceivable that one's imagination should not be degraded by his image, for life." Ah! Weimar, Weimar! All these apings of French manners appear so foreign to the genuine merits of the Germans! It is not an imitation of Paris that I like to find abroad; it is original, native character. In short, in two months I will be back with your Highness; it seems to me that I should be already with you. I am to dine with the Prince Louis, at Madame de Berg's. Afterwards I will give you my impressions more in detail; for till now nobody has been able to talk with me except about ballets. Pardon the confusion of this letter. I write on awaking, my head filled with the sounds of cymbals and trumpets.'[3]

[2] The dramatic author and courtier, who was assassinated by the student Sand.

[3] *Coppet et Weimar*, ii.

At Berlin began her friendship with Augustus William Schlegel, the greatest critic of his age. His learning was prodigious, even for a German. An exact classical scholar, he was also familiar with all the literatures of modern Europe; and, in every department of his multifarious knowledge, he was a critical, if not an indisputable authority. He was a poet of high merit. As a linguist he was of the first order, and, not only one of the very earliest leaders in Sanscrit and Indo-European studies, but he became an oracle of them, consulted by scholars from Paris, Oxford, Cambridge, and all places where that newly opened but marvellously fruitful field of research was cultivated. He was at home in mediæval literature, and contributed effectively to its just appreciation by modern students. With his vast acquisitions he combined the insight, and, it must be acknowledged, some of the infirmities of genius. He could be malicious; in his old age he was vain, and even pedantic; but remained, nevertheless, a supreme authority. He was withal a superior talker, and Madame de Staël, who ever liked a rival in this brilliant faculty, was irresistibly attracted to him. She received him into her family as instructor of her children, where he remained many years, liberally compensated by a salary of twelve thousand francs, with abundant leisure for his literary labours, opportunities for extensive travel with his patroness, and the freedom and luxuries of an opulent home.

Madame de Staël remained six weeks in Berlin, the idol of its highest society. It was there that she first heard of one of the foulest crimes of her persecutor—one which the world will never forgive nor palliate, and which might well add to the intensity of her apprehensions of his growing power and his personal enmity against herself. 'I lived,' she says, ' on the quay of the Spree, and my apartments were on the ground floor. I was awakened early one morning, and told that Prince Louis Ferdinand[4] was on horseback under my window, with important news for me.' It was the news of the execution of the Duc d'Enghien. 'What folly!' she exclaimed, 'it is a false report, started by the enemies of France.' The Prince sent her the 'Moniteur,' reporting the 'judgment,' and the terrible crime could not be doubted. It struck her, as it struck all Europe, with astonishment and horror. She hastened to Vienna. A letter from her father, the last she ever received from him, denounced in the strongest terms the murder of the Duke, but assured her of his own continued health. Two letters soon followed, intimating his dangerous illness. The courier who brought them actually knew that he was dead ; the sad news was withheld from her, but she instinctively surmised it. She wrote to the Duchess

---

[4] Who fell gallantly, two years later, at the battle of Saalfeld, and whose brother, Prince Augustus, found an asylum at Coppet, and was smitten there with a life-long passion for Madame Récamier.

of Saxe-Weimar: 'I am going home—leaving Vienna, where my happiness ends. I preserve for you the most tender gratitude. If I return to life, I will return to you, but every day will deepen the wound of which I may die, sooner or later. Sympathise with me in your palace, in your noble solitude. Think sometimes of the broken heart in which the memory of you will still live.'

She immediately directed her course homeward. On the route her father's death was revealed to her. 'A sentiment of inexpressible terror,' she says, 'was joined to my despair. I saw myself without support on earth, forced to sustain my soul by my own little strength against the misfortunes of life. I felt that thenceforward my heart could no more be happy as it had been; and no day has passed, since April 1804, in which I have not referred all my sufferings to this event.'

All the strength of that unsurpassed filial affection which had bound her to her father now burst forth in convulsive agonies. Madame Necker de Saussure received from her a letter of 'twelve pages, exceeding all imagination in its frightful, terrible, and yet touching wailings.' Accompanied by her husband, and the youngest son of Madame de Staël, she set out to meet her; they found her at Zurich in profound suffering, and conducted her homeward. 'I will not describe,' says her cousin, 'the cruel scenes which followed. It is not when grief overwhelms the soul that genius is recognisable.

The violent sufferings of a desolate heart are the same with all our poor human race. On this journey, it was only in brief intervals, of calmness, that I could recognise the real Madame de Staël, and never have I been more struck with what was marvellous in her nature than in these intermissions of her anguish. When the exhaustion of suffering had subdued her violent emotions, she entreated us to converse in the carriage, apparently because the sound of words helped her to command herself. She indicated to Schlegel a subject for discussion. He developed a great quantity of novel ideas, and, when the conversation became animated, she sometimes suddenly launched into it, resuming all her talents. Speaking of Germany, of men, of systems, of society, she displayed a fire of thought and a beauty of language altogether extraordinary; a thousand splendid pictures succeeding one another, until, reseized by violent grief, she sank again under the thought of her bereavement. It was like the illumination of lightning in a storm, suddenly extinguished by winds and rain. Her thoughts could not be completely distracted; even when most carried away by our discussions, a trembling, a contraction of the lips, showed that she had not ceased to suffer, and that she spoke under the weight of her grief. In the midst of her desolation, when we arrived at Coppet, singular affections of the imagination seized her; she sunk under a sort of vertigo. Believing that she had lost the guardian of all that was necessary to her being, it seemed to her that the general ties of all things were dissolved. She imagined that her fortune would be lost; that her children would never be educated; that her people would no longer obey her; that nothing could go on without her father.' 'I have lost my father!' was her exclamation in answer to every remonstrance. The strong brain was overwhelmed by the stronger heart. 'It would be necessary,' continues her cousin, 'to describe each day of her life, at this time, if we would show the place of her father in her heart. She never ceased to live with him; she always felt herself protected, consoled, succoured by him. Later she invoked him in her prayers, and no happy event occurred without her saying "My father has obtained this for me."' She bore his miniature on her person the remainder of her life. It was an object of superstition to her; only once did she part with it; she imagined that it might console her daughter in a period of sickness as it had consoled herself, and, giving it to her, said, 'Gaze upon it, gaze upon it, when you are in pain.' [5]

Necker died after an illness of nine days, invoking, with his hand upon his failing heart, blessings upon his absent daughter, and repeating many times, with all his remaining force, 'She has loved me dearly! She has loved me dearly!' His last words were, 'Great God, my Judge and my Saviour, receive Thy servant, hastening down to death.'

[5] *Notice &c.* ii.

On his death-bed he had written, with a trembling hand, a letter to Bonaparte, assuring him that his daughter was not responsible, in any way, for his last book, and entreating him to have compassion on her sufferings. This last letter, from the dying hand of one of the most notable men of the times, in behalf of his only child, the most notable woman of the times, was received by Napoleon, but was treated with silent contempt.[6] 'Magnanimity,' she says, alluding to his conduct in this instance, 'magnanimity always appeared to him affectation, and he spoke of it as melodramatic. Had he been able to appreciate the ascendency of this virtue, he would have been both a better and an abler man.'

A good man, and in many respects a great man—one of the few who have not been corrupted by wealth or power—Necker, after a long and stormy life, found peace at last amid the tranquil scenery of the family cemetery at Coppet, where he was laid to rest by the side of his remarkable wife, at whose grave he had not failed, during ten years, daily to meditate and pray. His daughter placed on their tomb a touching bas-relief, by Canova, representing a being, aerial as if already glorified, leading towards the sky another figure, which looks back compassionately on a young woman who is veiled and prostrate on a grave.

Time, which rectifies all things, will probably,

[6] *Dix Années*, i. 16.

sooner or later, rehabilitate Necker in the history of France. It cannot be doubted that, in the corrupt times of the Revolution and of the First Empire, if not since, his almost anomalous moral character rendered him incomprehensible to his critics, and impaired his rank as a statesman. Had the American Revolution failed, Washington's own character, as well as his fame, would have been different in the judgment of the world. Necker, before the unavoidable failure of the Revolution, was the great man of his times. Not merely were his talents acknowledged, but his opinions were enthusiastically approved, except by the corrupt ruling classes and a few Radicals. 'Men of extraordinary genius,' says Emerson, 'acquire an almost absolute ascendant over their nearest companions. The Count de Crillon said to M. d'Allonville, with French vivacity, "If the universe and I professed one opinion, and Necker expressed a contrary one, I should be at once convinced that the universe and I were mistaken."'

The men who defeated Necker defeated the Revolution. No impartial thinker can doubt that, had France followed the guidance of Necker (whatever may have been the fallacy of some of his opinions, as of those of all around him) she would have escaped the atrocities and failures of the Revolution. History may yet have a word to say on that subject.

The only survivor of his personal acquaintances

whom I have been able to discover, writes: 'The hour has not yet come for impartial justice to be done to this venerable man, who combined with so many eminent gifts such severe virtues. The writer who could trace with the same pen the "Compte-Rendu," the "Cours de Morale Religieuse," and the "Bonheur des Sots,"—the Minister of State who, without accepting any reward, put into the treasury two millions of his own property, with hardly a hope of receiving it again—the man who had the courage, at the Court of Versailles, to be, at that time, a defender of religious sentiments, a faithful husband, and a devoted parent—who from 1780 to his death in 1804 avowed, as his political motto, the utmost liberty compatible with order,—such a man merits that his memory be held in honour by every nation which is capable of appreciating true worth. The creator of the Provincial Assemblies in France, an institution which (as M. de Lavergne has shown) might, if rightly appreciated, have saved France, deserved the national gratitude. His trial before the tribunal of history is not yet finished.'[7]

Curiously enough, the chief hostile criticism on Necker's policy has had reference to a principle which the advancing liberalism of our own times zealously recognises. He wished the largest possible consideration of the national problem by the national mind. He therefore provided that the *Tiers Etat*,

---

[7] Pictet de Sergy's unpublished *Souvenirs*.

the people, should be represented in the States-General by as many deputies as the two other orders united ; for the two others were virtually one : the Church being a part of the State constitution, the clergy were functionaries of the State ; the nobles and the clergy formed the aristocratic class ; both claimed immunities from taxation which could no longer be tolerated by the burdened people. What remedy could the latter command without equal representation? This sympathetic concession to the people has been considered by Necker's critics his great crime ; in our day it should be esteemed his great virtue.

He has been further condemned for not guaranteeing, in his programme of the States-General, the separate action of the nobles and clergy on the one hand, and the deputies of the people on the other. The latter were substantially the nation. They were the sufferers whose wrongs were to be redressed. The problem was a financial one. Increased resources could alone save the State. The nobles and the Church had brought it to ruin by their financial excesses and exemptions. They had obstinately refused to share in the taxation proportionately with the people, down to the time of the States-General, when the gathering storm compelled them to make favourable avowals, which the people could not, or would not, trust. Necker did not dictate to the deputies on the question of their separate or united action. He left that for their own decision, though his sympathies were on the side of the people. The nobles and the clergy resisted, during six tumultuous weeks, the attempts of the popular representatives (led chiefly by Mirabeau) for a combined Assembly for the verification of their powers. They met separately down to June 17, 1789, when the deputies of the people, after some additions to their number from the other orders, declared themselves to be the 'National Assembly,' announcing that, 'after the verification of their powers, they discovered the Assembly to be already composed of representatives which were sent directly by at least ninety-six hundredths of the nation.'[8] It was the obstinacy of the aristocratic classes that thus roused the popular passions, till they at last swept the nobility and the Church out of the bankrupt country. The ruling classes and the Church were responsible for the long degradation of the people, by which they were rendered capable of the ferocities which ensued; and they were responsible also for the immediate provocation which aroused and maddened the people. Neither Necker nor any other man could have anticipated the popular excesses. Hitherto, throughout French history, the people had been too humbly submissive; the higher classes had led the way in almost every national disruption, and they

[8] *Hist. de la Révolution*, &c., i. 6, par Bertrand de Moleville. Paris, 1801.

wished now to control the nation without sharing materially in the financial sacrifices necessary for its salvation. They wrangled at Versailles till their hour was passed; the nation was wrecked; and they who provoked the disaster have found it convenient to charge Necker with their own responsibility for it.

CHAPTER XXI.

LIFE AT COPPET.

Moral Effect of the Death of her Father—Her Religious Views—Letter to Gouverneur Morris—Her Sketch of Necker's Character and private Life—Society at Coppet—Bonstetten—Schlegel—Müller, the Historian—Her Opinion of him—Madame Necker de Saussure—Letter to Madame Récamier.

THE death of her father made a moral epoch in Madame de Staël's life. The baptism of sorrow purified her nature. Always predisposed to religious sentiments, she had, nevertheless, hitherto felt more or less the relaxing influence of the prevalent moral ideas of her times. Though they could not change her principles, they could not fail to affect the sentiments, and, to some extent, the life of a being so susceptible. Her cousin says that from this time 'her religious opinions were more pronounced, her sentiments of piety more constant and more active. The vagueness of a poetic faith could no longer suffice for her heart.' Not a poetic faith, indeed, but still hers was always a faith of the heart rather than of the head. It was more difficult, in that age than even in ours, to accept the traditional, the definitive dicta of the Church. The genius, the spirit of Christianity, now became,

more than ever, precious to her; but she found it
not in speculative dogma or formula, or sectarian
arrogations. She found it in all sects, underlying
their petty discriminations; in the sincere but
eccentric fervour of Madame de Krüdner, as we
have seen and shall hereafter more fully see; in the
Moravians, to whom she devotes a chapter of her
'Allemagne;' in the mediaeval Mystics, notwithstanding their reveries; in the Protestant sects
generally; and in select Roman Catholic minds.
'Who,' she asks, 'is not profoundly affected in reading the spiritual writings of Fénelon? Where else
do we discover more light, more consolation, more
charity? Here is no fanaticism, no austerity other
than that of virtue, no intolerance, no exclusiveness.
The diversities of Christian communions cannot be
felt at this height, which is above all the accidental
forms that time creates and destroys. We have
no control over our birth or our death, and more
than three-fourths of our destiny is determined
by these events. No one can change the primary impressions of his birth, his country, his
age. No one can acquire features or genius
which he has not received from nature; and
how many other circumstances enter irresistibly
into the composition of life! If our fate depend
upon a hundred different lots, there are ninety
and nine which depend not upon ourselves; and
all the force of our will bears upon the feeble
portion which seems yet in our power. The action

of the will, even on this feeble portion, is singularly incomplete. The single act of man which can always attain its object, is *the accomplishment of duty*. The issue of all other resolutions depends on accidents with which even prudence can do nothing. The greater proportion of men never obtain that which they most strongly desire; and prosperity, even if they attain it, comes to them often in an unexpected way.'[1] We have heretofore seen, in her remarkable conversation with Lacretelle, the historian, and shall hereafter see in an equally remarkable one, reported by Ritter, the distinguished Berlin professor, how completely she relied on the instincts of the heart in matters of religion. But the intuitions of the heart were, with her, the highest logic,—higher than the deductions of the reason, and always in harmony with the latter when it is right. She believed that the instincts, which in lower creatures are so sure, ought to be surer in man, in whom they are aided by reason; they are indeed but a quicker, a spontaneous logic, and, in matters of the heart, man's most infallible resource. Religion was, with her, supremely a matter of the heart; and dogma and formula important only so far as they ministered to the needs of the heart.

In her present affliction her genius, as usual in the great trials of her career, remained unimpaired, and rose to loftier altitudes; and her greatest

---

[1] *L'Allemagne*, iv. 6.

works were to follow. Thenceforward life was to her more serious, more sacred. For some time her grief seemed inconsolable. Four months after the death of Necker she wrote to her American friend, Gouverneur Morris: 'The pain of his loss deepens every day in my heart. Ah! tell me, in your America, where they love mankind—in your America, where they believe in God, how do you endure the sorrow of death? When souls have been so intimately united, is there no communication between the living and the dead? I have friends, I have duties, but he was in the centre of my heart; there, where no one else has penetrated —where no one else ever can penetrate. I weep bitterly in writing; sympathise with me, for my heart is broken.'

Bonstetten was now with her, to comfort her. 'She is frightfully depressed,' he writes to Frederica Brun; 'we have done nothing but weep together. What eloquence! What sentiment! What profound love for the father who loved her so much! She is now independent, with an income of a hundred thousand livres; and God only knows if she will be happy, with all her earthly advantages; the world is too little for her soul of fire.'[2]

She turned to her habitual means of relief in times of trouble—to work; and prepared a sketch of the 'Character and Private Life of Necker,'[3] to

---

[2] Steinlen's *Bonstetten*, ch. vi.
[3] *Du Caractère de M. Necker et de sa Vie privée: Œuvres complètes*, ii.

accompany a volume of his fragmentary writings which she soon published, with the title of his 'Manuscripts,'—that palpitating record of grief and affection, that heart-touching lament, which Benjamin Constant says is 'the best revelation of her own character; for her whole mind and heart are displayed in it. The delicacy of her perceptions, the astonishing variety of her thoughts, the ardour of her eloquence, the strength of her judgment, the reality of her enthusiasm, her love of liberty and justice, her passionate sensibility, the melancholy which often marked even her purely literary productions,—all these are here devoted to express a single feeling, to call forth the sympathy of others in a single sentiment. Nowhere else has she treated a subject with all the resources of her intellect, all the depths of her feeling, and without being diverted by a single thought of a less absorbing nature.'[4] There is probably not to be found in all literature a more sincere and affecting disclosure of the heart of woman, or a more perfect expression of filial affection, than in this introduction to the 'Manuscripts.' It is limited to the personal character and private life of Necker; for to her, in this time of sorrow, the subject was too sacred for politics; she makes but passing allusions to them. She projected, however, a vindication of his public life, and left it at her death, twelve years later, incomplete,

[4] Constant's *Mélanges* &c. viii.

but splendid with her best ability, in her elaborate work on the French Revolution.

Occupation mitigated her grief; her friends gathered sympathetically and numerously around her; and we are assured that the summer of 1804 was one of the most brilliant seasons at the château.[5] Schlegel, Constant, Sismondi, Bonstetten, entertained her by their conversation. Müller, the historian, joined them—a living library—'crushing under the weight of his erudition, as well as his historic good sense, the two sceptics'—Constant and Schlegel. 'Sismondi was astonished and confounded by this rattling fire of ideas. Bonstetten was gay, elegant, full of fine amiability. The good angel of the house, Madame Necker de Saussure, quite up to the intellectual level of these men, tempered their disputations by her sweet gravity and masculine judgment; in the midst of them all, the queen, the mistress of these enchanting scenes, Corinne, powerful and vivid, electrified the circle, though death was in her heart. "I go," she said to them, " to bear the burden of life into Italy, where, they say, one forgets existence." It was a spectacle worthy of profound and melancholy interest.'

Bonstetten in midsummer wrote: 'Madame de Staël becomes daily greater and better; but souls of great talent have great sufferings: they are solitary in the world, like Mont Blanc.' In his letters to Frederica Brun he has left us many

[5] Steinlen's *Bonstetten*, ch. vii.

interesting allusions to Coppet at this period. 'I like Schlegel very much,' he says. 'He is a man full of ideas, of spirit, of great and solid learning. It is hardly possible to have more intellect than he has: he attacks everything, and his French-German is so amusing, so droll, so biting, that any adversary is disarmed in ten minutes. He has an agreeable countenance, an expression of kindliness; but in excitement it becomes as sharp as a sword: his gestures are so characteristic, that I cannot help laughing at him. Madame de Staël plunges into his disputes; all old French opinions enter the lists by turns, and are thrust from the saddle like dismounted cavaliers. Schlegel, when not in gentle mood, is unmercifully severe; and the most beautiful sight in the scene is Madame de Staël charging herself with the blame of our quarrels; and she has three times as much intellect as he. Schlegel responds to her, now with the finest thought, and then with the finest gallantry. Everybody is delighted with the combat. They make breaches into the poor French party every day; Madame de Staël helps to demolish it. Albertine [Madame Necker de Saussure] is a convert. Müller is always the same: gay, accomplished, a devourer of books; we are to each other what we were twenty years ago.' 'I returned yesterday with Müller from Coppet. I feel fatigued, as by a surfeit of intellect. There is more mind expended at Coppet in a day than in many countries in a year. But I am half dead; and my chamber at Geneva seems a tomb.' Again: 'I was yesterday at Coppet, with Sismondi, Müller, and Mallet; the *beaux esprits* of all Switzerland united there. Müller fought Schlegel; the latter denied, at the table, the personality of Moses, of Homer, and of Ossian; Müller responded that he would some time or other take the pen and demonstrate, in a learned work, that Charlemagne never existed. Then he gave us an analysis of the first two books of Moses, chapter by chapter, which imposed silence on Schlegel and Constant. They dared not open their mouths again. The good Sismondi was quite stunned; he has declared to me that they all seemed steeped in clownish ignorance. I tried to console him. He wished to go to Germany, to see, himself, its great geniuses; I counselled him rather to go to Greece.'

Madame de Staël, with whom sentiment was infinitely superior to erudition, heartily appreciated Müller, who combined both. 'He is,' she says, 'the most learned of historians, and is truly a poet in his manner of painting events and men—a scholar, and a writer of grand talent. He is a man of incredible knowledge; and his powers, in this respect, really alarm us. One cannot conceive how the head of man can contain such a world of facts and dates. The six thousand years known to us are all perfectly arranged in his memory; and his studies have been so profound, that they are as astounding as his personal recollections. There is not a village of Switzerland, not a noble family, the history of which he does not know. One day, in consequence of a bet, they demanded of him the series of the sovereign Counts of Bugey. He named them instantly, save that he could not recall whether one of them had been regent or reigned by title, and he seriously reproached himself for such a failure of memory. Men of genius among the ancients were not subject to this immense labour of learning, which augments as time goes on; their genius was not fatigued by erudite studies. It costs more to distinguish oneself in our days, and we ought to respect the formidable labour now requisite for the mastery of almost any subject. The death of such a man as Müller is an irreparable loss; something more than a man seems to perish when such faculties are extinguished. He is the classic German historian, reading habitually, in the original, the Greek and Latin authors; he cultivates literature and the arts in the service of history; his boundless erudition, instead of impairing his natural vivacity, is the ground whence his imagination takes its flight, and the living truth of his pictures is founded in their scrupulous fidelity.'[6]

Bonstetten makes an excursion with Müller to Valeyres. 'We are again,' he says, 'the old, or rather the young friends. He is joyous as a child; but here the people seem to me frightfully prosaic. In four days I shall be in Coppet, where I shall find

[6] *L'Allemagne*, ii. 29.

myself prosaic, at least till my wings grow again.' In August he and Müller are again at Coppet. He is not in good mood, and qualifies his opinions somewhat. Of Madame de Staël he says (still to Frederica Brun), 'She has an extreme kindness; no person has more mind; but she is destitute of some of your excellences. She lacks appreciation of art; for her the beautiful exists only in intellect, or eloquence. No one has more practical wisdom, less for herself, it is true, than for her friends; but Schlegel is insupportable to me. He has not been able to discipline himself enough to attain a little reason.' Nothing, however, could change Bonstetten's good opinion of Madame Necker de Saussure. 'She is an angel,' he writes a little later; 'she criticises my labours with severity, and makes excellent remarks to me; for she understands metaphysics and languages better than her cousin.' 'Nevertheless,' remarks Steinlen, his biographer, 'Madame de Staël was always the literary star around which moved the thoughts of Bonstetten—she was the Muse who was able to awaken ideas.'

Though conversation and labour afforded to Madame de Staël the most effectual reliefs from suffering, she could not yet rise above the dejection occasioned by the death of her father. Coppet was still too sad a place for her stricken heart and restless genius. She planned a tour in Italy (which was to enable her to give to the world her best-known work), and on the eve of her departure wrote to Madame Récamier (November 2, 1804), 'Dear and beautiful Juliette, you give me the hope of seeing you, next July, on my return from Italy; then only can I believe myself no more exiled. I will receive you in the château, where I have lost what I loved the most in the world. You will bring a sense of happiness here, where it no longer exists. Beg M. Récamier to afford me this consolation. Adieu, dear Juliette, I embrace you. I love you more than any other woman in France.'[7]

[7] *Coppet et Weimar.*

CHAPTER XXII.

ITALY—ART.

Madame de Staël goes to Italy—Her Love of Music—Schlegel's connection with her Works—Her Italian Tour—Observations on Art—'Corinne.'

NECKER died on April 8, 1804; by the end of October his daughter's sketch of his 'Character and Private Life' was finished. Her mind now recoiled upon itself; every local scene that recalled her father recalled her bereavement. Her health began to fail, and she was ordered by her physician to the more genial climate of the South. In November she was on her way to Italy, accompanied by nearly all her family—her domestics, her three children, and Schlegel; and, part of the way, by Sismondi. She could have no better guide among the classic monuments of that country than the learned German, who was familiar with every allusion to them in the Latin writers, and whose cultivated, artistic taste could assist her own.

Hitherto music had been to her the chief of the arts. She was skilful at the piano, and a good singer; and music was a necessity of her nature, not merely as a relief from study or trouble, but as an expression of her exuberant sensibility. For many years an Italian musician, Pestosa, was a member of her household, not only as an instructor, but as a sort of family minstrel.[1] The other arts she could appreciate only by her instinctive good taste; the conversation of Schlegel led her to more critical appreciation of them. Nominally the instructor of her children, he was, practically, her own also, and doubtless we owe, in part, the splendid superiority of her subsequent works to his aid. The chief merits of her 'Allemagne' have been claimed for him; he unquestionably was the best of authorities, and she used him as other authors would use the best of accessible libraries. All her writings were submitted to the criticism of the cultivated *coterie* of Coppet; but Schlegel himself denied that he had given more than critical revision to the 'Allemagne,' and acknowledged that, instead of making her books, he had himself learned from her how to write so as to interest the European public.[2] No reader of her essay on Literature can doubt her ability to write the 'Allemagne;' and, whatever aid she might have received from Schlegel, as from books or other sources, in gathering the materials for her 'Corinne,' its magnificent descriptions, its wealth of

---

[1] *Coppet et Weimar*, iii.
[2] P. de Golberg's article on Schlegel in the *Nouvelle Revue Germanique*, Sept. 1832.

sentiment and of thought, its superabundant genius in all respects, prove it to have been all her own. No man could have written it; its faults, as well as its excellences, indicate the sex of its author.

She was an apt scholar for Schlegel's instructions in the arts; for, if hitherto unskilled in their technical criticism, her genius was ever in sympathy with them. To her, beauty was the highest utility. Rigorous analysis, so important in the sciences and practical arts, she would apply cautiously to the fine arts. 'Analysis,' she says, 'can examine only by dividing. It is applicable, like the scalpel, to dead nature, but it is a poor instrument for the knowledge of that which lives; and if it is difficult to define, by words, the animated conception which represents to us objects in their completeness, it is precisely because such a conception belongs to the very essence of things. To divide in order to comprehend is, in philosophy, a sign of weakness, as to divide in order to conquer is, in politics.' Speaking, in her 'Allemagne,' of the sentiment, the enthusiasm, which characterised the art criticism of Winckelmann, she remarks: 'It is thus only that we can comprehend the beautiful arts. It is necessary that the attention which they excite should spring from love, and that we discover in the great works of genius, as in the features of a cherished being, a thousand charms, revealed by the sentiments which they inspire.' Though the sentiment of the beautiful was ever strong with her, yet, as with the Greeks, it had hitherto found its gratifications more in humanity, in living rather than in inanimate nature. What we call the 'fine arts' were, in her native language, called the beautiful arts—*beaux arts*. 'The beautiful,' she says, 'considered only as agreeable, would be confined to the sphere of the sensations, and, in consequence, be subject to differences of taste; it could not merit that universal assent which is the true proof of beauty. The beautiful, defined as perfection, demands a sort of appreciation similar to that on which esteem is founded. The enthusiasm which the beautiful ought to inspire belongs neither to the sensations nor the judgment: it is an innate disposition, like the sentiment of duty and the primary notions of the understanding. We recognise the beautiful, when we see it, because it is the exterior image of the ideal, the type of which is in our minds. Diversities of taste can apply to that which is agreeable, because the sensations are a source of this kind of pleasure; but all men admire what is really beautiful because they have, in their souls, sentiments of celestial origin which beauty awakens, and which it enables them to enjoy.'

It is to be regretted that we have but few details of her Italian travels. The first part of the 'Ten Years of Exile' ends at her return from Germany, in 1804, and the narrative is not resumed till after an interval of nearly six years.

We learn from her son, the Baron de Staël,[3] that her mind, oppressed by grief, revived under the genial sky of Naples; that the vivid impressions of the scenery, the art, and the poetic life of the South, reawakened her genius, restoring her power to think and write. She was treated by the diplomatic agents of Napoleon without favour, but also without injustice. Letters of introduction from Joseph Bonaparte gave her access to the best society in Rome, but she wrote to Bonstetten that she found in it little nourishment for either her mind or heart. William Humboldt was her best companion there. The Roman princes seemed stupid to her. 'I got along better,' she says, 'with the cardinals, who, though they tyrannise a little, have a wider range of thought. But how little need has one of men here, where things speak so powerfully! Yesterday I was received at the Arcadian Academy with indescribable applause. All Rome, with its princes, cardinals, &c. was present. I spare you a dozen sonnets, in which I am made a new star.'[4]

She appreciated the capabilities of the people and the evils which repressed their spirit. 'In the present state of the Italians,' she says, 'the glory of the beautiful arts is the only intellectual passion allowed them. They discern genius, in the arts,

---

[3] *Avertissement*, by Baron de Staël, to second part of the *Dix Années* &c.

[4] Morell's *Karl von Bonstetten*, viii. Winterthur, 1864.

with an enthusiasm which ought to produce many great men, if applause alone sufficed to produce them—if a strong life, grand interests, and national independence, were not necessary for their existence.'

She observes that even the humour of the people is tinctured with the artistic spirit : 'The true gaiety of the Italians is not mockery, it is imagination ; their comedy is not the picture of manners, but poetic exaggerations. It is Ariosto, not Molière, that can amuse Italy.' 'The people of the South are readily fatigued by prose, they paint their true sentiments only in poetry.' She recognised much originality, much individuality, in their spirit as in their poetic, though not in their prose literature. The limitations imposed by political oppression on the range of inquiry and speculation rendered the prose writers tame and monotonous, but the poets had more freedom in their imaginative sphere. She discerned in the general mind much 'national colour,' with abundant individual variations. And this intellectual character is, in her estimation, a good ground of hope, 'for,' she adds, 'genius is essentially creative, it bears the character of him who possesses it. Nature, which wills that no two leaves shall be alike, has placed still more diversity in souls ; and imitation is only a species of death, as it deprives one of his natural existence.'

The climate and scenery especially charmed her senses and tranquillised her mind. 'The nightingales repose among the roses, and the purest music mingles with the sweetest odours. All the charms of nature seem here to attract one another. But that which is, above all, refreshing and inexpressible, is the balminess of the atmosphere. When we contemplate a beautiful view, in the North, the climate always mars a little the pleasure that we feel. The slight sensations of cold and humidity, which turn our attention more or less from what we see, are like false notes in a concert; but, in approaching Naples, you experience so perfect a sense of well-being, so intimate a friendship of nature for you, that nothing lessens your agreeable sensations. The relations of man, in our climates, are mostly with society. Nature in the warm countries places him in relation with exterior objects, and his feelings flow spontaneously forth upon surrounding scenes. The South has, indeed, its melancholy: in what place does not the destiny of man produce it? But there is, in this melancholy, neither discontent, nor anxiety, nor regret. Elsewhere it is life, such as it is, that suffices not for the faculties of the soul; here the faculties of the soul suffice not for life. One's superabundant sensations inspire indolent reveries, of which the mind hardly troubles itself to take account. There is, in this nature, at once a life and a repose which satisfy entirely the varied cravings of existence.'

To such a mind the great works of art could

not fail to be unusually suggestive. She wandered through the miles of galleries, in Florence, Rome, and Naples, crowded with such works, or rather their classic ruins—with delight mixed with awe. In the Vatican, 'one seems to see,' she remarks, 'the battle-field where time has warred against genius, and these mutilated members attest its victory, and our loss.' She was struck by the air of repose which the classic masters impressed on their statues and busts, 'the images of heroes and gods, in which the most perfect beauty, in eternal serenity, seems to enjoy itself. What poetry in these visages, where the sublime expression is forever fixed, where the greatest thoughts are clothed with an image so worthy of them! The courageous support of the suffering of our times, in the midst of a social state so cold and so oppressive, is now what is most noble in man; and, in our days, he who has not suffered knows not how to feel, or think. But there was, in antiquity, something more noble than suffering: it was calm heroism; it was the sentiment of force, which could develop itself amidst free and liberal institutions. The most beautiful statues of the Greeks nearly always indicate repose. The Laocoon and the Niobe are the only ones which express violent suffering; but it is the vengeance of heaven which they recall, not passions born in the human heart. Human nature had, with the ancients, an organisation so healthy, the air circulated so freely in their large lungs, their political order was so much in harmony with their faculties, that there seldom existed souls ill at ease, as in our days. We hardly discover in their statues any traces of melancholy. The head of Apollo, in the Justinian palace, and another of Alexander dying, are the only ones in which dispositions of the soul for reverie and suffering are indicated; but they both appertain, according to all appearance, to times when Greece was subjugated. After the loss of liberty there were no longer that pride, that tranquillity of soul, which produced, among the ancients, the chief works of sculpture, and of poetry composed in the same spirit.'

The tombs, the sarcophagi, had to her mind a peculiar significance, in accordance with the classic times. 'They recall only heroic or agreeable ideas. On the multitude of those in the Vatican one sees battles and sports represented in relief. The memory of the activity of life was the most beautiful homage that the classic ancients believed they could render to the dead. Nothing enfeebled, nothing diminished, their forces. But the statues in sleep, or only in an attitude of complete repose, presenting an image of eternal tranquillity, accord most marvellously with the general effect of the South on man. It seems as if the beautiful arts are here the spectators of nature; and that genius itself, which so agitates the soul in the North, is, under a beautiful sky, but an added harmony.'

The obelisks, hoary with antiquity and aspiring in form, pleased her imagination. 'Their summits, lost in the air, seem to bear even to heaven a great thought from man.'

St. Peter's—'the greatest edifice that man has ever raised,' was, to her, the most sublime monument in Rome, and the more so that it at first baffles and disappoints the mind. 'One reaches the sublime only by degrees. Infinite distances separate it from that which is only beautiful. St. Peter's is a work of man which produces on the mind the effect of a marvel of nature. It is the only work of art on earth which has the kind of grandeur that characterises the immediate works of creation. In it the genius of man is glorified by the magnificence of nature.' 'The view of such a monument is as a fixed and never-ceasing strain of music—ready to do you good whenever you approach it.'

She was hopeful, even then, of the destiny of the Italians. They needed but unity, nationality, and liberty, with their consequent ameliorations, for the successful activity of the repressed genius which she discerned in them. Prophetically she says, 'There is so much soul in their beautiful arts, that, perhaps, the day may come in which their character may equal their genius.' A land which, since her day, has produced both a Cavour and a Garibaldi—which was the first to initiate the

Renaissance, and which, during ages of oppression, has never failed to produce great individual minds in science and philosophy, as well as in poetry and the arts, need never despair.

Her Corinne shows how thoroughly she studied Italian life and character, and how minutely she observed the scenery and monuments of the country. Even in our day, it is one of the best handbooks for the traveller, in Rome; if not for the topographical features of the city and its vicinity, yet for local descriptions, and especially for the artistic and poetic appreciation of classic ruins, and of life; for, while it pictures real scenes truthfully, it expresses also their ideal suggestions—those poetic inspirations which all intelligent travellers feel, but which few can well define to themselves, and fewer can express to others. Our best impressions of grand or beautiful sights are always enhanced by their communication to sympathetic and appreciative minds. 'Let us pause here,' said Oswald to Corinne, as they stood in view of the tomb of Adrian and St. Peter.s.' 'I know not if I am deceiving myself,' replied Corinne, ' but it seems to me that we become dearer to one another, in admiring together monuments which speak to the soul by a true grandeur.' Genius never looked through clearer eyes on the marvels of Italy than in the person of Madame de Staël; and the pen has never more enchantingly described them.

Abundantly supplied with observations on the life and art of the South, she returned to the North, to embody them in her most popular, though not her most able book.

END OF THE FIRST VOLUME.

LONDON : PRINTED BY
SPOTTISWOODE AND CO., NEW-STREET SQUARE
AND PARLIAMENT STREET

www.ingramcontent.com/pod-product-compliance
Lightning Source LLC
Chambersburg PA
CBHW032032220426
43664CB00006B/453